KV-555-197

The Dragonflies of Great Britain and Ireland

Cyril O. Hammond FRES

THE DRAGONFLIES OF GREAT BRITAIN AND IRELAND

With enlarged illustrations of all the British species in colour by the author and an illustrated key to the aquatic larval stages by the late A. E. Gardner

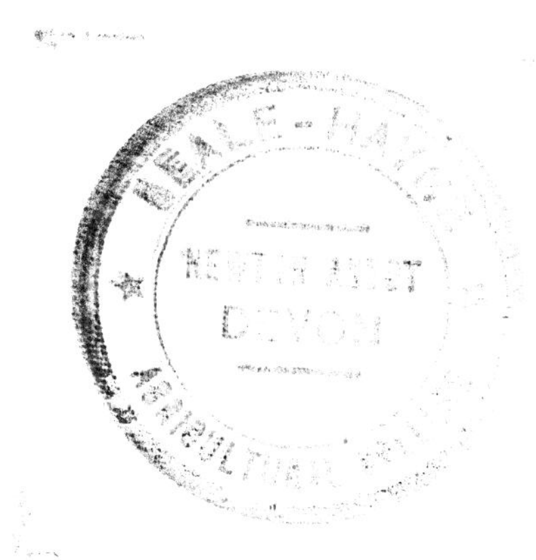

Curwen Books
The Curwen Press Ltd

Curwen Books, The Curwen Press Ltd, London

Printed at The Curwen Press, England
on Hi-speed Blade Cartridge 115gsm

Set in Monotype Plantin (110)

Case bound in Winterbottom Caxton Kingsway
at The University Printing House, Cambridge

Book and jacket designed by James Shurmer

ISBN 0 902068 06 7

Contents

Foreword by Cynthia Longfield

This is the Dragonfly book of the Century. All the British species are portrayed on twenty fully coloured plates more than life-sized, and in several critical species showing varieties in colour and pattern.

Cyril Hammond is supremely endowed with the skill to give us just exactly what is needed for the identification between genera and species. Also the reader is helped by the keys and the text, skilfully researched.

The enlarged maps from John Heath and his team at B.R.C., Monks Wood, Hunts, have brought up to date the reports on distribution and are large and clear enough to be used for continuous recording. Although the 1960 New Naturalist Volume on Dragonflies pioneered the concept of live colour photographs and maps on distribution, this present volume has enlarged and improved on both.

Owing to the previous publishers deciding not to reprint the various British Isles handbooks, we have been left with a terrible two year vacuum. Nobly, Cyril Hammond has filled the gap and produced a book which provides every clue to the identity of our British species, mostly in beautifully executed colour plates. The student should not omit reading the skilfully compiled keys. The shapes of the anal appendages and the secondary copulation genitalia are diagnostic. Also the venation of the adult wings is different in every genus. The novice should not overlook the chapters and diagrams depicting how to recognise a dragonfly at any stage in its life history.

Grateful Odonatists, north to south, east to west, are enormously indebted to Mr. Hammond for undertaking such a major task and fulfilling it so triumphantly. Many people lent a hand and provided the specimens needed for detailed illustrations and for mapping local distribution and also helped in collecting fresh specimens. Sadly some species are already rare or even extinct since the latest published surveys.

Alas, one very important part of a dragonfly's life history, from egg to adult, we no longer can have, as a part II volume to Mr. Hammond's book the larvae were to be contributed by our old friend and wizard breeder, Eric Gardner. He wrote so happily only a month before his sudden death, of being able to impart all the unpublished information he still could have added. Cyril Hammond and Eric Classey (owner of the copyright) arranged instead to include in this volume Gardner's *A Key to the Larvae of the British Odonata*, dating from 1954 but nowhere surpassed.

We are exceedingly grateful to the Publishers and Mr. Basil Harley for producing such a superb volume.

Cynthia Longfield, April 1977

Preface

Over three-quarters of a century have passed since W. J. Lucas produced his masterly work, *British Dragonflies*, in 1900. In 1922 the present author became interested in the Odonata and later had the good fortune to meet W. J. Lucas in person at the meetings of the Royal Entomological Society of London.

Lucas's second book, *The Aquatic (Naiad) Stage of the British Dragonflies*, again displayed his artistic skill as an illustrator and clearly showed that accurately drawn illustrations still surpass the best photographs for identification purposes.

Although three good books on British dragonflies have appeared since then, none has illustrations of both male and female of all the species. The present work was undertaken to fill that gap and to provide colour illustrations of sufficient magnification to show clearly the details necessary to ensure correct identification.

It is hoped that this book will stimulate interest and study, especially among young students, in much the same way as *Flies of the British Isles* (Colyer & Hammond, 1951) was successful in increasing the number of dipterists in the country.

It was intended to produce a second volume on the aquatic larval stages by A. E. Gardner but his untimely death in February 1976 has made this impossible. However, I am pleased that we are able to include his illustrated keys which were published in 1954, 1955. I am grateful to E. W. Classey for permission to include them here.

The author is indebted to Miss C. Longfield for help received at the British Museum (Natural History) when she was responsible for the Odonata collection and for being given the happy task of illustrating, from live specimens, a damselfly new to the British list which she discovered in 1946, forming the frontispiece of *The Dragonflies of the British Isles* (Longfield, 1949). He is also in her debt for having contributed most of the Irish records on the distribution maps.

Grateful thanks are due to the Trustees of the British Museum (Natural History) and to Dr. P. Freeman, Keeper of Entomology, for facilities to study some of the rarer species, and to Peter Ward, also at the Museum, for helpful suggestions during the preparation of the book.

Thanks are also due to Dr. M. G. Morris, Institute of Terrestrial Ecology, Furzebrook Research Station, Professor J. D. Gillett, Brunel University and A. Rodger Waterston OBE of the Royal Scottish Museum, Edinburgh for valuable assistance; to Alan Stubbs, Peter Chandler and Raymond Uffen for help in collecting and for many delightful trips in the field; to John Ismay of the Castle Museum, Norwich for arranging and supervising the Nature Conservancy Council survey of the dragonflies of the Norfolk Broads in 1975; to Dr. D. A. L. Davies for the gift of a pair of the rare *Aeshna caerulea* which was most useful for comparison with other specimens of the same species; to J. L. Banks for sending a live male of the same species for colour assessment; to Bill Parker for obtaining a live specimen of *Gomphus vulgatissimus* from the River Thames for me; to Raymond Fry, Warden of Thursley Common Nature Reserve, Surrey, with whom I have spent many pleasant hours recording the species; to David Chelmick who kindly escorted me over some of the best localities in Sussex; to the late A. E. Gardner for many years of exchanging information on records and distribution and for the gift of a pair of the very rare *Coenagrion armatum*; to Miss Eanna ni Lamhna and the staff of the Irish Biological Records Centre, Dublin for collating the Irish records; to John Heath, Biological Records Centre, Institute of Terrestrial Ecology, Monks Wood Experimental Station, who supplied the up-dated distribution maps and to Basil Harley for making the publication of this work possible and for his great help in piloting the book through the press; and finally to the many colleagues at the British Entomological and Natural History Society and other friends who also gave me every encouragement as the work progressed.

Cyril O. Hammond

Introduction

'Horse-stingers' and 'Devil's Darning Needles' they were called years ago; nowadays the former are known as dragonflies, the latter as damselflies. The term dragonflies is applied to the larger and more robust species belonging to the Anisoptera and damselflies to the smaller, slender-bodied species belonging to the Zygoptera, but in the literal sense they are all dragonflies belonging to the order Odonata.

Possibly the dread of these insects results from their ferocious appearance and their size and often the formidable array of spots and stripes enhances this. Let it be stated emphatically that these lovely insects are harmless to humans, having no sting as is commonly believed even today. When caught, although they will curl the abdomen round to touch the captor's hand, suggestive of a sting, they may be handled with impunity. Similarly, if the holder places the tip of his finger against the mouth of even the largest species, only a slight nip will be experienced from the powerful mandibles.

The haunts of dragonflies are many and varied; ponds and lakes, canals and lily pools, slow and fast running streams, sphagnum bogs and marshes, ditches and dykes and glades in woods or along hedgerows. Many species are shy and wary and make off hastily on being approached, but the large *Aeshna cyanea* is curious and will come within a yard of the still observer. It is this close approach which has led some people to accuse the insect of 'dive-bombing'. The collector would wish that all the species were as inquisitive.

Their legs are suitable for grasping and so well-proportioned that when bent for catching their prey all the six claws meet together at the mouth. They are not, however, suitable for walking, although damselflies, which rest on the marginal vegetation, use them for climbing, and will sometimes turn and face the onlooker so that the body is behind the stem at which the observer is looking.

It is not unusual to see a male and female flying in tandem, the male grasping the female round the neck or prothorax with its anal appendages (claspers) in the case of the Zygoptera (Fig.1a) or by the back of the head or by the head and neck in the case of the Anisoptera. This is the stage primary to mating. The reproductive organs of the male are unique in the insect world. The genital opening for the sperm is situated, as in other insects, near the tip of the abdomen, underneath the ninth segment; but the accessory copulatory apparatus of male dragonflies is below the second and base of third segments. Thus the male must transfer the sperm from the ninth to the second segment by bending its abdomen in a curve and charging the accessory apparatus with sperm prior to copulation. From the in tandem position the male curves his body downwards and the female upwards to copulate, as shown in Fig.1b. The majority of species fly to the nearest herbage, shrub or tree to complete the process which may last many minutes. *Libellula* species, however, copulate for only a few seconds in the air.

Egg laying follows almost immediately and may be effected in one of two ways – from

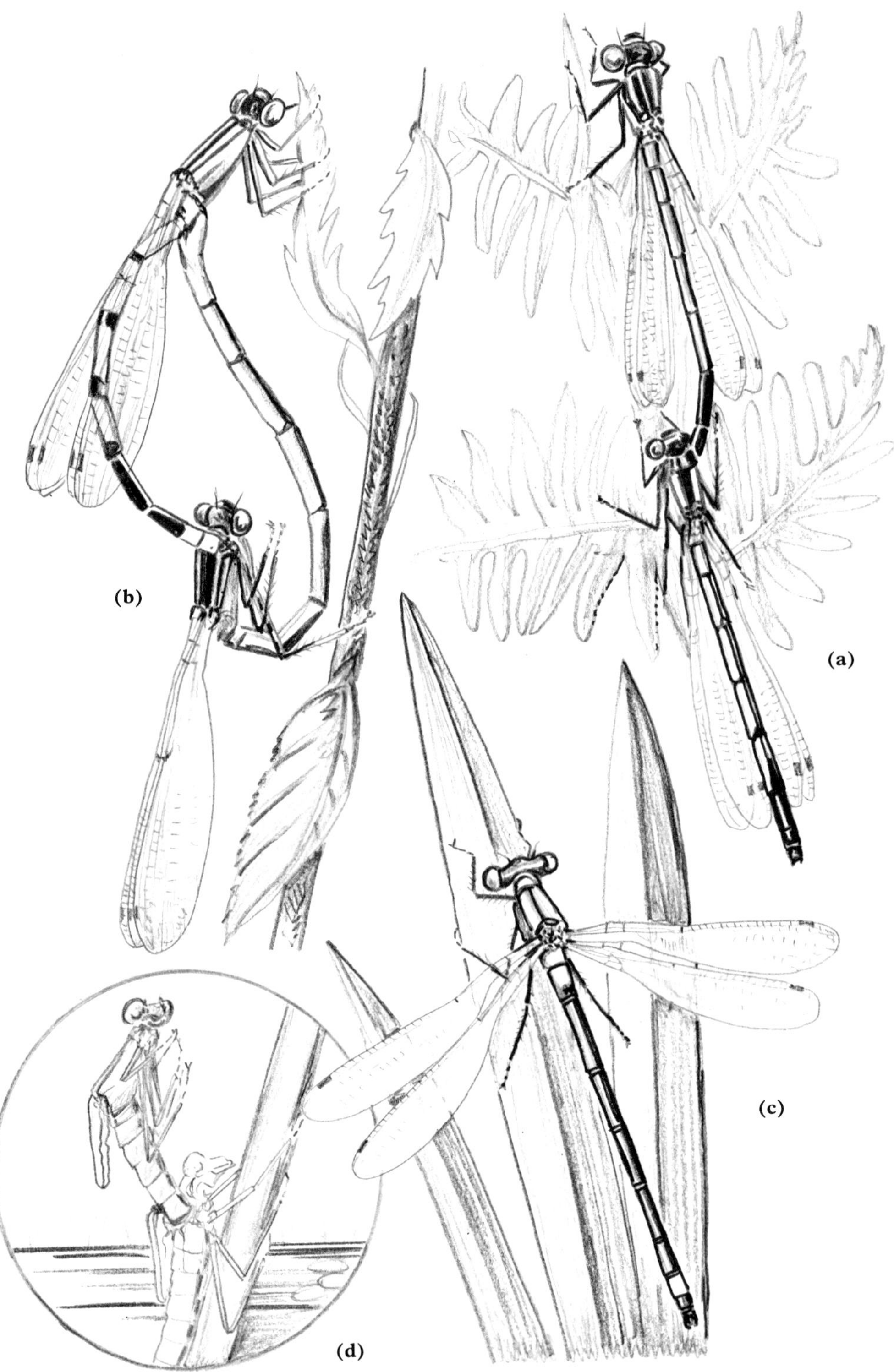

Figure 1. (a,b) Mating positions of Zygoptera. **(c)** Zygoptera at rest. **(d)** Upright rest position, usual in the Zygoptera during final moult.

above or below the surface of the water. The majority of Anisoptera use the former method, flying low over the water and flicking the surface with the end of the abdomen to wash off the eggs singly or in a gelatinous mass. The male is sometimes in attendance also, either helping in tandem or hovering above the female. Most species of the Aeshnidae settle on floating vegetation and dip the abdomen well into the water to oviposit in plant tissues, except *Aeshna mixta* which deposits its eggs in wet mud by the bank. *Cordulegaster boltonii*, which has a long ovipositor, stabs the mud repeatedly, laying an egg each time. The Zygoptera, which also have well-developed ovipositors, lay their eggs in incisions they make in the stems of water plants. To do this, the females of some species lower themselves into the water and become completely submerged for several minutes and may even be accompanied by the male in tandem ready for a quick take off. Other species glue their eggs to the undersides of the floating leaves of aquatic plants.

In those damselflies and aeshnas which lay in plant tissues (endophytic oviposition), the eggs are elongate (Fig.3e, page 20). In those which lay in mud (*Cordulegaster boltonii* and *Somatochlora metallica*) or freely in water or on the surface of aquatic plants (exophytic oviposition) the eggs are round or oval and are sometimes enclosed in a gelatinous coat (*Cordulia* and *Libellula*) which may help in attaching them to objects as well as preserving them from desiccation. Eggs may hatch in less than a fortnight or may take up to eight weeks, according to the species.

Metamorphosis is incomplete – there is no pupal stage. The larvae, like the adults, are carnivorous. A full account of the larval (or nymphal) stages of dragonflies is given in the section by Gardner (page 72). The emergence of the adult is accomplished in five stages. First, the mature larva climbs up a rush or reed out of the water and fastens itself to a perch, ensuring that the legs have a secure hold (Fig.2a). The skin splits behind the neck and the insect withdraws the thorax and part of the abdomen to hang head downwards (Fig.2b). This 'rest' position is held for some while to allow the legs to harden, and when this has occurred, the insect gives a vigorous upward heave and attaches itself by its legs to the top of the larval skin (Fig.2c). The abdomen is now withdrawn to hang downwards and the wings are expanded (Fig.2d). The final stage is the lengthening of the abdomen. The 'rest' stage in the Zygoptera is usually upright (Fig.1d).

The colours of the newly-emerged adult are drab compared with the resplendent brilliance of the mature insect. Most species have a dull creaminess which will not disappear until the insect has made many flights and had several meals. The metallic species attain their true colours most quickly. Colour change is gradual throughout life so that the colourings selected for the illustrations in this book are indicative of the insect at its brightest. Just how long an individual may live depends mainly on weather conditions and feeding, and the average life (apart from predators) may be from four to eight weeks, according to the species. A prolonged summer will provide unusually late dates for the species and produce some remarkable colour changes. In the extended summer of 1975 I captured what I took to be a very worn male *Orthetrum cancellatum* (24th August), but on examination it was a female which had assumed the male coloration – the abdomen was completely blue! It is not unusual for other species to do the same. Female *Anax imperator* change from the normal green to blue with age, and female *Sympetrum striolatum* may have a band of red down the back of the abdomen. The beginner will therefore have much to remember in identifying the insects in all their stages.

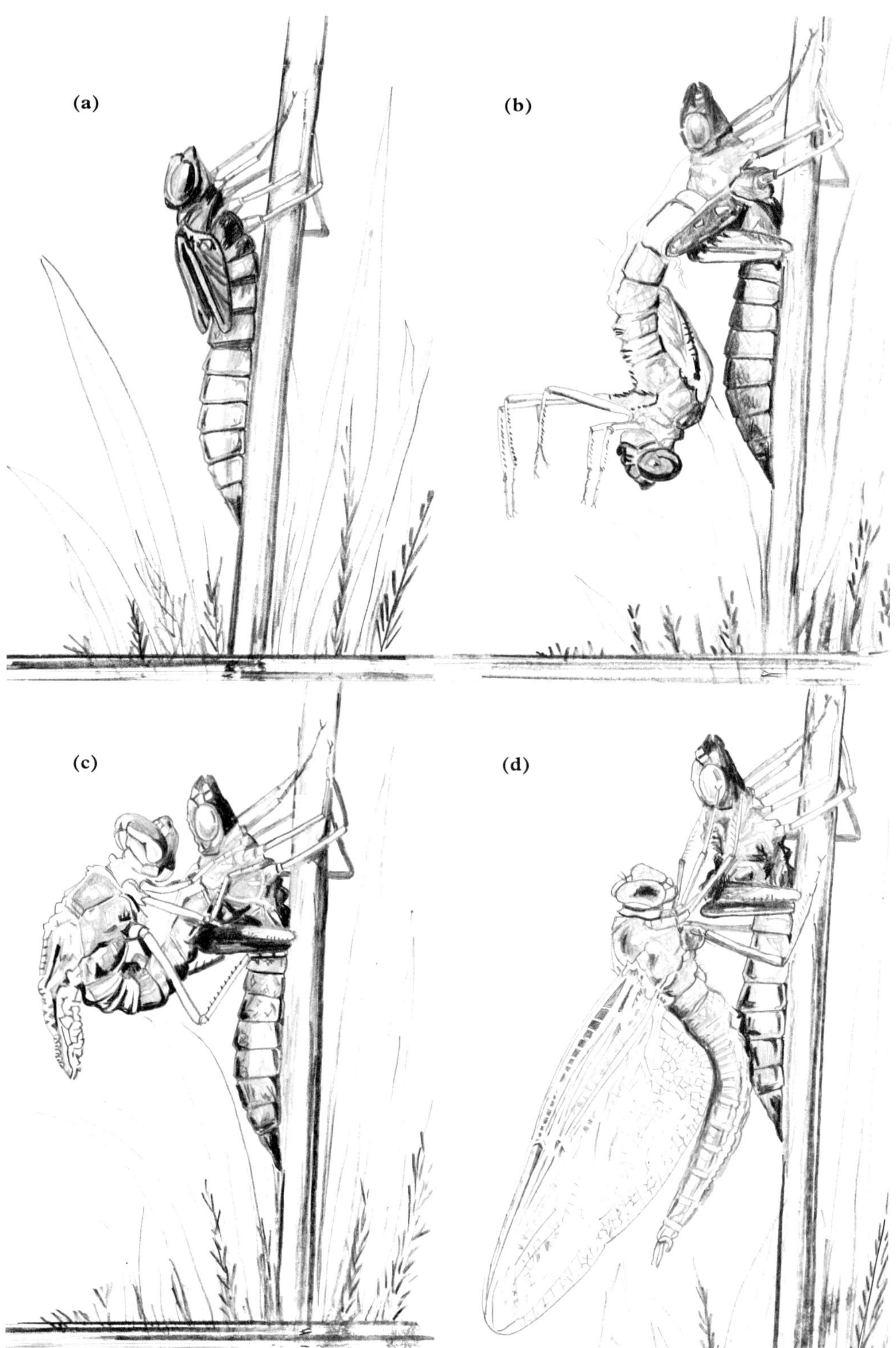

Figure 2. Stages in the emergence of a Hawker Dragonfly (*Aeshna sp.*).

Colourful as dragonflies are, their brilliance fades with their death. Left on the setting board with no treatment, the large aeshnas quickly become discoloured, and in some cases, almost black. This may account for the fact that the dragonflies have less appeal to collectors than Lepidoptera which, on the whole, retain their colours.

Entomologists intending to make a study of dragonflies will find the white nylon butterfly net used by lepidopterists quite suitable for capturing damselflies and most of the large dragonflies; but the darter dragonflies, especially *Leucorrhinia dubia*, are easily startled when approached by anything white, so it is advisable to use a black net to ensure success. This also applies to *Cordulia* and *Somatochlora* which, when hawking near the edge of a pond, are extremely adept at avoiding white nets and are less likely to be aware of a black net swept quickly in the line of their path.

When captured, the insects are best taken home alive. For all damselflies, small glass tubes with cork or plastic stoppers are the most suitable means of transport. Larger glass tubes will accommodate the small and medium dragonflies but on no account should the round glass-topped boxes favoured by lepidopterists be used, since the insects can easily damage or break their wings by continued battering. The largest dragonflies should have their wings folded over their backs and then be placed in paper or transparent envelopes to prevent struggling. They may be sent through the post in this way with cotton wool packing in a cardboard box.

If it is desirable to send live specimens of damselflies through the post, a glass tube with a wad of cotton wool at the bottom to which the insect can cling will ensure its staying alive till arrival. The author sent specimens of the very rare *Coenagrion scitulum* to F. C. Fraser: the females arrived well enough to oviposit, thus enabling the species to be bred and the life history to be studied.

A wad of cotton wool soaked with ethyl acetate appears to be the most efficient method of killing specimens, but the insects should not be left in the vapour as their colours quickly deteriorate. For students unable to obtain ethyl acetate, a similar solution known as 'killing fluid' is obtainable from entomological dealers. Chloroform quickly spoils colours and should never be used. The usual type of setting board may be used, but the grooves should be wide enough to accommodate the legs. If the grooves are too deep (for damselflies) then a small piece of card may be wedged in and a hole punched ready for the pin holding the specimen to be secured.

The abdomen of the larger dragonflies should be eviscerated before setting; this is accomplished by laying the insect on its back and slitting the abdomen with sharply pointed scissors, starting as near the second segment as possible in the males and ending near the eighth segment in the females. The abdomen can then be gently opened and the gut removed with tweezers. Any remaining liquid may be absorbed with small plugs of cotton wool rolled between the finger and thumb. Unless this is done, colours will rapidly deteriorate and patterns may be obliterated.

Several methods of colour preservation have been tried. Keeping specimens in absolute alcohol in glass tubes will ensure that the markings are always retained, though colours may fade after long periods. F. C. Fraser recommended immersion in methylated spirits for four hours and setting immediately afterwards. From results obtained, the best method to date is that developed by D. A. L. Davies, *Entomologist* (1954, **87**: 34–36) and known as freeze-drying. The dragonfly is first starved to allow the gut to be evacuated of its contents. It is then killed and set and rapidly frozen in a deep-freeze at $-10°C$. Then it is placed in a glass desiccator over concentrated sulphuric acid and the air pumped out to a pressure of less than 0.05mm. Hg. The ice crystals evaporate and the moisture is absorbed by the concentrated acid.

Dragonfly recording is not so rewarding as it was earlier in the century. In the thirties, I saw twenty-six species by the Basingstoke canal at Byfleet; twenty-one of these were regularly found each year. My last visits in 1974 produced four species in the same stretch of canal. In 1908 F. W. Campion listed twenty-one species for Epping Forest; now the list is less than half that number. At the present time the entomologist may consider he has found a good locality if the day's activities yield ten species. Even in the New Forest one is hardly likely to encounter more than a dozen species in any one day.

Search for the rarer species entails much travel. It is feared that two species are no longer with us: *Coenagrion scitulum* which has not been recorded since its habitat was spoiled by the sea encroachment of 1953, and *Coenagrion armatum* due to pollution of its habitat.

Dragonflies, like butterflies, make beautiful photographs – perhaps this is the best way of remembering them – and photographs of the best localities are sure to provide pleasing pictures as reminders of pleasant days well spent.

Books for further reading

Corbet, P. S., Longfield, C. & Moore, N. W., 1960. *Dragonflies.* (New Naturalist) Collins, London.

———, 1962, *A Biology of Dragonflies.* Witherby, London.

Fraser, F. C., 1956. Odonata. *Handbk Ident. Br. Insects,* 1 (10). Royal Entomological Society, London.

Longfield, Cynthia, 1949. *The Dragonflies of the British Isles* (Edn 2). (Wayside & Woodland) Warne, London.

Lucas, W. J., 1900. *British Dragonflies (Odonata).* Upcott Gill, London.

———, 1930. *The Aquatic (Naiad) Stage of the British Dragonflies.* Ray Society, London.

All the above are at present out of print.

EXTERNAL FEATURES AND CLASSIFICATION

The *head* (Fig.3) is transversely wide, broader than the thorax and has large globular *compound eyes* (*E*) on each side; three simple eyes or *ocelli* (*Oce*) usually in the form of a triangle with the anterior ocellus larger than the two laterals lie on the flattened *vertex* (*V*) or dorsal part of the head; the *antennae* (*Ant*) are short and thread-like with seven tapering joints of which the two basal segments are stouter than the rest and are situated laterally and in front of the vertex; the mouth is on the lower side and consists of the *labium* (*Lbm*) or lower lip and the *labrum* (*Lbr*) or upper lip, which enclose the mandibles and the palps; above the labrum is the epistome or clypeus which is divided transversely into *anteclypeus* (*Acl*) and *postclypeus* (*Pcl*); above this is the *frons* (*Fr*) or forehead; behind the eyes is the *occiput* (*Occ*) which varies considerably in shape in the two suborders. The thorax consists of a separate narrow collar-like *prothorax* (*Pr*) bearing the forelegs and joined by a membrane to the large *synthorax* (*Sth*) in which the meso- and metathorax are fused. The synthorax is obliquely constructed by the anterior pleurites (or side plates) expanding forwards and upwards to meet in a keel, the *middorsal carina* (*mdc*) forming a false 'dorsum' or back and carrying the wings rearwards; at the same time the middle and hind pairs of legs have been carried forwards and brought close together. The dorsum of the synthorax may be marked with brightly coloured stripes, an *antehumeral stripe* (*Ast*) about midway between the middorsal carina and the *humeral suture* (*Hs*) and a *humeral stripe* (*Hst*) close to the anterior margin of the humeral suture; two lateral sutures may be present distal to the humeral suture dividing the sides of the synthorax into three panels which may also have coloured stripes.

The *legs* which are used for perching, climbing and for catching flying insects consist of two small basal joints the coxa and trochanter, two longer segments *femur* (*Fe*) and *tibia* (*Ti*) and three terminal segments forming the foot or *tarsus* (*Ta*) ending in a pair of bifid claws. The length and thickness of the spines on the leg joints vary considerably in the different genera, the spines on the femora and tibiae becoming quite long in some species and forming a basket for catching prey when the legs are clasped together.

The two pairs of elongate wings (Fig.4) are usually hyaline but may be in part or wholly coloured. The wing membrane is strengthened by a series of longitudinal veins, stoutest in the basal half and tapering towards the apex and linked by numerous cross-veins which form a fine supporting network. The arrangement of the principal veins and crossveins is characteristic for all the main genera and many of the species, providing most useful characters for the identification of specimens which have lost their natural colours.

The principal longitudinal veins are as follows: the *Costa* (*C*) which forms the anterior margin of the wing from base to apex; the *Subcosta* (*Sc*) extending from the base to below the notch or *Nodus* (*N*) about the middle of the costa; the *Radius* extending from wing base where it is united to the *Medius* ($R+M$) as far as the apex near which it is united to the costa by a chitinised coloured cell the *Pterostigma* (*Pt*) whose proximal corner is linked posteriorly to *R2* by a strong oblique crossvein the *Brace* (*Br*); the medius (*MA*) is basally fused with the radius but soon diverges turning down and posteriorly to form the *Arculus* (*Arc*) before running outwards as the lower *sector of the arculus* (*Sa*); the upper sector of the arculus or *Radial sector* (*Rs*) gives off three or four branches *R2*, *R3*, *R4* and *R5*, the last two being fused into a single vein; in the Anisoptera *Rs* runs outward to the subnodus and turns posteriorly as an *oblique vein* (*o*) which continues outwards as *IR3* and basad to meet *Rs* as a brace vein the *bridge* (*B*); next the *Cubitus* ($Cu+A$) runs out from the base to the arculus and continues curving into the hind margin; last is the *Anal vein* (*A1*) which runs parallel to the cubitus from base to the posterior margin. Between *MA* and *Cu2* near the base of the wing lies the *triangle* (*t*) or discoidal cell (of Anisoptera) or *quadrilateral* (*q*) (in Zygoptera); above *t* lies the

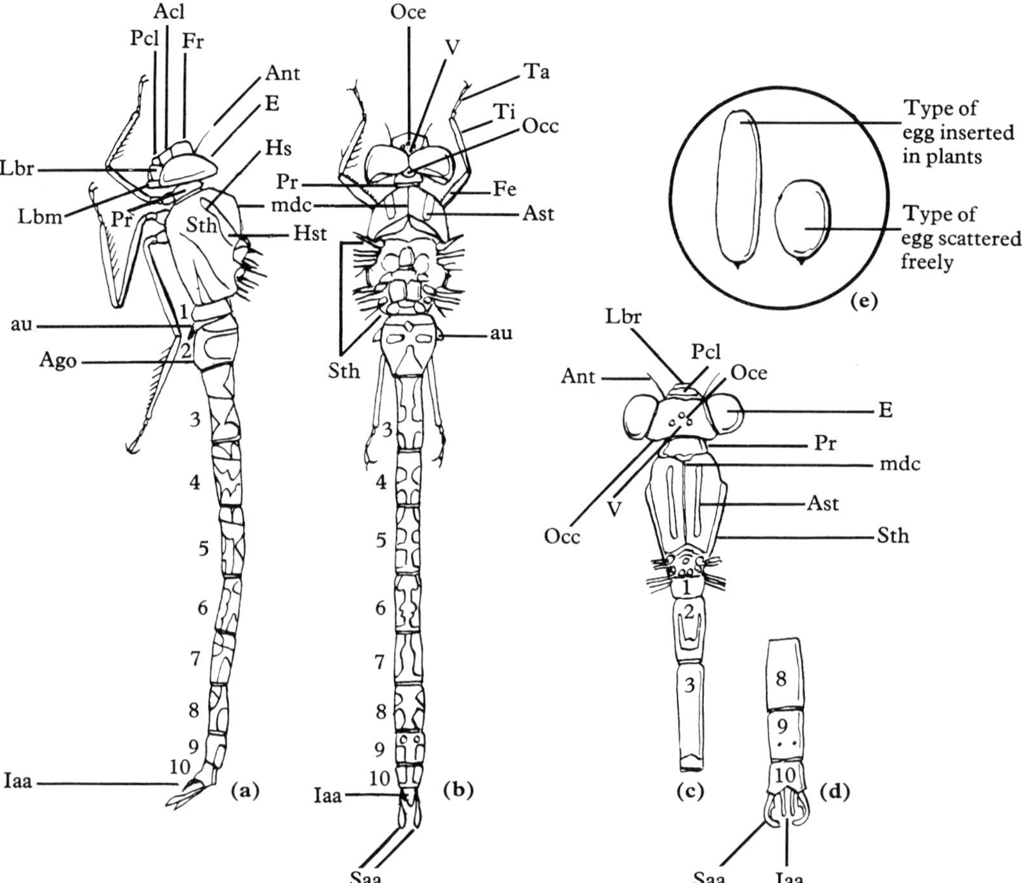

Figure 3. External features of male dragonflies. **(a)** and **(b)** a hawker (*Aeshna*) in left side and dorsal views; damselflies **(c)** *Coenagrion* and **(d)** *Lestes* in dorsal view. *Acl*, anteclypeus; *Ago*, accessary genital opening; *Ant*, antennae; *Ast*, antehumeral stripe; *au*, auricle; *E*, compound eye; *Fe*, femur; *Fr*, frons; *Hs*, humeral suture; *Hst*, humeral stripe; *Iaa*, inferior anal appendage; *Lbm*, labium; *Lbr*, labrum; *mdc*, middorsal carina; *Occ*, occiput; *Oce*, ocellus; *Pcl*, postclypeus; *Pr*, prothorax; *Saa*, superior anal appendages; *Sth*, synthorax (fused meso- and metathorax); *Ta*, tarsus; *Ti*, tibia; *V*, vertex. The abdominal segments are numbered 1–10. **(e)** (inset) types of egg.

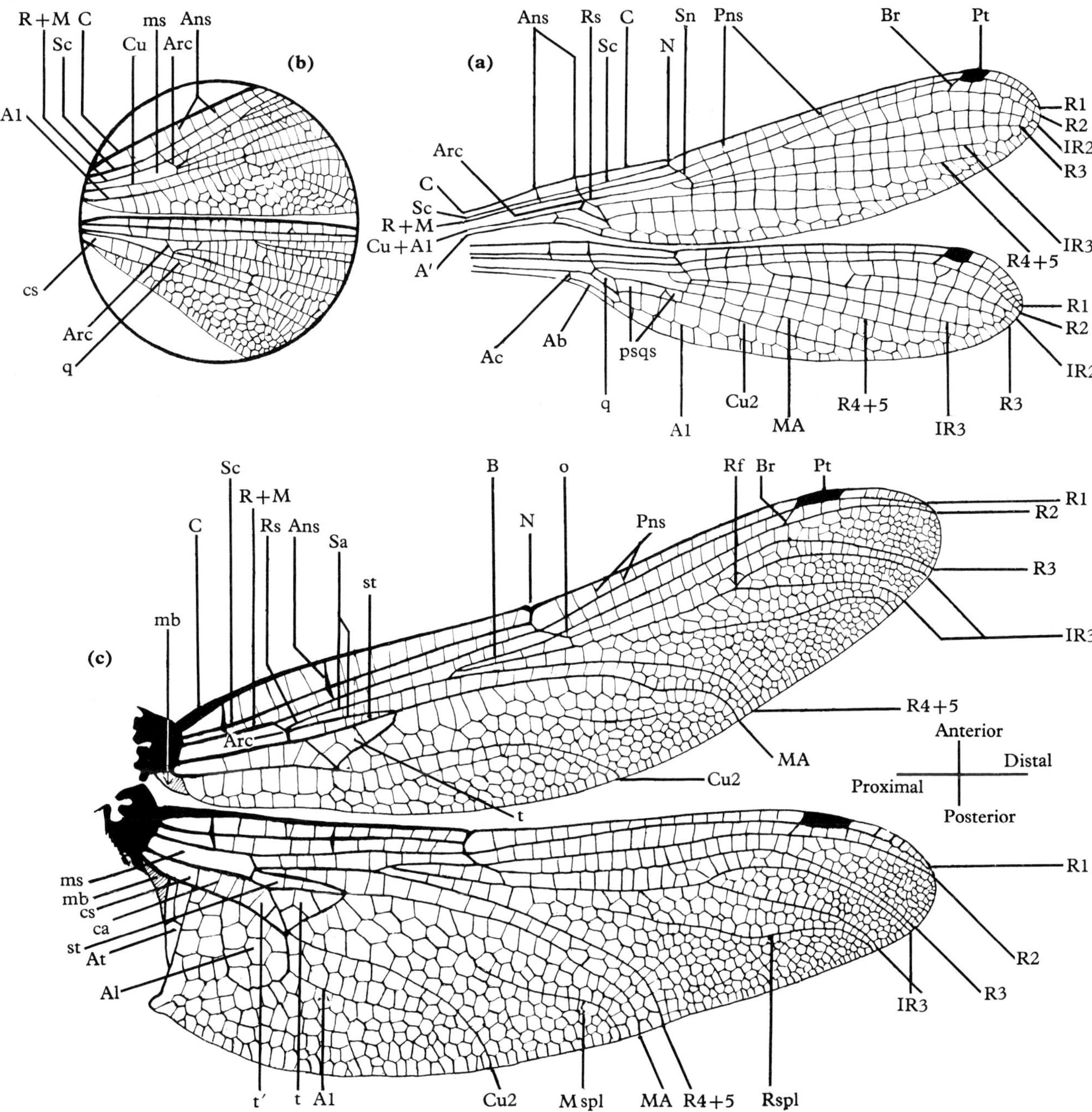

Figure 4. (a) Zygopterous wings, large red damselfly, *Pyrrhosoma nymphula*. **(b)** (Inset) base of wings of the banded demoiselle, *Agrion splendens* (Zygoptera). **(c)** Anisopterous wings of the southern hawker, *Aeshna cyanea*. *Ab*, anal bridge; *Ac*, anal crossing; *Al*, anal loop (hindwing, Anisoptera); *Ans*, antenodals, including the two thickened primary antenodals; *Arc*, Arculus; *At*, anal triangle; *A1*, first anal vein; *A′*, second anal; *B*, bridge; *Br*, Brace; *C*, Costa; *ca*, cubitoanal crossveins; *Cu*, Cubitus; *Cu+A1*, cubitoanal; *Cu2*, second cubital; *cs*, cubital space; *MA*, medius or anterior median vein; *mb*, membranule; *ms*, median space; *Mspl*, median supplement; *N*, Nodus; *o*, oblique vein; *Pns*, postnodals; *psqs*, postquadrilateral cells; *Pt*, Pterostigma; *q*, discoidal or quadrilateral (in Zygoptera); *R1*, Radius; *R2*, *R3*, *R4+5*, branches of radius; *R+M*, Radius and Medius fused at base of wing; *Rf*, radial fork; *Rs*, Radial sector; *Rspl*, radial supplement; *IR2*, *IR3*, intercalated branches of radius; *Sa*, sectors of arculus; *Sc*, subcostal; *Sn*, subnodus; *st*, supratriangle; *t*, discoidal cell or triangle (in Anisoptera); *t′*, subtriangle (in Anisoptera).

supratriangle (*st*) and there may be a *subtriangle* (*t'*) on the inner side of *t* in the Anisoptera; in the Anisoptera the triangle may be free or crossed by one or more veinlets and in the Zygoptera the quadrilateral is either a long narrow rectangle crossed by numerous veinlets (Agriidae) or trapezoidal and always uncrossed (Lestidae, Platycnemididae and Coenagriidae).

Between the distal side of the quadrilateral and the subnodus in Zygoptera lies a short series of *postquadrilateral cells* (*psqs*) which are of value in the classification of genera. In the *costal space* between the costa and radius there is usually a series of crossveins of which those proximal to the nodus are called *antenodals* (*Ans*) and those distal the *postnodals* (*Pns*); two of the series of antenodals are thickened and are known as the *primary antenodals* and these alone form the antenodal series in the zygopterous families Lestidae, Platycnemididae and Coenagriidae. The *cubital space* (*cs*) between the cubital and anal veins encloses several crossveins the *cubitoanals* (*ca*) (Anisoptera and Agriidae) and in the remaining Zygoptera there is only one crossvein the *anal crossing* (*Ac*). Anisopterous wings also have at the base a short pigmented *membranule* (*mb*) and in the hindwings of males of some genera an *anal triangle* (*At*) and often a well-marked cluster of cells – the *anal loop* (*Al*); intercalary veins may also occur posterior to *IR3* forming the *radial supplement* (*Rspl*) as well as to *MA* forming the *medial supplement* (*Mspl*); in some aeshnas *IR3* divides before the pterostigma producing the *radial fork* (*Rf*).

The *abdomen* (Fig.3) is long and narrow in most species but shorter and broad in the libellulids and always has ten segments the last bearing one or more pairs of appendages. Each segment consists of a convex dorsal surface (*tergite*) which is continued ventrally to meet the narrow flat underside (*sternite*). In many anisopterous males, segment two bears a pair of lateral *auricles* (*au*) which seem to serve to guide the female to the accessory genitalia which are situated on the underside of this segment and the base of the third. The male accessory genitalia lie in a deep pit (*Ago*) which accommodates a three-segmented penis, its hood-like sheath and two pairs of hooks (*hamules*) which help to link the partners in copulation. The actual opening of the sperm ducts is on the underside of the ninth segment.

The female abdomen is generally more cylindrical than that of the male and the genitalia are situated in the sternites of segments eight and nine. Zygopterans and aeshnas which lay their eggs in the tissues of aquatic plants have a strong ovipositor protected with lateral valves. *Cordulegaster* which lays in mud has a long ovipositor but the rest of the dragonflies have no ovipositor and their eggs are extruded into water.

Anal appendages. In anisopteran males the abdomen terminates in two *superior anal appendages* (*Saa*) and one *inferior anal appendage* (*Iaa*) which are situated above the anus whereas zygopteran males have a pair of inferior as well as a pair of superior anal appendages and the former are situated below the anus. These anal appendages vary in size and shape and provide useful characters for the diagnosis of species. The male uses these appendages for seizing the female by the head (Anisoptera) or the prothorax (Zygoptera) when making in tandem flight and when copulating. Females have only a single pair of anal appendages which may be as long as or longer than segment ten (some Anisoptera) or rudimentary as in many damselflies.

CLASSIFICATION

The keys following are partly based on Fraser (1956).

BRITISH ODONATA Key to suborders

Fore- and hindwing similar in shape, folded back vertically over the abdomen when in repose (except *Lestes* which rests with wings half open). Radius straight, discoidal cell a simple quadrilateral, no oblique vein or bridge (except *Lestes*). Eyes widely separated, projecting at sides of head. Males with two superior and two inferior anal appendages, females with two superior anal appendages and ovipositor complete...**ZYGOPTERA**

Fore- and hindwing differing in shape, the hindwing considerably broader at the base. Wings held horizontally or depressed in repose. Radius curved, oblique vein and bridge present, discoidal cell comprising a triangle and supratriangle with sometimes a subtriangle. Eyes meeting or almost so (except *Gomphus*). Males with two superior and one inferior anal appendages; females with no inferior anal appendage and ovipositor variable...........**ANISOPTERA** (p.24)

ZYGOPTERA Key to families

1 Numerous antenodals (Fig.4b, p.21), wings heavily tinted; no pterostigma in male, false pterostigma in female; body metallic blue or green...............AGRIIDAE (Pl.13, p.57)

— Only 2 antenodals, wings clear, pterostigmata present in both sexes..........................2

2(1) Body metallic green; in the mature male segments 1–2 and 9–10 of abdomen with a bluish white pruinescence; superior anal appendages caliper-like and longer than segment 10...LESTIDAE (Pl.14, p.59)

— Body not metallic green; superior anal appendages not prominent..........................3

3(2) Discoidal cell almost rectangular, only 2 postquadrilateral cells (*psqs*) before subnodus; hind tibiae of male flattened and feather-like......PLATYCNEMIDIDAE (Pl.15, p.61)

— Discoidal cell irregular, sharp pointed distally, 3 or 4 *psqs* before subnodus; legs normal... ....COENAGRIIDAE (Pls.15–20, pp.61–71)

AGRIIDAE Only one genus and two species..........................*Agrion* (Pl.13, p.57)

LESTIDAE Only one genus and two species.............................*Lestes* (Pl.14, p.59)

PLATYCNEMIDIDAE Only one species...............*Platycnemis pennipes* (Pl.15, p.61)

COENAGRIIDAE Key to genera

1 Head bronzy-black above without pale postocular spots, eyes (in life) red; wings with 3–5 *psqs*: females without ventral apical spine on abdominal segment 8.......................2

— Head with pale postocular spots, eyes blue or green; wings with 3 *psqs*: females with or without a ventral apical spine on abdominal segment 8....................................4

2(1) Abdomen dull black pruinosed grey, segments 9–10 blue in male, greenish and with shallow 'V' shaped notch dorsally on 10 in female, superior anal appendages in male as long as segment 10; wings with 4–5 *psqs*, *Ac* shorter than basal portion of *Ab*, two rows of cells between costa and radius beyond *Pt* as well as between sectors at apex of hindwing, 20 or more cells between *A1* and hind margin of wing............*Erythromma* (Pl.15, p.61)

— Thorax and abdomen black and orange or largely red; only one row of cells between costa and radius beyond *Pt*..3

3(2) Larger species (overall length 36mm), frons evenly rounded; thorax with prominent yellow or red antehumeral stripes, legs black; abdomen red and black, anal appendages in male subequal and as long as segment 10; in female segment 10 deeply cleft dorsally; forewing with 3–4 *psqs*, hindwing with 3 *psqs*, *Pt* brown longer than subtending cell, about 20 cells between *A1* and hind margin of wing Fig.4a....... *Pyrrhosoma* (Pl.16, p.63)

— Smaller species (overall length 31mm), frons flattened above with transverse crest; thorax bronzy-black with at most a vestigial antehumeral stripe, legs red; abdomen red or with segments 4–10 bronzy; wings with 3 *psqs*, *Pt* as long as subtending cell, *Ac* longer than basal portion of *Ab*, 15 cells or less between *A1* and hind margin of wing.............. .... *Ceriagrion* (Pl.16, p.63)

4(1) *Pt* of forewing bicolored black basally whitish apically; abdomen bronzy-black with segments 8 or 9 blue, and apex of 10 produced dorsally into turretlike tubercle in male; females polychromatic with small ventral apical spine on segment 8........................ .... *Ischnura* (Pl.17, p.65)

— *Pt* black in both wings; abdomen largely blue with black markings; females duller, greyish or bluish green, with or without ventral apical spine on segment 8.....................5

5(4) Generally two rows of cells between costa and radius distal to *Pt* in hindwing; apical black mark on segment 2 in male a dot or small vase-shaped mark without lateral extensions basad; females with a strong ventral apical spine on segment 8....................... .... *Enallagma* (Pl.18, p.67)

— Only a single row of cells between costa and radius distal to *Pt*, apical black mark on segment 2 in males produced laterally basad; females without a ventral apical spine on segment 8... *Coenagrion* (Pls.18–20, pp.67–71)

ANISOPTERA Key to families

1 Two primary antenodals very obvious (Fig.4c, p.21); antenodals in costal and subcostal spaces generally not aligned...2

— No conspicuous antenodals; those in costal and subcostal spaces usually in alignment....4

2(1) Eyes widely separated; ocelli arranged transversely...........GOMPHIDAE (Pl.5, p.41)

— Eyes touching or nearly so; ocelli arranged in a triangle......................................3

3(2) Eyes just meeting at a point; triangles of similar shape in fore- and hindwing. Female with a long ovipositor projecting well beyond segment 10 and short anal appendages...... .... CORDULEGASTERIDAE (Pl.4, p.39)

— Eyes touching for some distance; triangles dissimilar in fore- and hindwing. Female with rather long anal appendages and ovipositor similar to the zygopteran type............ .... AESHNIDAE (Pls.1–3,5, pp.33–37,41)

4(1) Base of hindwing angular in male; auricles present on segment 2 of abdomen in male; body metallic, dark or brilliant green or copper-bronze... ....CORDULIIDAE (Pls.8–9, pp.47–49)

— Base of hindwing rounded in both sexes; auricles absent on segment 2 of male. Body nonmetallic .... LIBELLULIDAE (Pls.6–7,10–12, pp.43–45,51–55)

GOMPHIDAE Only one species.......................... *Gomphus vulgatissimus* (Pl.5, p.41)

CORDULEGASTERIDAE Only one species........ *Cordulegaster boltonii* (Pl.4, p.39)

AESHNIDAE Key to genera

1 Base of hindwing rounded in both sexes, anal triangle absent, *Rs* arising close to *R1* at *Arc*, *Rspl* and *Mspl* 5–7 cell rows below *IR3* and *MA* respectively; abdomen in male with auricles, unspotted with black mid-dorsal pattern on a blue or green ground.............. .... *Anax* (Pl.4, p.39)

— Base of hindwing of male angular and anal triangle present, *Rs* arising near middle of *Arc*, *Rspl* and *Mspl* 1–4 cell rows below *IR3* and *MA* respectively; abdomen spotted and with auricles in male 2

2 Pterostigma (*Pt*) very narrow, usually only two cubitoanal veins, *IR3* symmetrically forked proximal to *Pt*; *Rspl* and *Mspl* straight each one cell row below *IR3* and *MA* respectively; thorax densely hairy .... *Brachytron* (Pl.5, p.41)

— Pterostigma long, moderately wide, three or more cubitoanal veins, *IR3* asymmetrically forked proximal to *Pt*, *Rspl* and *Mspl* curved 3–4 cell rows below *IR3* and *MA* respectively; thorax moderately hairy .... *Aeshna* (Pls.1–3, pp.33–37)

CORDULIIDAE Key to genera

1 Wings amber-tinted at base; hindwing with a single cubitoanal vein, base of discoidal cell slightly basal to arculus and discoidal cell without crossvein; thorax densely hairy, body bronzy or coppery metallic; inferior anal appendage in male deeply cleft with strong lateral tooth .... *Cordulia* (Pl.8, p.47)

— Wings clear at base; hindwing with two cubitoanal veins 2

2 Discoidal cell usually without crossvein in both wings; subtriangle of forewing a single cell; base of discoidal cell in hindwing distal to level of arculus; body metallic green with dorsal row of chrome yellow spots; in male superior anal appendages with strong ventral subbasal spine, inferior appendage deeply cleft without lateral teeth................ .... *Oxygastra* (Pl.8, p.47)

— Discoidal cell of both wings traversed by crossvein; subtriangle of forewing usually three-celled; base of discoidal cell of hindwing in line with arculus; body entirely metallic green; in male superior anal appendages without ventral spine, inferior appendage entire tapering to a point .... *Somatochlora* (Pl.9, p.49)

LIBELLULIDAE Key to genera

1 The most distal antenodal complete extending to radius; *MA* and *Cu2* in forewing diverging distally at wing margin; base of wings with triangular blackish brown marking (except in *Orthetrum*)................ 2

— The most distal antenodal incomplete and very oblique extending only to subcosta; arculus situated between 1st and 2nd antenodals; *MA* and *Cu2* in forewing converging distally at wing margin; base of wings clear .... *Sympetrum* (Pls.10–12, pp.51–55)

2(1) Not more than 9 (usually 8) antenodals in forewing; arculus situated between 1st and 2nd antenodals; pterostigma short and broad; *R3* not sinuous; abdomen parallel sided with mid-dorsal spots .... *Leucorrhinia* (Pl.10, p.51)

— More than 10 antenodals in forewing; pterostigma elongate and narrow; *R3* sinuous and undulated; abdomen not parallel sided and unspotted................ 3

3(2) Arculus is proximal to 2nd antenodal its sectors separate at origin; base of hindwing with conspicuous blackish brown marks; one or more supplementary crossveins in bridge, triangle with crossvein in both wings................ *Libellula* (Pl.7, p.45)

— Arculus is level with 2nd antenodal its sectors fused in short stem at origin; base of hindwing clear; no supplementary crossveins in the bridge; triangle with one crossvein in forewing free in hindwing .... *Orthetrum* (Pl.6, p.43)

CHECK LIST

ORDER ODONATA

Suborder ZYGOPTERA

Family PLATYCNEMIDIDAE

Platycnemis Burmeister, 1839

pennipes (Pallas, 1771), White-legged damselfly

Family COENAGRIIDAE

Ceriagrion Selys, 1876

tenellum (de Villers, 1789), Small red damselfly

Erythromma Charpentier, 1840

najas (Hansemann, 1823), Red-eyed damselfly

Coenagrion Kirby, 1890

armatum (Charpentier, 1840), Norfolk coenagrion, Norfolk damselfly

hastulatum (Charpentier, 1825), Northern coenagrion, Northern damselfly

mercuriale (Charpentier, 1840), Southern coenagrion, Southern damselfly

puella (Linnaeus, 1758), Common coenagrion, Azure damselfly

pulchellum (van der Linden, 1825), Variable coenagrion, Variable damselfly

scitulum (Rambur, 1842), Dainty coenagrion, Dainty damselfly

Enallagma Charpentier, 1840

cyathigerum (Charpentier, 1840), Common blue damselfly, Common damselfly

Pyrrhosoma Charpentier, 1840

nymphula (Sulzer, 1776), Large red damselfly

Ischnura Charpentier, 1840

elegans (van der Linden, 1820), Common ischnura, Blue-tailed damselfly

pumilio (Charpentier, 1825), Scarce ischnura, Scarce blue-tailed damselfly

Family LESTIDAE

Lestes Leach, 1815

dryas Kirby, 1890, Scarce green lestes, Scarce emerald damselfly

sponsa (Hansemann, 1823), Green lestes, Emerald damselfly

Family AGRIIDAE

Agrion Fabricius, 1775

splendens (Harris, 1776), Banded agrion, Banded demoiselle

virgo (Linnaeus, 1758), Demoiselle agrion, Beautiful demoiselle

Suborder ANISOPTERA

Family GOMPHIDAE

Gomphus Leach, 1815

vulgatissimus (Linnaeus, 1758), Club-tailed dragonfly

Family AESHNIDAE

Brachytron Selys, 1850

pratense (Müller, 1764), Hairy dragonfly

Aeshna Fabricius, 1775

caerulea (Ström, 1783), Blue aeshna, Azure hawker

cyanea (Müller, 1764), Southern aeshna, Southern hawker

grandis (Linnaeus, 1758), Brown aeshna, Brown hawker

isosceles (Müller, 1767), Norfolk aeshna, Norfolk hawker

juncea (Linnaeus, 1758), Common aeshna, Common hawker

mixta Latreille, 1804, Scarce aeshna, Migrant hawker

Anax Leach, 1815

imperator Leach, 1815, Emperor dragonfly

Family CORDULEGASTERIDAE

Cordulegaster Leach, 1815

boltonii (Donovan, 1807), Golden-ringed dragonfly

Family CORDULIIDAE

Cordulia Leach, 1815

aenea (Linnaeus, 1758), Downy emerald

Somatochlora Selys, 1871

arctica (Zetterstedt, 1840), Northern emerald

metallica (van der Linden, 1825), Brilliant emerald

Oxygastra Selys, 1870

curtisii (Dale, 1834), Orange-spotted emerald

Family LIBELLULIDAE

Orthetrum Newman, 1833

cancellatum (Linnaeus, 1758), Black-lined orthetrum, Black-tailed skimmer

coerulescens (Fabricius, 1798), Keeled orthetrum, Keeled skimmer

Libellula Linnaeus, 1758

depressa Linnaeus, 1758, Broad-bodied libellula, Broad-bodied chaser

fulva Müller, 1764, Scarce libellula, Scarce chaser

quadrimaculata Linnaeus, 1758, Four-spotted libellula, Four-spotted chaser

Sympetrum Newman, 1833

flaveolum (Linnaeus, 1758), Yellow-winged sympetrum, Yellow-winged darter

fonscolombei (Selys, 1840), Red-veined sympetrum, Red-veined darter

nigrescens Lucas, 1911, Highland darter

sanguineum (Müller, 1764), Ruddy sympetrum, Ruddy darter

scoticum (Donovan, 1811), Black sympetrum, Black darter

striolatum (Charpentier, 1840), Common sympetrum, Common darter

vulgatum (Linnaeus, 1758), Vagrant sympetrum, Vagrant darter

Leucorrhinia Brittinger, 1850

dubia (van der Linden, 1825), White-faced dragonfly, White-faced darter

Note. The check list gives first the scientific names and then the Longfield popular name. A second vernacular name is given by the author in a number of cases for the benefit of those who wish to use wholly English names. It is as well to remember that the Latin names are the only ones recognised internationally and should always be used by the serious student.

		A	M	J	J	A	S	O	N
Aeshna	*caerulea*	......	....	::□■■	■■□□	::::......	....	....	......
	cyanea	......	....	...::□□	□□■■	■■■■	■■■■	□□::::	......
	grandis	......	....	...::::::	□□■■	■■■■	■■□□	□□::::	......
	isosceles	......	.........::	□■■■	□::......	....	....	....	......
	juncea	......	....	::::□□	□■■■	■■■■	□□::::	::::......	......
	mixta	......	....	....	......::□	□□■■	■■■■	□□□::	......
Agrion	*splendens*	......	...::::□	□□■■	■■■■	■□□□	□□□::	::::......	......
	virgo	...::	□□□□	■■■■	■■■□	□::::...	....	....	......
Anax	*imperator*	......	......::□	□□■■	■■■■	■□□□	::::......	....	......
Brachytron	*pratense*	...::	□□■■	■■■□	::::::...	....	....	....	......
Ceriagrion	*tenellum*	......	.........::	::□□■	■■■■	■■□□	::::::::	::.........	......
Coenagrion	*armatum*	......	......□■	■□......	....	....	....	....	......
	hastulatum	......	....	...::□□	■■■■	□::......	....	....	......
	mercuriale	......	...::□□	□□■■	■■■■	□::......	....	....	......
	puella	......	::□□■	■■■■	■■■■	■□□::	::::......	....	......
	pulchellum	......	...::□□	■■■■	■■■■	□::......	....	....	......
	scitulum	......	....	......□■	■■■□	::.........	....	....	......
Cordulegaster	*boltonii*	::::	::::::□	□■■■	■■■■	■□□□	::::::::	::.........	......
Cordulia	*aenea*	......	...::□■	■■■■	■■□□	::::::::	::::......	....	......
Enallagma	*cyathigerum*	...::	::□□■	■■■■	■■■■	■■■■	□□□::	::::......	......
Erythromma	*najas*	......	::□□■	■■■■	■■■■	■□□□	::::::::	::.........	......
Gomphus	*vulgatissimus*	......	...::::■	■■■□	::::::::	....	....	....	......

Figure 5

The flight period given is the most satisfactory time for the species to be observed from the teneral to fully adult stages.

In the Flight Tables the black squares refer to the best time to observe the species: the open squares earlier and later times when the species may be teneral or very adult: the dotted squares show exceptional dates due to a forward spring or a prolonged summer.

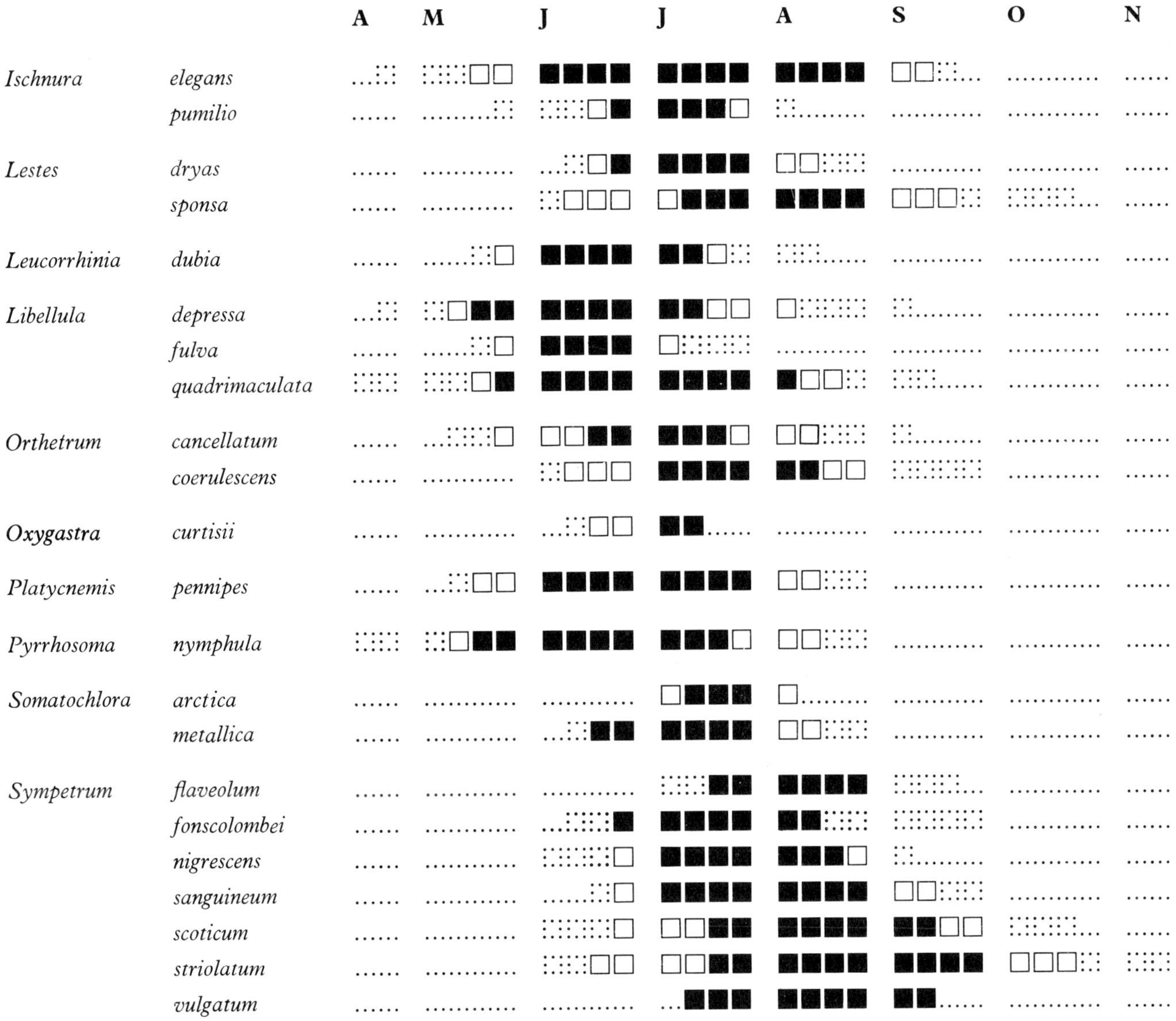

		A	M	J	J	A	S	O	N
Ischnura	*elegans*	...⁞	⁞⁞□□	■■■■	■■■■	■■■■	□□⁞...	....	......
	pumilio	......	.........⁞	⁞⁞□■	■■■□	⁞........	....	....	......
Lestes	*dryas*	......	....	...⁞□■	■■■■	□□⁞⁞	....	....	......
	sponsa	......	....	⁞□□□	□■■■	■■■■	□□□⁞	⁞⁞⁞...	......
Leucorrhinia	*dubia*	......	......⁞□	■■■■	■■□⁞	⁞⁞......	....	....	......
Libellula	*depressa*	...⁞	⁞□■■	■■■■	■■□□	□⁞⁞⁞	⁞.........	....	......
	fulva	......	......⁞□	■■■■	□⁞⁞⁞	....	....	....	......
	quadrimaculata	⁞⁞⁞	⁞⁞□■	■■■■	■■■■	■□□⁞	⁞⁞......	....	......
Orthetrum	*cancellatum*	......	...⁞⁞□	□□■■	■■■□	□□⁞⁞	⁞.........	....	......
	coerulescens	......	....	⁞□□□	■■■■	■■□□	⁞⁞⁞⁞	....	......
Oxygastra	*curtisii*	......	....	...⁞□□	■■......	....	....	....	......
Platycnemis	*pennipes*	......	...⁞□□	■■■■	■■■■	□□⁞⁞	....	....	......
Pyrrhosoma	*nymphula*	⁞⁞⁞	⁞□■■	■■■■	■■■□	□□⁞⁞	....	....	......
Somatochlora	*arctica*	......	....	....	□■■■	□.........	....	....	......
	metallica	......	....	...⁞■■	■■■■	□□⁞⁞	....	....	......
Sympetrum	*flaveolum*	......	....	....	⁞⁞■■	■■■■	⁞⁞⁞...	....	......
	fonscolombei	......	....	...⁞⁞■	■■■■	■■⁞⁞	⁞⁞⁞⁞	....	......
	nigrescens	......	....	⁞⁞⁞□	■■■■	■■■□	⁞.........	....	......
	sanguineum	......	....	......⁞□	■■■■	■■■■	□□⁞⁞	....	......
	scoticum	......	....	⁞⁞⁞□	□□■■	■■■■	■■□□	⁞⁞⁞...	......
	striolatum	......	....	⁞⁞□□	□□■■	■■■■	■■■■	□□□⁞	⁞⁞⁞
	vulgatum	......	....	....	...■■■	■■■■	■■......	....	......

THE PLATES

Notes on Measurement

Measurements are given in millimetres. Those for the abdomen include the anal appendages. Where sexes differ considerably measurements are given for both. Overall length is measured from the frons to the tip of the abdomen and is the average for a species. Wingspan is measured with the front edge of the hind wings at right angles to the body and is also an average measurement.

Flight Period

The months cover the normal flight period for each species. However, in the case of a widespread species it is likely to occur later in the north of its range than in the south. Similarly, seasonal differences may affect the emergence of the imagines and advance or retard their appearance on the wing. For more detailed information about the best time within this flight period to study a species, refer to the chart (Fig.5) on pages 28–29.

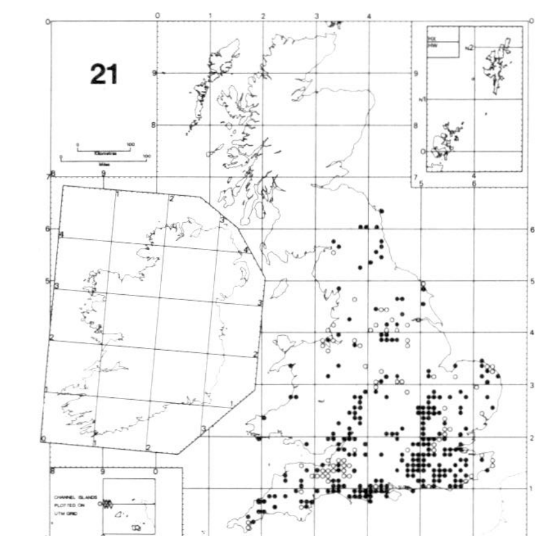

Aeshna cyanea

Aeshna juncea

Aeshna cyanea (Müller, 1764)

The Southern Aeshna, The Southern Hawker

1 ♂ Thorax has a pair of broad apple-green antehumeral stripes.
Spots on segments 1–7 are green.
Spots on segment 8 are blue.
Anal triangle has 3–6 cells (usually 3).

2 ♂ Blue bands on segments 9–10.

3 ♀ Note the conspicuous yellow triangle on segment 2 as in the male.

4 ♀ Note complete bands on segments 9–10.

Size. Wingspan 100mm; hindwing length 43–50mm. Average overall length 70mm; abdomen length ♂51–60mm, ♀52–58mm.

Flight period. Mid-June to mid-October.

Flight and habitat. The most inquisitive of all the aeshnas, approaching within a yard or two of the observer, usually near the ground but sometimes from above. A lover of country lanes and hedgerows and shady spots in woods. Frequently seen around small ponds in gardens. Flies till dusk and sometimes on moonlit nights in suitable weather. Territorial in behaviour.

Status and distribution (Map 21, also page 103).
Very common in the southern counties; less common in the Midlands and scarce farther north.

Aeshna juncea (Linnaeus, 1758)

The Common Aeshna, The Common Hawker

5 ♂ The eyes are confluent for a distance longer than the length of the occipital triangle.
The fork of *IR3* is well defined and the membranule is white at the base and apically grey.
Spots on all segments are blue.
No conspicuous yellow triangle on segment 2.

6 ♂ Spots on segments 9–10 in place of bands on *A.cyanea*.

7 ♀ No conspicuous yellow triangle on segment 2.

8 ♀ Spots on segments 9–10 in place of bands on *A.cyanea*.
Scottish examples may have a much darker abdomen and in some, the spots may be blue, leading to confusion with *A.caerulea* (Pl.3, figs.4,5).

Size. Wingspan 95mm; hindwing length 40–47mm. Average overall length 74mm; abdomen length ♂53–58mm, ♀50–54mm.

Flight period. Mid-June to mid-September.

Flight and habitat. Flies high over well-reeded ponds in circles while hawking, or on a definite beat along a stream or dyke. Has a preference for coniferous woodland in England. In Scotland settles among heather or bracken in dull weather but is active as soon as sunshine appears when it will hawk well above the observer.

Status and distribution (Map 24, also page 104).
The most widely distributed of all the aeshnas, being found from the southern counties of England to the most northerly counties of Scotland, where it has a strong foothold.

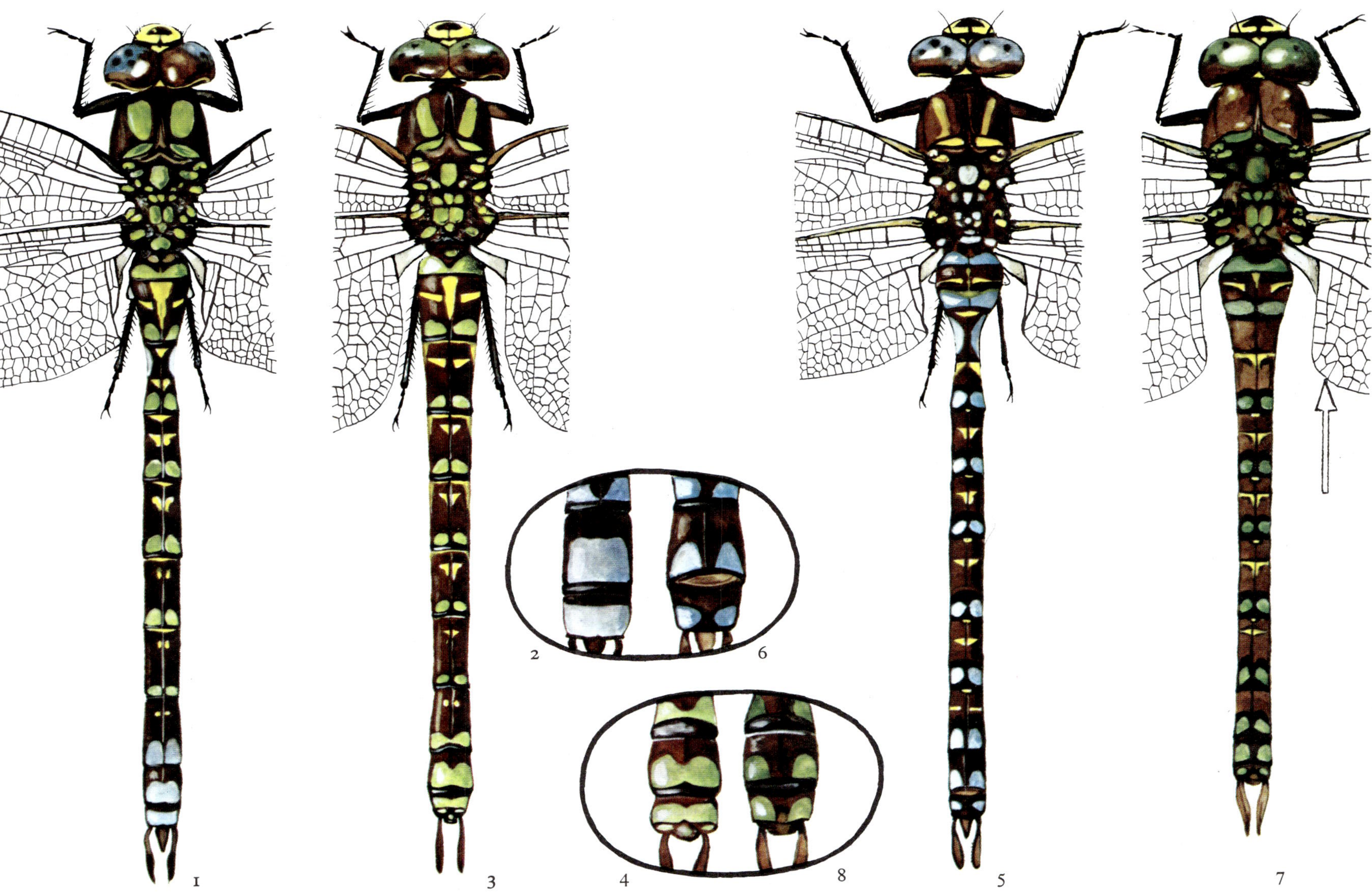

(×2 approx) Plate I

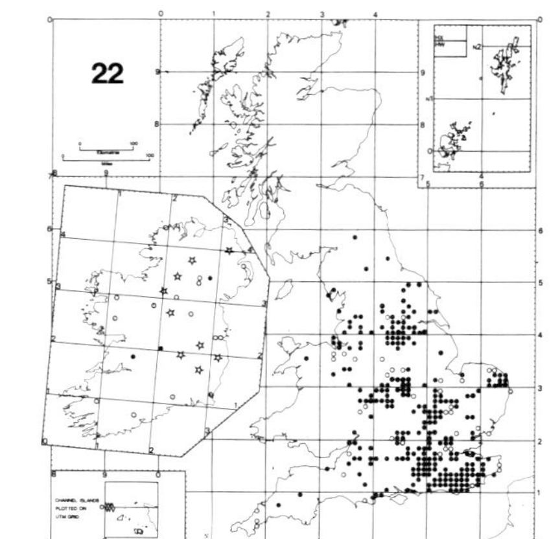

Aeshna grandis

Aeshna isosceles

Aeshna grandis (Linnaeus, 1758)

The Brown Aeshna, The Brown Hawker

1 ♂ Our only aeshna species with brown wing venation and pale amber-tinted membrane.
The pterostigma is also brown, the anal triangle is 2-celled and the membranule is short.

2 ♂ Note blue spots on segments 2–3.

3 ♀ No blue spots on segments 2–3 as in the male.
This species has an all over brown appearance when in flight.

Size. Wingspan 102mm; hindwing length 41–49mm. Average overall length 73mm; abdomen length ♂54–60mm, ♀49–54mm.

Flight period. Beginning of July to mid-October.

Flight and habitat. Has a strong preference for hawking around the edge of a pond or along the centre of a canal or stream. Strictly territorial and antagonistic to other males. Flight usually directly backwards and forwards on a special beat. Prefers open ground to woods. Flies from early morning till after dusk.

Status and distribution (Map 22, also page 103).
Very common in the south and south-eastern counties; less common in the Midlands and absent from the north.

Aeshna isosceles (Müller, 1767)

The Norfolk Aeshna, The Norfolk Hawker

4 ♂ Easily distinguished from *A.grandis* by the transparent wings. Note also the saffron suffusion at the base of the hindwing. The venation is mostly black and the anal triangle has 3–6 cells (usually 4). The membranule extends along the base of the hindwing. Pterostigma pale brown.

5 ♂ A conspicuous pale yellow triangle on segment 2, also present in the female.

6 ♀ Note the green eyes in both sexes.

Size. Wingspan 93mm; hindwing length 39–45mm. Average overall length 67mm; abdomen length ♂47–50mm; ♀49–54mm.

Flight period. End of May to mid-July.

Flight and habitat. Prefers keeping near water, hawking by bushes or trees at the edge of a broad, flying well above the observer; or flying along a broadland dyke quite low in search of a female.

Status and distribution (Map 23, also page 104).
Restricted to the Norfolk Broads, and although many colonies were destroyed by sea encroachment, the species was still found occupying several broads and dykes during a survey in 1975.

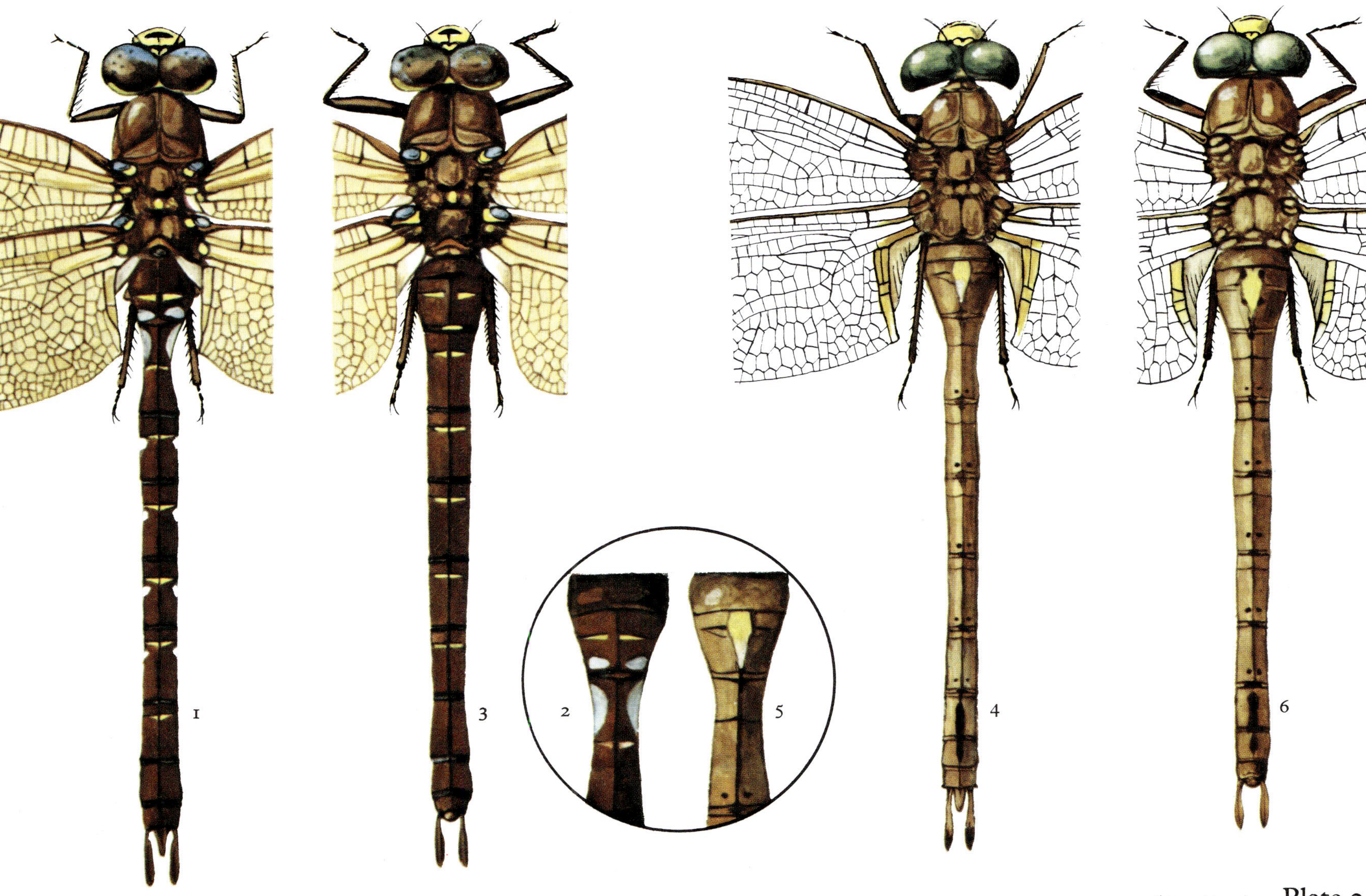

(× 2 *approx*) Plate 2

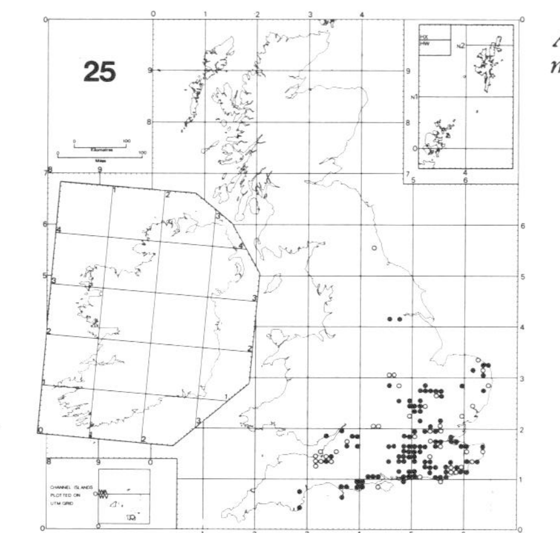

Aeshna *mixta*

Aeshna *caerulea*

Aeshna mixta Latreille, 1804

The Scarce Aeshna, The Migrant Hawker

1 ♂ The anal triangle in the male is 3-celled and the fork of *IR3* is well before the pterostigma.
In the specimen selected for illustration, the anal triangle in the left hindwing is aberrant, having five cells instead of the normal three as shown in the right hindwing.
All large spots on abdomen blue.

2 ♂ Note the cream marking on segment 3. In ageing specimens this gives way gradually to blue from the ventral surface upwards.
The 3-celled anal triangle in *A.mixta* is an additional useful character in separating the species from *A.juncea* which has only two cells.

3 ♀ Antehumeral stripes pale or absent.
Anal appendages longer than segments 9–10 combined – the longest of our six aeshnas.

Size. Wingspan 85mm; hindwing length 37–40mm. Average overall length 63mm; abdomen length ♂44–49mm, ♀45–48mm.

Flight period. Mid-July to end of October.

Flight and habitat. A high flier when hawking for insects. Not so territorial as the other aeshnas, three or more may be seen flying in a confined area without aggression. The male also flies low along the edges of ponds and in and out among clumps of reeds in search of the female. Easily disturbed and very wary.

Status and distribution (Map 25, also page 105).
Once considered a frequent immigrant but now obviously breeding in many south-eastern localities where it is found regularly every year and is not uncommon.

Aeshna caerulea (Ström, 1783)

The Blue Aeshna, The Azure Hawker

4 ♂ The eyes are confluent for a short distance about equal to the length of the occipital triangle. The fork of *IR3* is ill defined and the membranule is ashy grey. All thoracic markings and all spots on abdomen a beautiful azure blue.
Antehumeral stripes reduced or absent.
Spots on segments 9–10 almost rectangular.

5 ♀ Blue spots smaller and less conspicuous than in the ♂.
Note especially the almost rectangular spots on segments 9–10 in comparison with the rounded spots of *A.juncea* (Pl.1, fig.8) with which this species may be easily confused in Scotland.

Size. Wingspan 80mm; hindwing length 38–41mm. Average overall length 62mm; abdomen length ♂45–48mm, ♀42–44mm.

Flight period. Beginning of June to mid-August.

Flight and habitat. Essentially a sun loving insect; in dull weather sheltering among heather or low vegetation. Enjoys basking on large stones where it is extremely wary, or on tree trunks where it is more easy to catch. Prefers birch woodland to open moorland and more likely to be found in clearings in woods than elsewhere.

Status and distribution (Map 20, also page 102).
A Scottish species, nowhere common but distributed over a wide area.

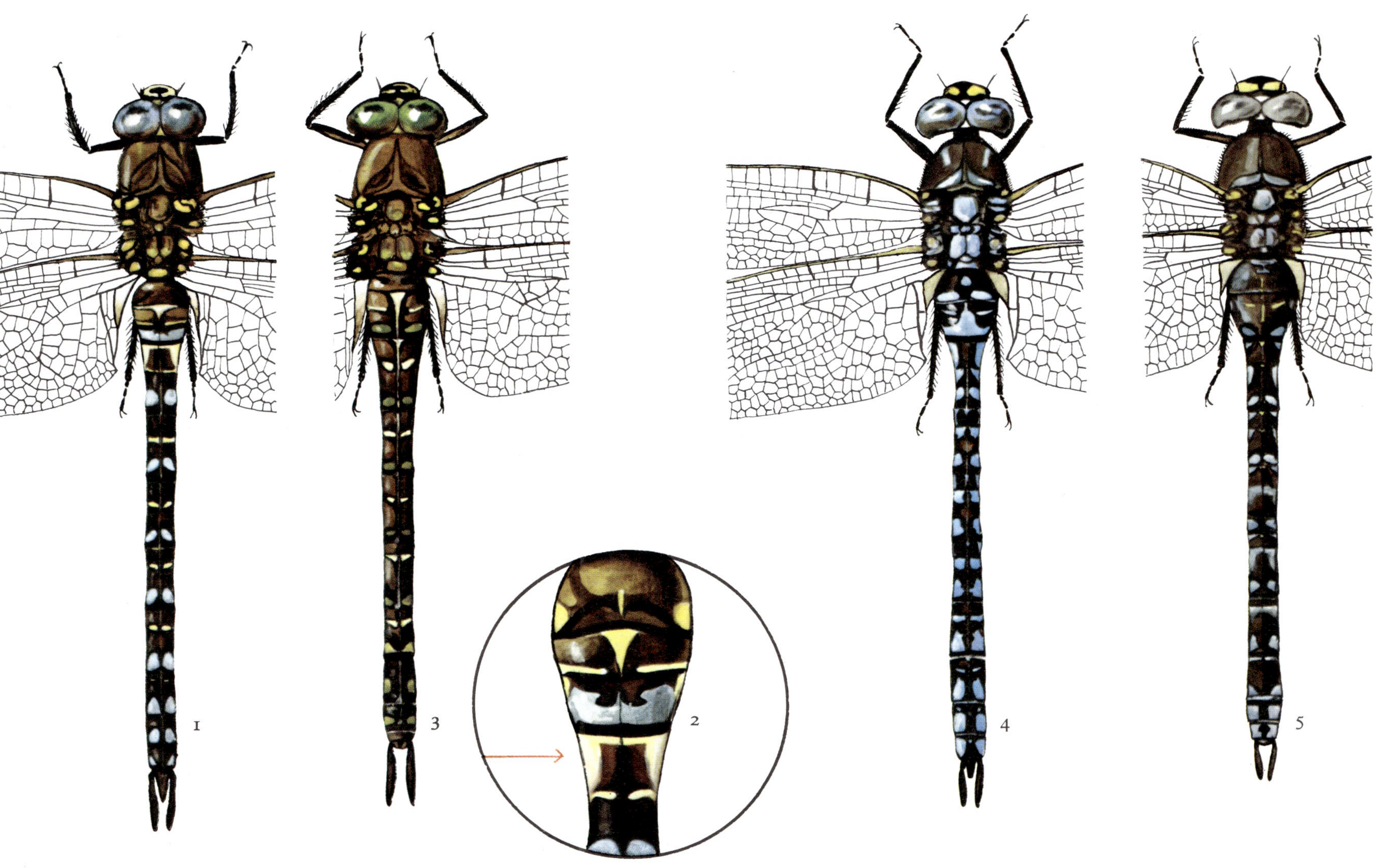

(× 2 *approx*) Plate 3

26

Anax imperator

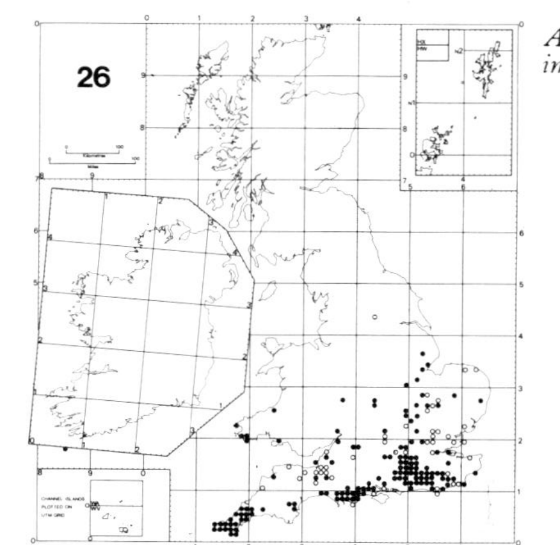

Cordulegaster boltonii

Anax imperator Leach, 1815

The Emperor Dragonfly

1 ♂ The largest of the hawker dragonflies.
The bright blue abdomen with the median black markings is sufficient to identify this species.
Note also the ♂ has the base of the hindwings rounded.
Compare with the aeshnas (Pl.1).

2 ♀ The normal abdomen is green with a brownish tip, but some very old adult females may attain the blue of the male.

Size. Wingspan 106mm; hindwing length 45–51mm. Average overall length 78mm; abdomen length ♂53–61mm, ♀49–51mm.

Flight period. End of May to end of August.

Flight and habitat. Usually found flying in the vicinity of large ponds or canals and keeping well out over the water. A tireless flier. When hawking around the outer edge of a reed-bed or making a sudden quick circle a little inland it is extremely wary and difficult to catch. Usually settles on a reed but may soar to the treetops.

Status and distribution (Map 26, also page 105).
Mainly a southern species. In good years it is not uncommon.

Cordulegaster boltonii (Donovan, 1807)

The Golden-ringed Dragonfly

3 ♀ Note the unique long ovipositor, making this species the longest bodied of the hawker dragonflies.

4 ♂ The conspicuous yellow bands on a black background serve at once to identify this large species.

Size. Wingspan 101mm; hindwing length 41–46mm. Average overall length ♂74mm, ♀84mm; abdomen length ♂54–60mm, ♀60–64mm.

Flight period. End of May to end of August.

Flight and habitat. Patrols low along streams flying strongly and direct. It is not easily disturbed and since its flight path is predictable it may be readily caught. Rests on reeds, boulders or heather and it may be seen well away from water.

Status and distribution (Map 27, also page 106).
More common in the southern counties and Wales than in the Midlands. Absent from the east in England and widely distributed in Scotland.

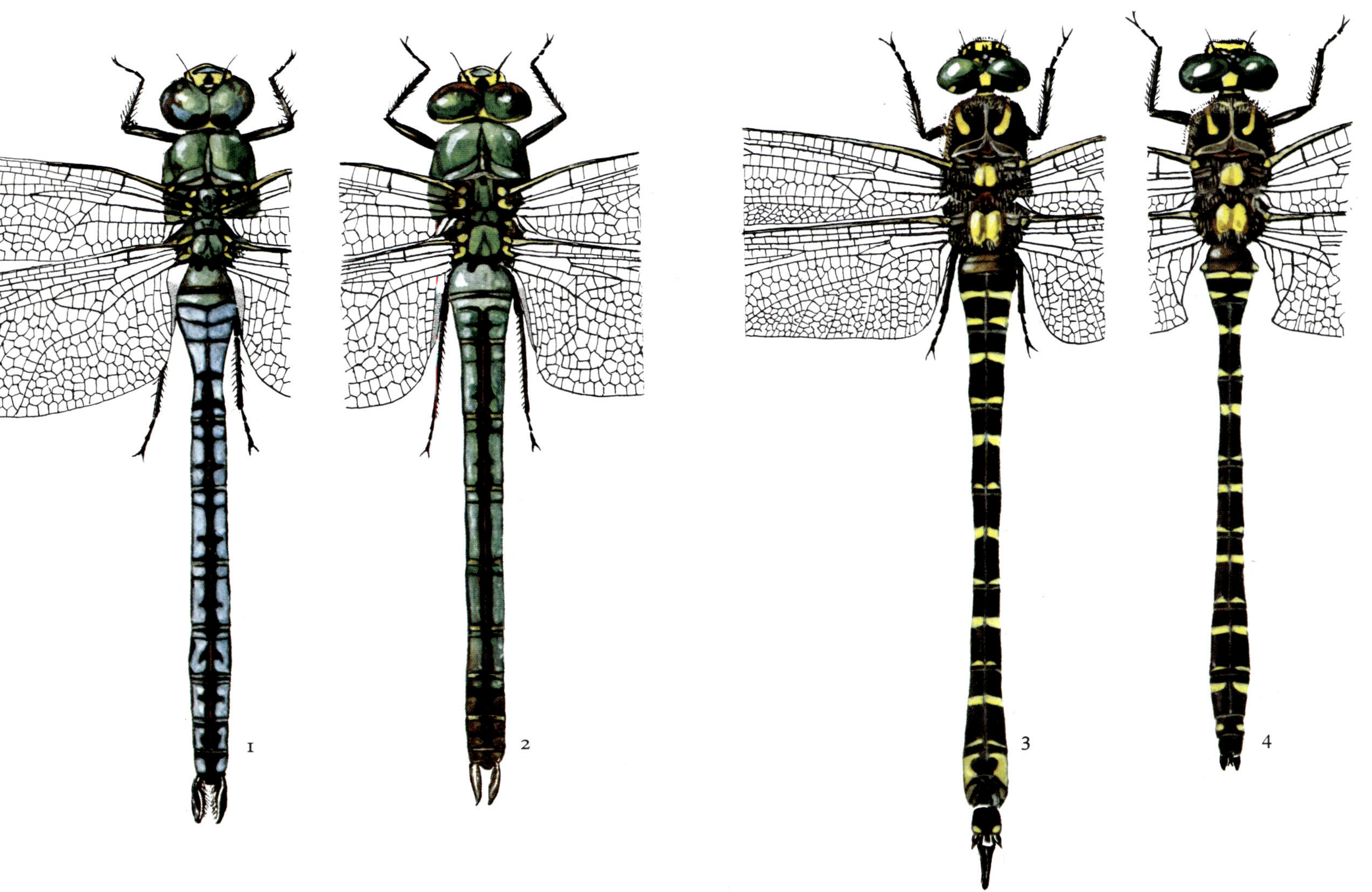

($\times 1\frac{1}{2}$ *approx*) Plate 4

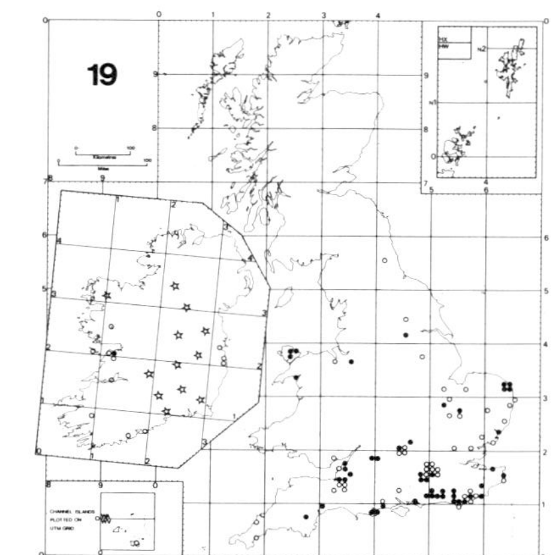

Brachytron pratense

Gomphus vulgatissimus

Brachytron pratense (Müller, 1764)

The Hairy Dragonfly

1 ♂ The thorax is the most hairy of all British dragonflies.
Antehumeral stripes conspicuously green.
Base of hindwings rounded.

2 ♀ Abdomen very hairy as well as the thorax.
Wings suffused with saffron at the base.
Antehumeral stripes inconspicuous.

3 ♂♀ Pterostigma extremely narrow in both sexes.

Size. Wingspan 72mm; hindwing length 34–37mm. Average overall length 55mm; abdomen length ♂ 40–46mm, ♀ 38–42mm.

Flight period. Beginning of May to end of June.

Flight and habitat. The male flies strongly and swiftly, low along streams, dykes or canals, both hawking for insects or searching for the female which only approaches water to mate and oviposit.

Status and distribution (Map 19, also page 102).
Not common; usually seen singly where it occurs.
A broadland dragonfly extending to the south-eastern and southern counties.

Gomphus vulgatissimus (Linnaeus, 1758)

The Club-tailed Dragonfly

4 ♂ Note the wide distance between the eyes.
The base of the hindwing is strongly excised and the anal triangle has five cells.

5 ♀ The conspicuous pale green markings on a black background will readily identify this small robust hawker.
Eyes wide apart as in the male.
Base of hindwing rounded.

Size. Wingspan 64mm; hindwing length 28–33mm. Average overall length 50mm; abdomen length 32–37mm.

Flight period. End of May to end of June.

Flight and habitat. A slow-flying hawker with a short beat along a stream. Frequently hovers and settles on vegetation or on stones where its cryptic coloration makes it hard to see. Mating pairs may be knocked up from nearby vegetation.

Status and distribution (Map 18, also page 101).
Still well established in several localities along the Thames and also in Sussex, but apparently absent from some old haunts.

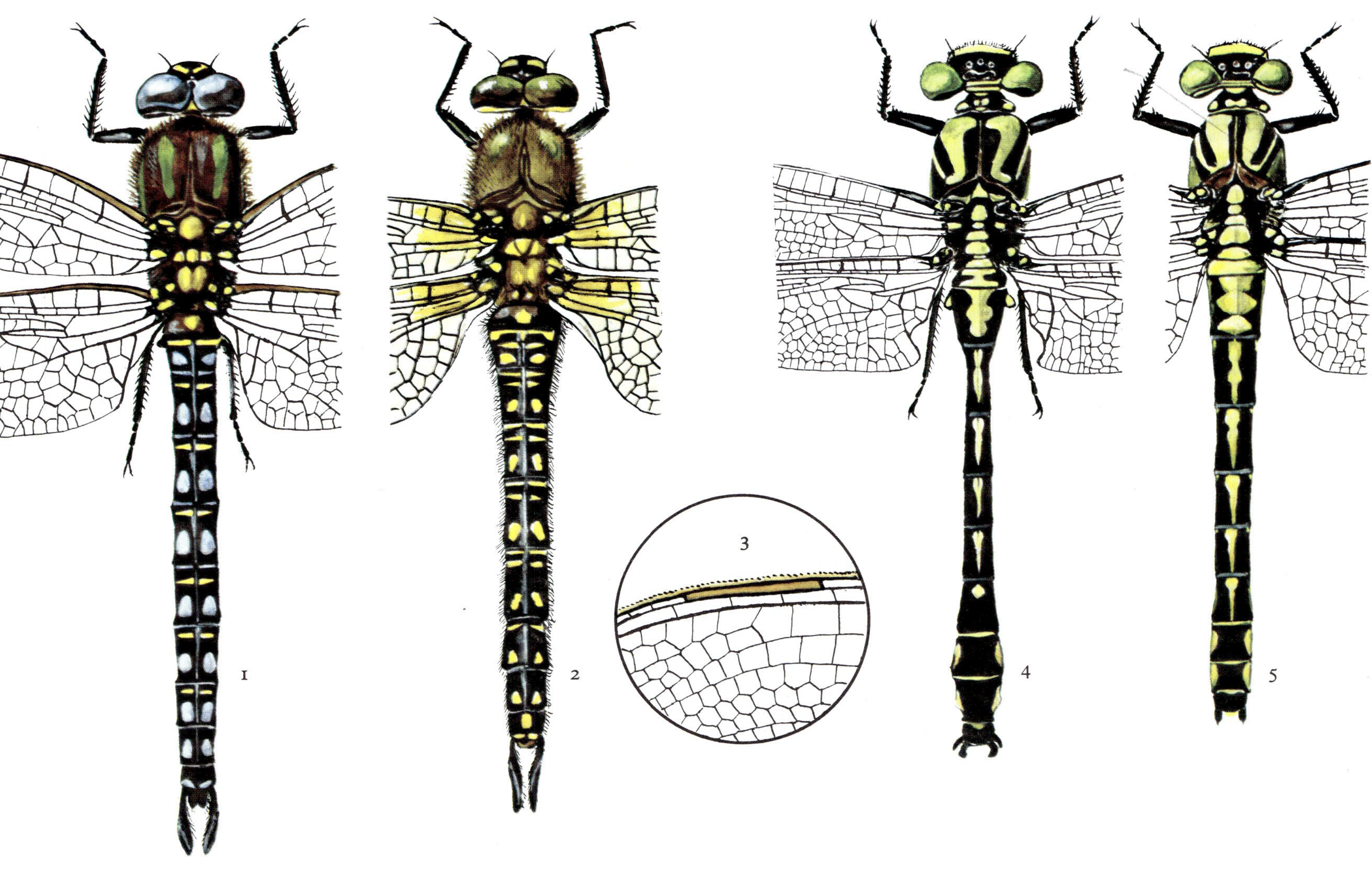

(×2 approx) Plate 5

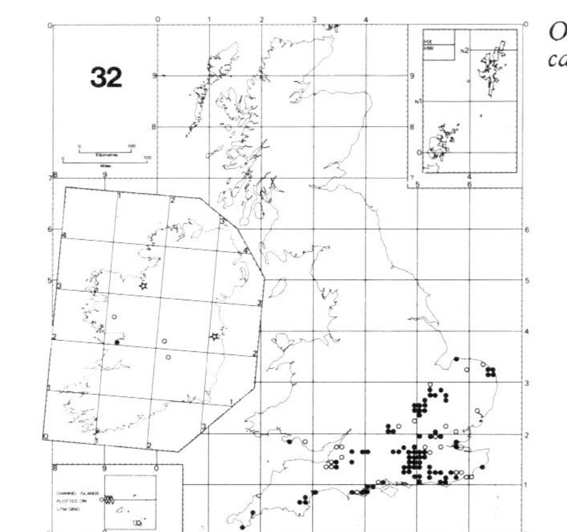

Orthetrum cancellatum

Orthetrum coerulescens

Orthetrum cancellatum (Linnaeus, 1758)

The Black-lined Orthetrum,
The Black-tailed Skimmer

1 ♂ The teneral male is yellow as is the female.
The blue pruinescence does not appear until the insect is fully adult as illustrated.
Later even the orange lateral markings may be obscured by blue.
Note the black tip to the abdomen, segments 8–10.

2 ♀ Females become much duller with age, turning a dirty grey and in good years some specimens may attain the blue male coloration. Wings are usually very worn if this stage is reached.

3 ♂♀ Pterostigma black in both sexes.

Size. Wingspan 77mm; hindwing length 35–40mm. Average overall length 50mm; abdomen length 30–35mm.

Flight period. End of May to mid-August.

Flight and habitat. The male flies swiftly just skimming the surface of the water. Settles for long periods on bare patches by the water's edge, repeatedly returning to the same spot.
Quickly colonises old gravel pits and wanders in search of new habitats. The female generally settles on reeds or nearby vegetation.

Status and distribution (Map 32, also page 108).
A south-eastern and southern species also found in the London area.

Orthetrum coerulescens (Fabricius, 1798)

The Keeled Orthetrum, The Keeled Skimmer

4 ♂ The teneral male resembles the female in colour.
The blue pruinescence of fully adult males extends over the abdomen to the tip.
Note the pale thoracic stripes, not obvious in *O.cancellatum.*

5 ♀ Wings slightly clouded; base suffused with amber – heavily so when teneral.

6 ♂♀ Pterostigma pale orange in both sexes.

Size. Wingspan 60mm; hindwing length 28–34mm. Average overall length 42mm; abdomen length 27–30mm.

Flight period. Mid-June to end of August.

Flight and habitat. Males fly swiftly and erratically over marshy ground where the species breeds. Very aggressive towards other males. Females settle amongst heather or long grass and do not fly far at a time.

Status and distribution (Map 33, also page 109).
Mainly a southern species but not uncommon where it occurs. It is very local in Scotland.

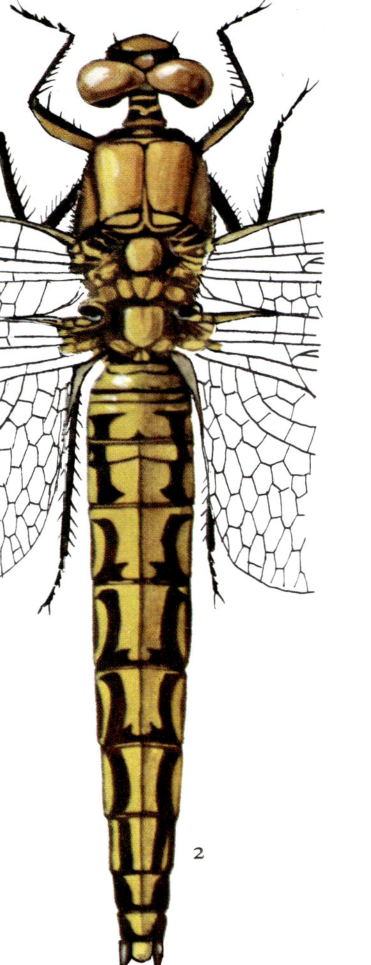

4

5

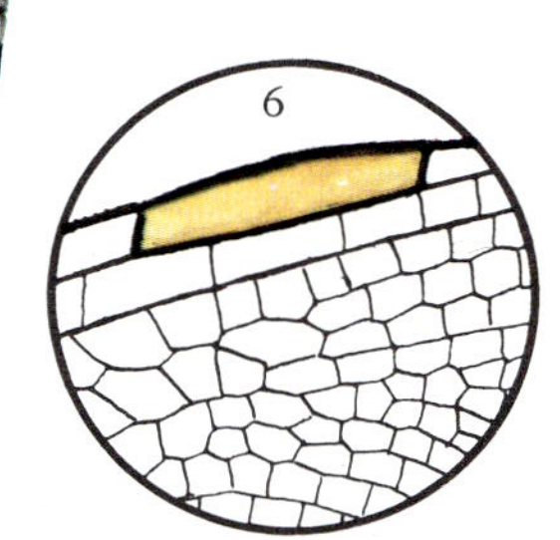

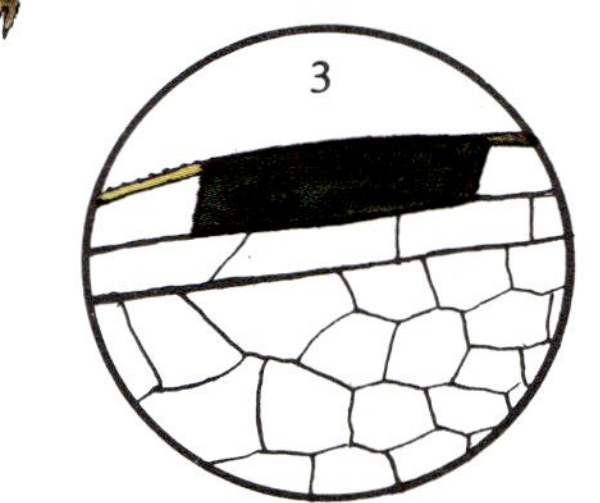

(×2½ *approx*) Plate 6

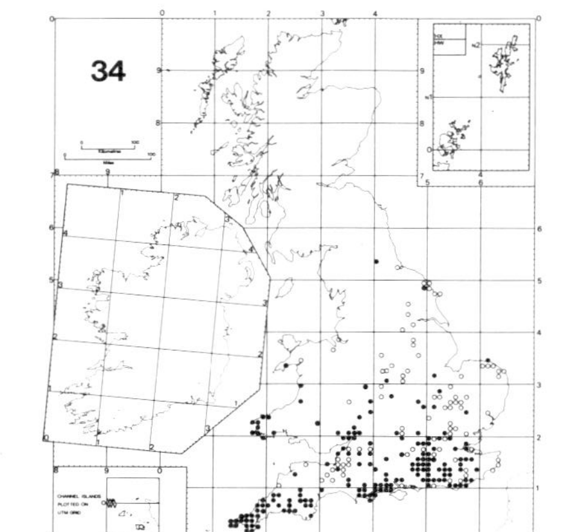

Libellula depressa

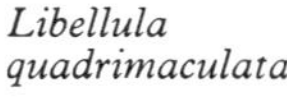

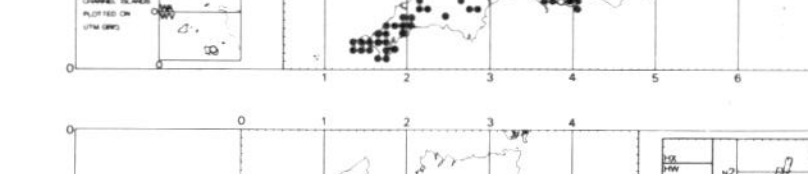

Libellula quadrimaculata

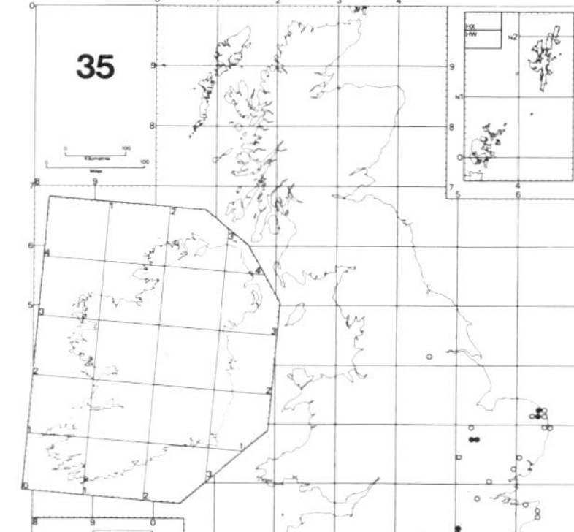

Libellula fulva

Libellula depressa Linnaeus, 1758

The Broad-bodied Libellula,
The Broad-bodied Chaser

1 ♂ Teneral coloration as in the female. The blue pruinescence appears when fully adult and covers all segments of the abdomen.
Dark brown patches at base of all wings in both sexes.

2 ♀ Yellow spots at sides of abdomen conspicuous.

Size. Wingspan 76mm; hindwing length 33–37mm. Average overall length 44mm; abdomen length 24–28mm.

Flight period. Mid-May to beginning of August

Flight and habitat. Males are extremely territorial, selecting the same perch on a twig or reed for days on end. They are very aggressive to other males and their flight is swift and erratic. The female settles on bushes by a pond for long periods and allows the observer to approach before making a sudden getaway. Pairing is in flight and soon over.

Status and distribution (Map 34, also page 109).
Not nearly so common as it used to be but well in evidence in some southern counties.

Libellula quadrimaculata Linnaeus, 1758

The Four-spotted Libellula, The Four-spotted Chaser

3 ♀ No dark markings at base of forewing but a deep amber coloration.
A dark patch at base of hindwing.

4 ♂ Anal appendages. The fully adult male is coloured as the female.
There is no blue pruinescence. Abdomen black tipped in both sexes.

5 ♂♀ A conspicuous dark spot at the nodus in both sexes. f.*praenubila* Newman has an additional dark patch on the wing below the pterostigma.

Size. Wingspan 75mm; hindwing length 32–40mm. Average overall length 43mm; abdomen length 27–32mm.

Flight period. Mid-May to mid-August.

Flight and habitat. Inhabits boggy pools where males will hawk for long periods, hovering and flying in circles. As the species is common, many males may be found sharing the same large pond but keeping to their own quarters unless challenged by a rival. Teneral specimens are usually found among heather where they may be suddenly knocked up only to settle a little farther on.

Status and distribution (Map 36, also page 110).
Widely distributed almost throughout the British Isles. Locally common in Scotland.

Libellula fulva Müller, 1764

The Scarce Libellula, The Scarce Chaser

6 ♀ Two dark streaks at base of forewing and a dark triangular spot at base of hindwing. Conspicuous black markings down the centre of the abdomen from segments 3–10.

7 ♀ Wing tips with a brown patch.

8 ♂ Teneral males coloured as female.
The blue pruinescence of adult males on segments 8–10 interrupted by black.

Size. Wingspan 74mm; hindwing length 35–38mm. Average overall length 44mm; abdomen length 26–29mm.

Flight period. End of May to beginning of July.

Flight and habitat. Males are extremely active, settling frequently. They are territorial and aggressive. Females prefer settling among tall grasses; in dull or wet weather or after early morning dew they may be picked up by hand.

Status and distribution (Map 35, also page 110).
Once abundant in the Norfolk Broads; now scarce owing to pollution, but present in 1975. Still holding its own in some southern counties.

1

2

3

6

8

5

4

7

($\times 2\frac{1}{2}$ *approx*)

Plate 7

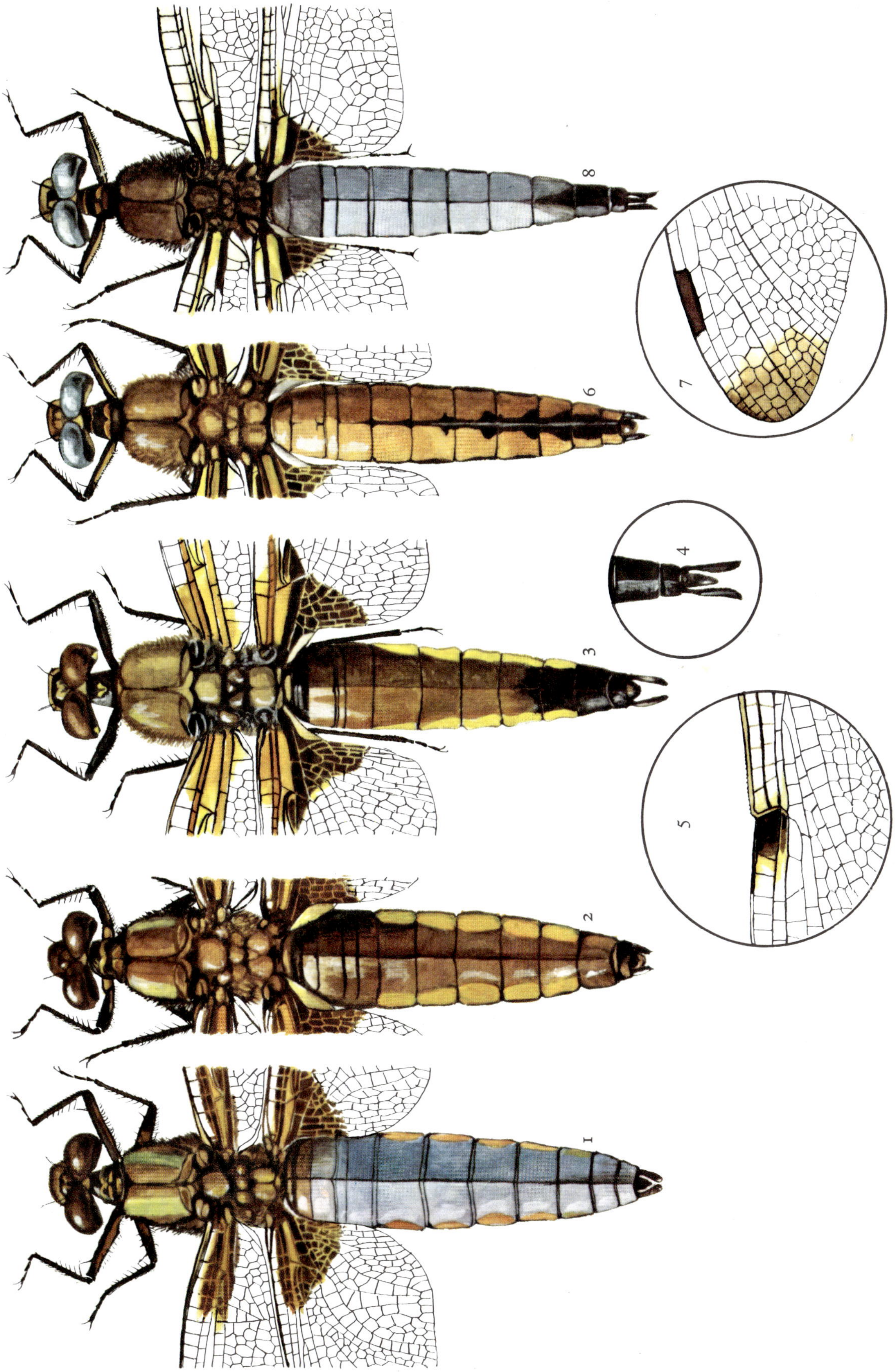

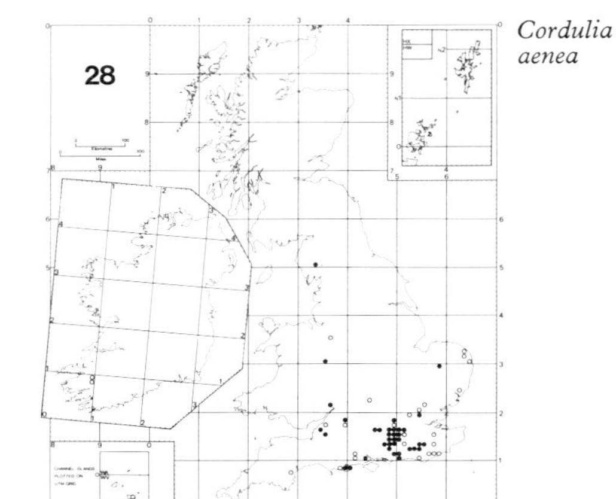

Cordulia aenea (Linnaeus, 1758)

The Downy Emerald

1 ♂ **2** ♀ The bright green eyes and brilliant metallic green of the downy thorax in contrast with the bronze-black abdomen render easy determination of this species.

3 ♂♀ Base of discoidal cell of male hindwing slightly basal to line of arculus.

Size. Wingspan 68mm; hindwing length 31–34mm. Average overall length 48mm; abdomen length 34–38mm.

Flight period. Mid-May to end of July.

Flight and habitat. A fast flier, keeping low above the surface of the water at the edge of a pond or canal, making a short but regular patrol. Very alert and quick at avoiding the net.

Status and distribution (Map 28, also page 106).
Still relatively common in the localities where it occurs, especially in south-eastern counties.

Oxygastra curtisii (Dale, 1834)

The Orange-spotted Emerald

4 ♂ The deep yellow spots in the centre of the abdomen on a green-bronze background at once identify this rare species.

5 ♀ Wings of the female deeply amber tinted.

6 ♂♀ Base of discoidal cell of male hindwing slightly distal to line of arculus.

Size. Wingspan 72mm; hindwing length 32–36mm. Average overall length 53mm; abdomen length 36–39mm.

Flight period. End of June to mid-July.

Flight and habitat. In its known localities this species seems to have a preference for fir and birch woods where it will make short flights over the heather and remain settled for a long time. A sun-loving insect with erratic flight in intersecting circles while hawking for insects. Very timid, making off at the careless approach of the observer and flying to a considerable height.

Status and distribution (Map 31, also page 108).
There are no recent records for this rare species once found by Moors River in Hampshire.

7 ♂♀ *Somatochlora metallica:* base of discoidal cell of male hindwing in line with arculus (see also Pl.9, fig.1).

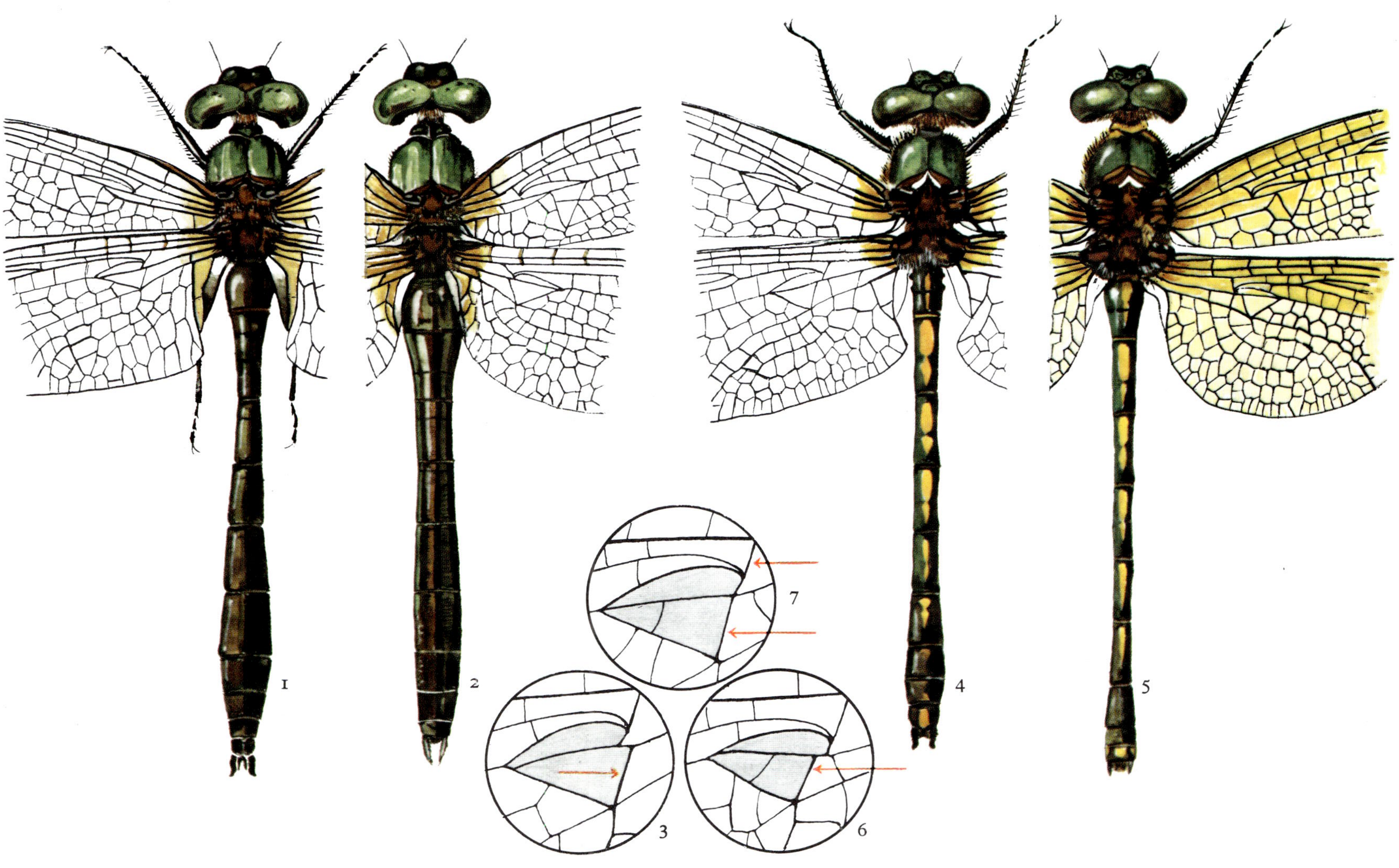

(×2 approx) Plate 8

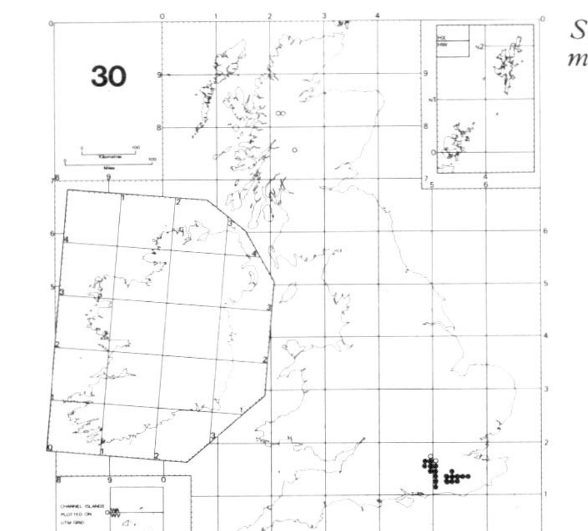

Somatochlora metallica

Somatochlora arctica

Somatochlora metallica (van der Linden, 1825)

The Brilliant Emerald

1 ♂ Brilliant metallic green thorax and abdomen.

2 ♂ Superior (upper) anal appendages widely separate at base with two lateral spines.

3 ♀ Wings suffused with saffron.

4 ♀ Vulvar scale very prominent in profile.
Anal appendages long and pointed.

Size. Wingspan 78mm; hindwing length 34–36mm. Average overall length 53mm; abdomen length 37–40mm.

Flight period. Mid-June to beginning of August.

Flight and habitat. With flying habits similar to *Cordulia aenea* (Pl.8, figs.1–3), with which it is often found. Only the more brilliant green will determine the species when in flight. The female prefers the neighbouring vegetation sometimes well away from the canal, pond or stream. After mating, the female selects a shady spot in which to oviposit, often under an alder bush overhanging the water.

Status and distribution (Map 30, also page 107).
A dragonfly which has extended its range in recent years, turning up in several new localities in Surrey, Sussex and Hampshire.

Somatochlora arctica (Zetterstedt, 1840)

The Northern Emerald

5 ♂ Dull black-bronze abdomen.

6 ♂ Superior anal appendages closely apposed at base and curving inwards to resemble calipers.

7 ♀ Wings almost clear.
Note the large orange spot on each side of the dorsum near the base of segment 3 of the abdomen.

8 ♀ Vulvar scale short and blunt in profile.

Size. Wingspan 68mm; hindwing length 32–36mm. Average overall length 50mm; abdomen length 37–40mm.

Flight period. Beginning of July to beginning of August.

Flight and habitat. Usually flies high with erratic spurts and figures-of-eight, soon making off at the approach of the observer. A false stroke of the net will send it off and it is soon high out of sight. The female is more likely to be encountered in woods and is easier to catch. It comes into the open to oviposit in peaty bogs, flicking the surface of the water with the abdomen.

Status and distribution (Map 29, also page 107).
Confined to the western and central counties of Scotland.

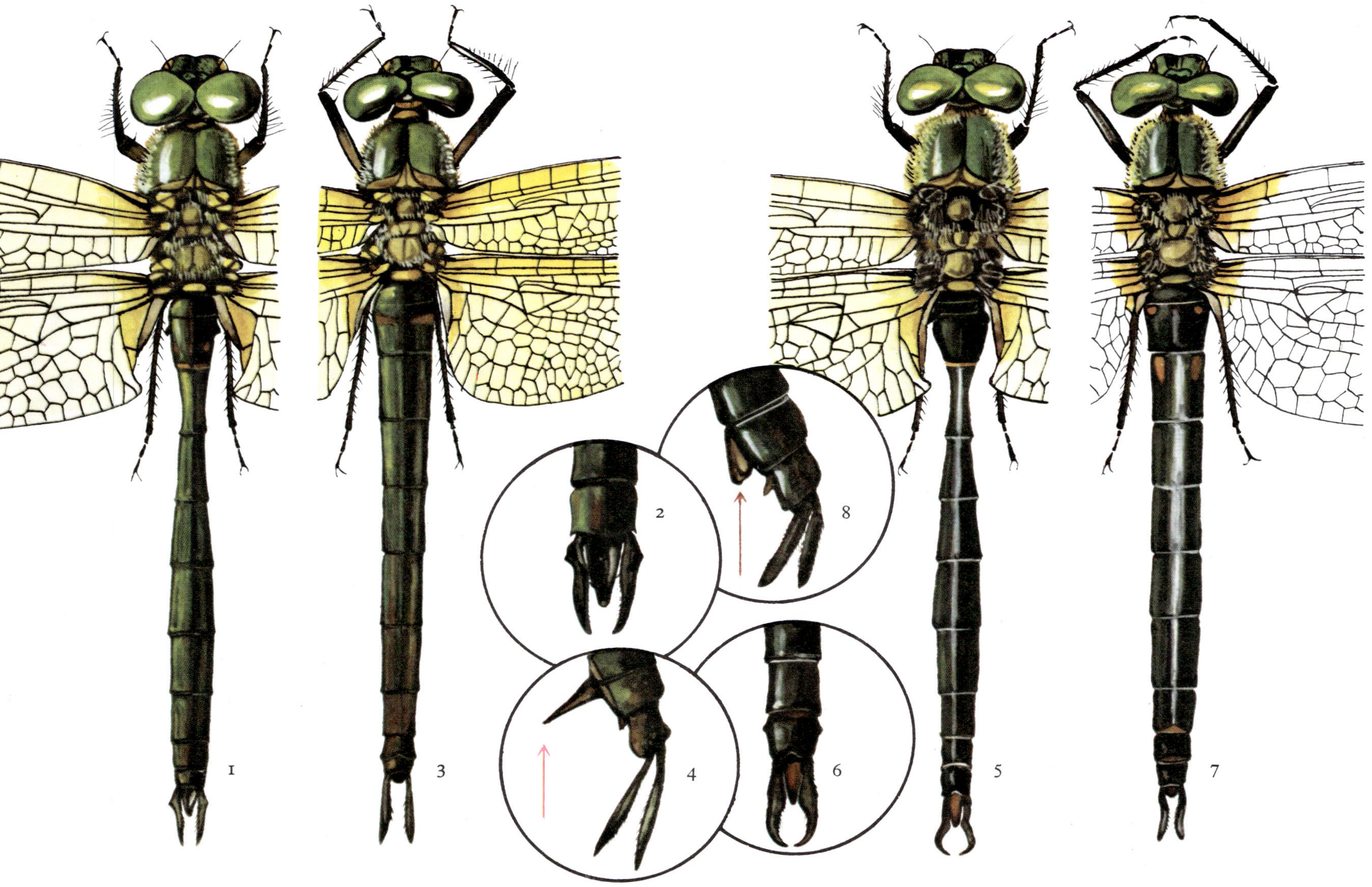

(× 2½ *approx*) Plate 9

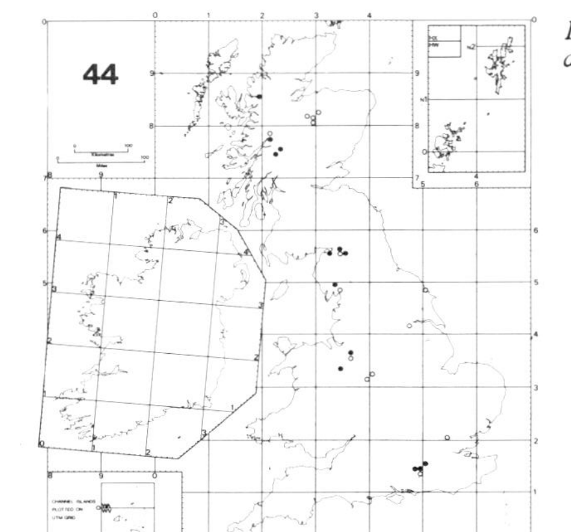

Leucorrhinia dubia

Sympetrum scoticum

Leucorrhinia dubia (van der Linden, 1825)

The White-faced Dragonfly, The White-faced Darter

1 ♂ Teneral males yellow as in the female.
The brown-black patch at the base of the hindwing separates this species from the genus *Sympetrum*.

2 ♀ Base of wings suffused with saffron.
A very rare form, *L.dubia* f.*lucasi*, Fraser, has the wings suffused with smoky saffron and bases amber yellow. This beautiful form is fully described in *Entomologist's mon.Mag.* **89:** 138.

3 ♂♀ The only dragonfly with a white face.

4 ♂♀ Pterostigma red-brown, rounded and robust.

Size. Wingspan 53mm; hindwing length 23–27mm. Average overall length 37mm; abdomen length ♂24–27mm, ♀22–24mm.

Flight period. End of May to mid-July.

Flight and habitat. A restless species, rarely settling for long and quickly off the mark when approached. Not given to long flights. Settles among the heather by peaty bogs where it breeds. Frequently hovers and an excellent darter. Soars high up if thoroughly disturbed.

Status and distribution (Map 44, also page 114).
Distribution determined by habitat but it is usually common where it occurs.

Sympetrum scoticum (Donovan, 1811)

The Black Sympetrum, The Black Darter

5 ♂ The only male sympetrum with a completely black body and black legs.

6 ♂ Note that in teneral males the abdomen may be confused with teneral males (or adult females) of *L.dubia*.

7 ♀ Teneral females are yellow and should be compared with *S.sanguineum* which also has black legs (Pl.11, fig.5).
Examination of the side of the thorax shows that *S.scoticum* has a heavy black band with three yellow spots, whereas *S.sanguineum* has only thin lines on a light background.
Note the black triangle on top of the thorax.

8 ♂♀ Pterostigma of both sexes black.

Size. Wingspan 46mm; hindwing length 22–26mm. Average overall length 32mm; abdomen length 20–24mm.

Flight period. End of June to end of September.

Flight and habitat. Frequents marshy spots or peat bogs, especially where there is heather, from which it may be swept on windy or rainy days. A restless species, flying for a few yards only before settling.

Status and distribution (Map 41, also page 113).
Usually common where it occurs. Widely distributed.

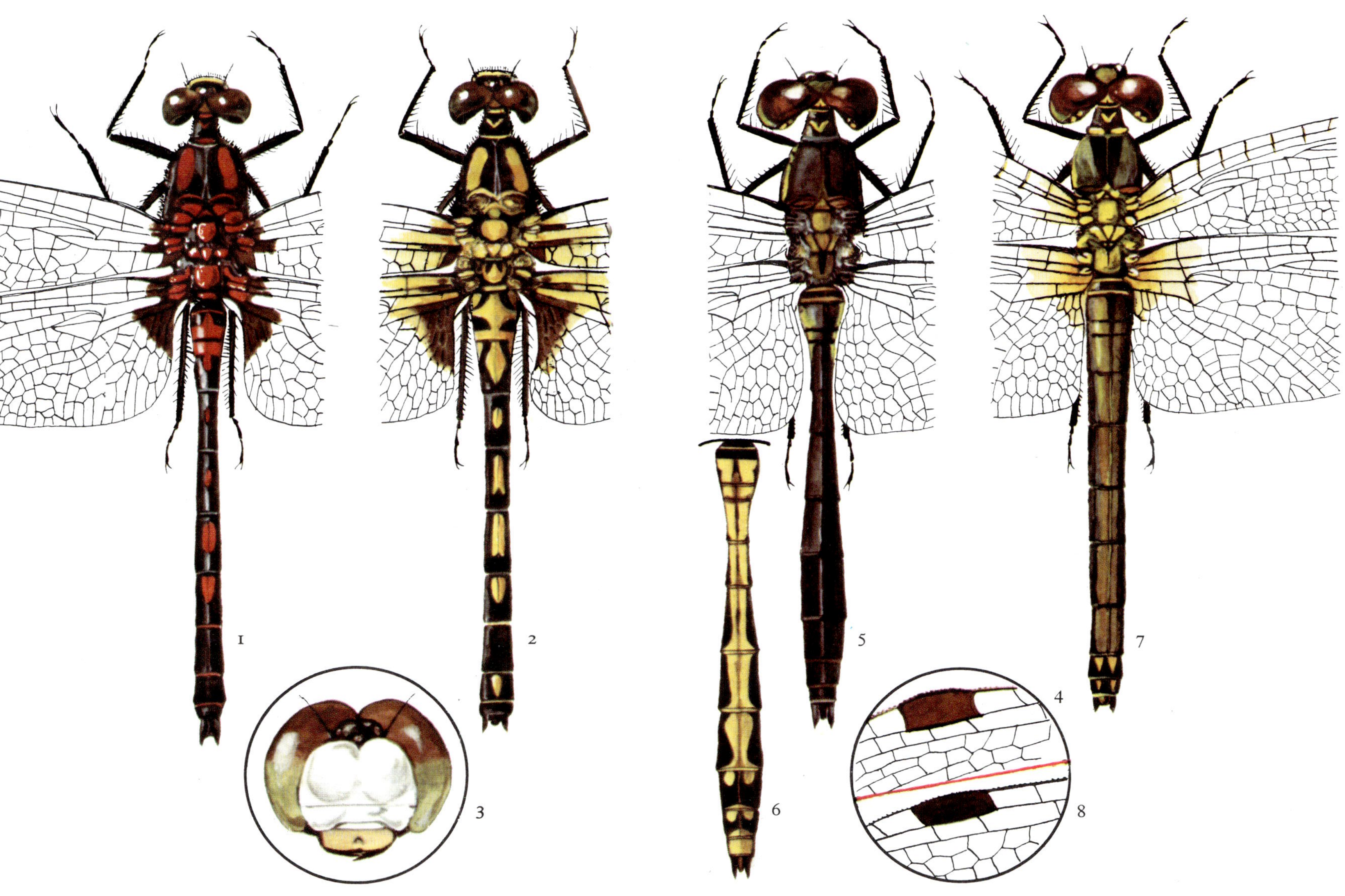

(×3 *approx*) Plate 10

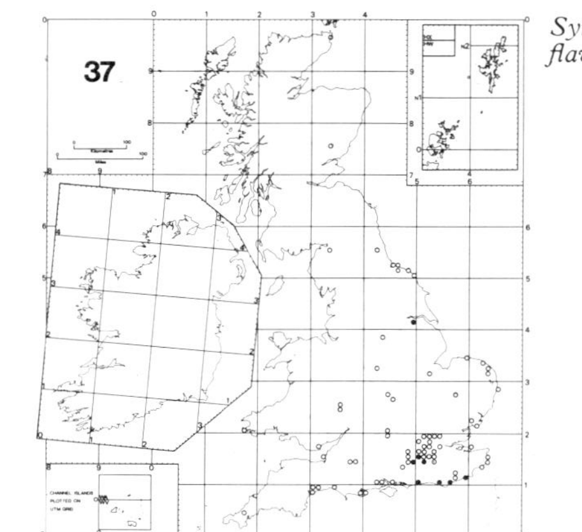

Sympetrum flaveolum

40

Sympetrum sanguineum

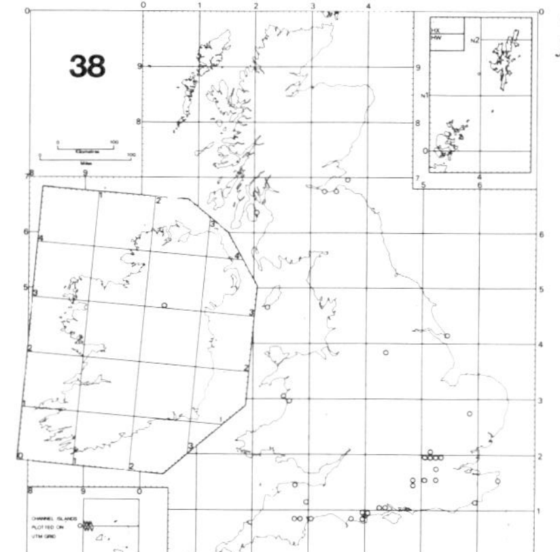

Sympetrum fonscolombei

Sympetrum flaveolum (Linnaeus, 1758)

The Yellow-winged Sympetrum,
The Yellow-winged Darter

1 ♂ **2** ♀ Wings of both sexes strongly suffused with saffron; in the male deeper on the hindwing and occupying about the basal third. Legs black with a yellow stripe.

3 ♂♀ Yellow patch at the node in most females.
In this genus the most distal antenodal (the one by the node – red arrow) is very oblique and between the costa and subcosta only.

Size. Wingspan 55mm; hindwing length 24–29mm. Average overall length 34mm; abdomen length 22–26mm.

Flight period. Mid-July to end of August.

Flight and habitat. When visiting Britain from overseas, this species selects ponds with copious rushy margins where the insects settle halfway down the rushes. When pursued, only short hopping flights are made, the insect making a fluttering flight or hovering before settling.

Status and distribution (Map 37, also page 111).
Most recent record August 1975. A fairly frequent immigrant more likely to be found in the south-eastern counties, Surrey and Hampshire seeming the most favoured.

Sympetrum sanguineum (Müller, 1764)

The Ruddy Sympetrum, The Ruddy Darter

4 ♂ A distinguishing feature of the male is the marked constriction of segments 3–5 of the abdomen.
The black markings on segments 8–9 are more prominent than in other British species of the genus.
Legs black in both sexes.

5 ♀ Sides of thorax pale with thin black lines.
No black triangle on the thorax as there is in *S.scoticum.*

Size. Wingspan 55mm; hindwing length 24–29mm. Average overall length 34mm; abdomen length 21–26mm.

Flight period. End of June to beginning of September.

Flight and habitat. A very quick darter which does not fly far before settling. It may be seen on sunny days basking on rushes or reeds with its wings depressed. At other times bare patches or logs are chosen. Likes well-reeded ponds on marshy ground or ditches with luxuriant vegetation.

Status and distribution (Map 40, also page 112).
Much less common than it used to be, perhaps because it is not so frequently reinforced by immigration.

Sympetrum fonscolombei (Selys, 1840)

The Red-veined Sympetrum, The Red-veined Darter

6 ♂ **7** ♀ Both male and female may be identified by the crimson costa and numerous red veins; only a few are black.
Legs black with a yellow stripe.

8 ♂♀ The pterostigma varies from pale yellow to pale pink with heavy black margins.

Size. Wingspan 60mm; hindwing length 27–31mm. Average overall length 40mm; abdomen length 24–26mm.

Flight period. End of June to mid-August.

Flight and habitat. On arrival in Britain this species has a preference for large lakes where it can patrol some distance away from the edge when the bright red body and bluish reflections from the wings make the insect a magnificent sight. At sunset the night is spent in tall grasses by the lake. In this way the very occasional female may be found.

Status and distribution (Map 38, also page 111).
An occasional immigrant arriving in fair numbers but mainly a male population.

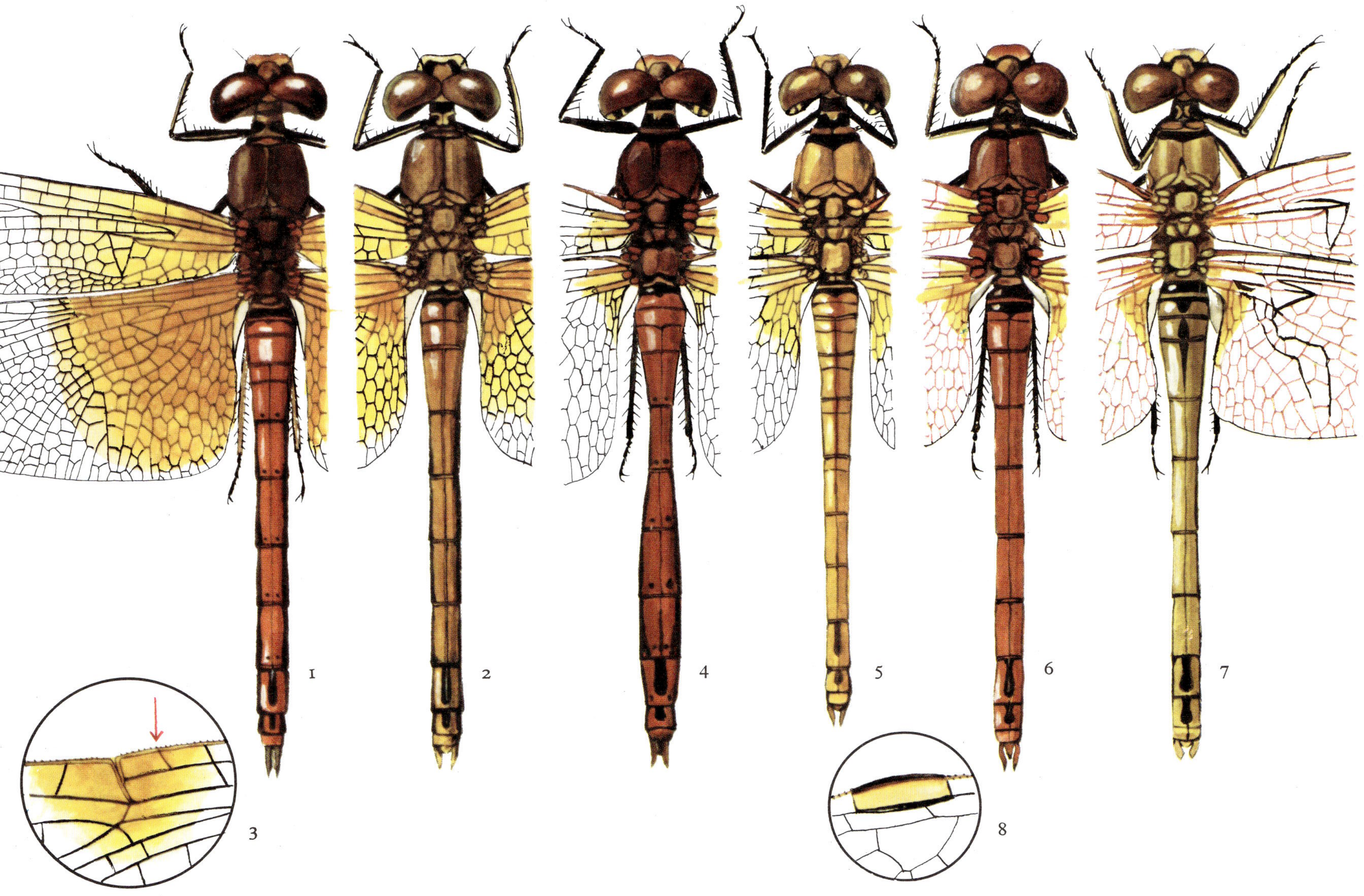

(×3½ *approx*) Plate 11

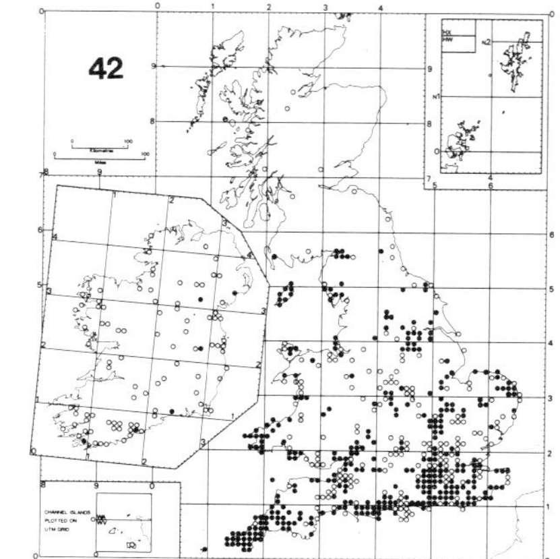

Sympetrum striolatum

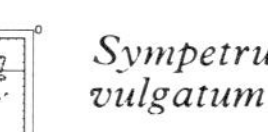

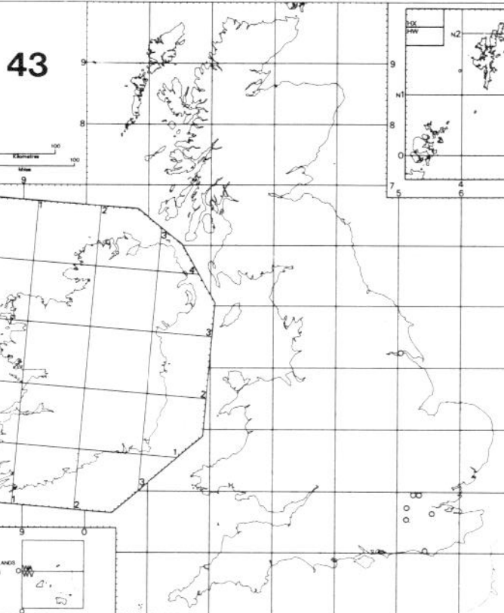

Sympetrum vulgatum

Sympetrum nigrescens

Sympetrum striolatum (Charpentier, 1840)

The Common Sympetrum, The Common Darter

1 ♂ The commonest member of the genus and the one most likely to be met with in England.

2 ♂ A remarkable aberration, taken by A. E. Gardner at Wood Walton Fen, 18.x.1959 – *S. striolatum* ab. *masoni* Gardner.

3 ♂♀ The narrow black band at the base of the frons is not continued down the sides of the eyes.

4 ♀ Ageing specimens frequently have a median red streak down the abdomen.

5 ♀ End of abdomen, lateral view, vulvar scale projecting at an angle of 30° below segment 9 of abdomen – (red dots).

Size. Wingspan 58mm; hindwing length 26–29mm. Average overall length 37mm; abdomen length 25–30mm.

Flight period. Mid-June to end of October.

Flight and habitat. Of all the genus *Sympetrum* this is the species which most frequently returns to the same spot to settle, a perch or a patch which it will occupy for several days. A fast darter and an excellent hoverer, it enjoys skirting ponds, but is equally at home in woods. It often settles on light coloured objects and bare patches of ground. When ageing, it becomes lethargic and stays for long periods basking in the sun.

Status and distribution (Map 42, also page 113).
Common and often abundant in its favoured localities. Frequently the last dragonfly to be seen in the year. The latest record is 20th November 1939 (Attlee, 1945. In *Rep.Proc.nat.Sci.archaeol.Soc.Littlehampton, suppl.*)

Sympetrum vulgatum (Linnaeus, 1758)

The Vagrant Sympetrum, The Vagrant Darter

6 ♂ Only eight specimens of this species have been recorded in Britain, mainly from the London area. The last recorded specimen was a male taken by the author, 8.vii.1946, at Trent Park, Barnet, the specimen illustrated.

7 ♂♀ The narrow black band at the base of the frons is continued down the sides of the eyes in both sexes.

8 ♀ End of abdomen, lateral view, vulvar scale projecting at right-angles and level with segment 9.

Size. Wingspan 60mm; hindwing length 26–28mm. Average overall length 36mm; abdomen length 24–28mm.

Flight period. Mid-July to mid-September.

Flight and habitat. Its habits are similar to *S. striolatum* and it should be specially looked for when there are immigrations of other sympetrums.

Status and distribution (Map 43, also page 114).
In early July 1946 when the last recorded specimen was taken, many *S. fonscolombei* (Pl.11, figs.6,7) were in the same spot and it could very well have arrived in company with that migrant.

Sympetrum nigrescens Lucas, 1911

The Highland Darter

9 ♂ This species is best identified from the side to show the dark band on the thorax and the very heavily marked abdomen. Legs black striped with yellow.

10 ♀ The black markings on the abdomen may lead to confusion with *S. scoticum*, but compare pterostigmata.

11 ♂♀ The black band across the base of the frons is continued a little way down the sides of the eyes.

12 ♂♀ Pterostigma of *S. scoticum*.

13 ♂♀ Pterostigma of *S. nigrescens*.

Size. Wingspan 55mm; hindwing length 25–30mm. Average overall length 34mm; abdomen length 24–28mm.

Flight period. End of June to mid-August.

Flight and habitat. Similar to *S. scoticum*. The female specimen (fig.10) was swept from heather on a sunny but windy day near Loch-an-Eilean. As a result of morphological studies, A. E. Gardner, 1955 (*Entomologist's Gaz.***6:** 86–107) showed that *S. nigrescens* was the correct name for this species and that *S. striolatum nigrifemur*, Selys 1884, with which it had previously been confused, was not a British insect.

Status and distribution (Map 39, also page 112).
The sympetrum most likely to be found in Scotland in place of *S. striolatum* which it closely resembles in the male, and females may be easily mistaken for *S. scoticum*.

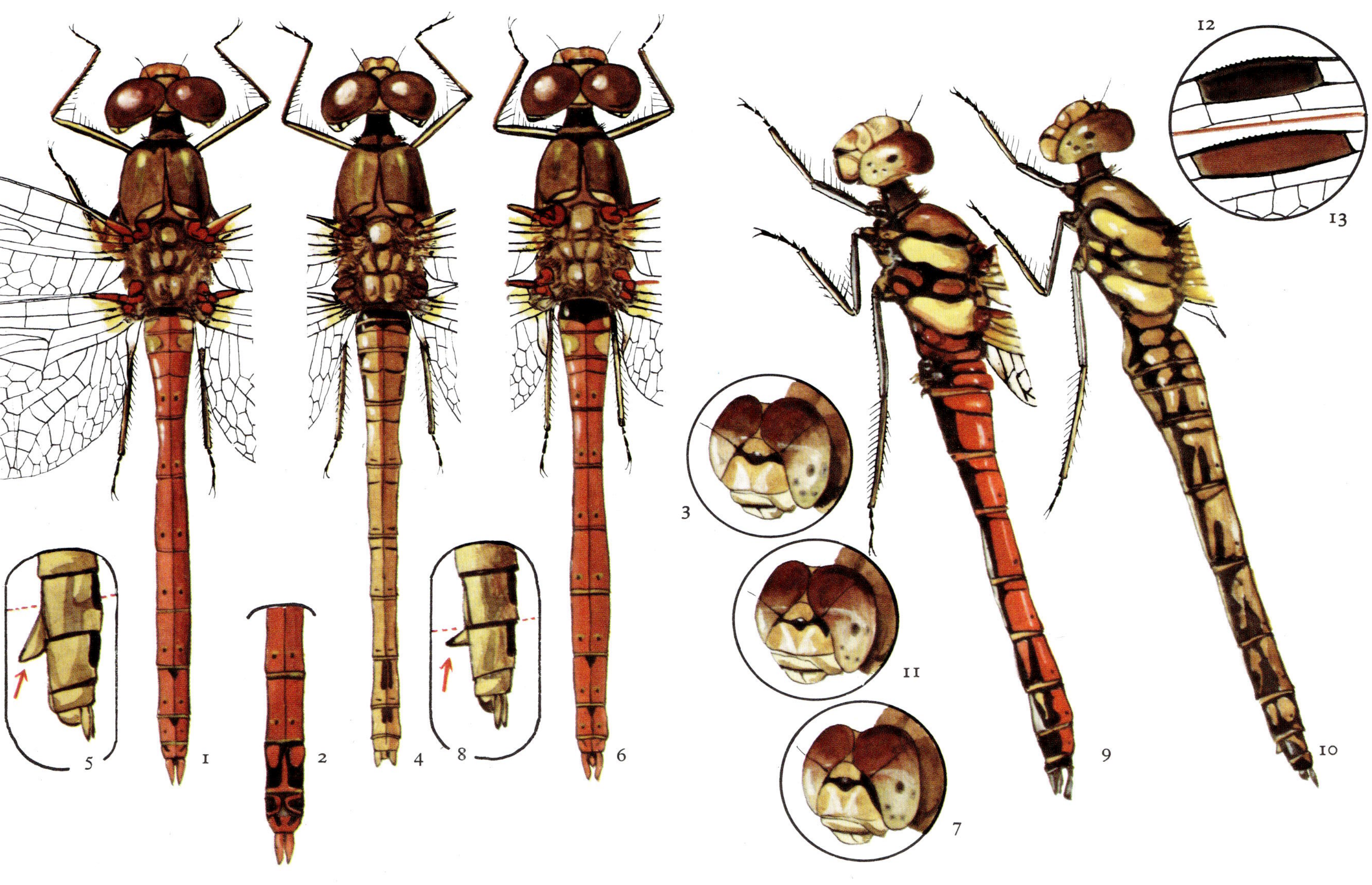

(×3 *approx*) Plate 12

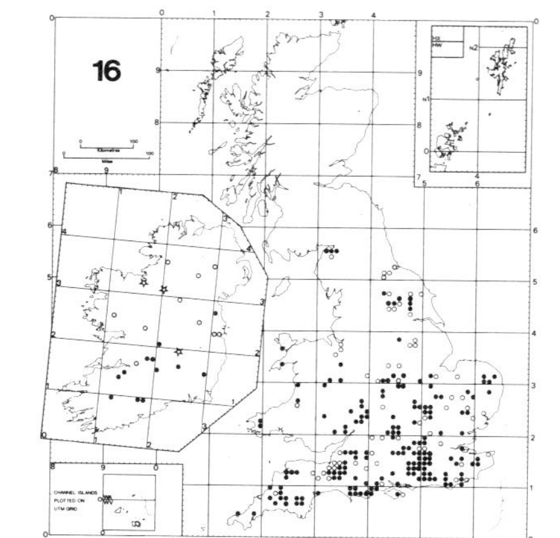

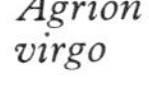

Agrion splendens

Agrion virgo

Agrion splendens (Harris, 1776)

The Banded Agrion, The Banded Demoiselle

1 ♂ The banded wing varies from light purple-brown to deep prussian blue according to age.
There is no pterostigma.

2 ♀ The wings give beautiful green reflections when in flight owing to the metallic green venation.
False pterostigma white; twice as large on the forewing as on the hindwing.

Size. Wingspan ♂61mm, ♀65mm; hindwing length 27–35mm. Average overall length 45mm; abdomen length 34–40mm.

Flight period. Mid-May to end of September.

Flight and habitat. This species prefers fast flowing streams, usually with muddy bottoms. Females have a feeble fluttering flight and usually settle on vegetation fringing the stream or on overhanging branches of trees. Males are much more active and engage in chasing one another and sometimes more than half-a-dozen may be seen involved in the chase which can last many minutes. Courtship is pretty to watch, the male vibrating his wings rapidly in front or above the female before flying with her in tandem.

Status and distribution (Map 16, also page 100).
Where this species is found, it is usually common and often abundant, frequently outnumbering any other damselflies present.

Agrion virgo (Linnaeus, 1758)

The Demoiselle Agrion, The Beautiful Demoiselle

3 ♂ In the male, almost all the wing is coloured purple-brown to deep blue-violet, according to age.
Pterostigma absent.

4 ♀ Wings dull purple-brown with dark venation which is finer than in *A.splendens*.
False pterostigma white; larger on forewing than on hindwing.

Size. Wingspan ♂58mm, ♀63mm; hindwing length 29–36mm. Average overall length 45mm; abdomen length 33–38mm.

Flight period. Beginning of May to mid-August.

Flight and habitat. Unlike *A.splendens*, this species prefers fast running clear streams with pebble bottoms such as are found in the New Forest. Slow fluttering butterfly-like flight in both sexes and flight not long sustained. Equally at home in sun or shade along the streams. Settling mainly on trees and bushes by the stream.

Status and distribution (Map 17, also page 101).
Although not so common nor so widely distributed as *A.splendens*, it is quite plentiful in its favoured localities, especially in the southern counties.

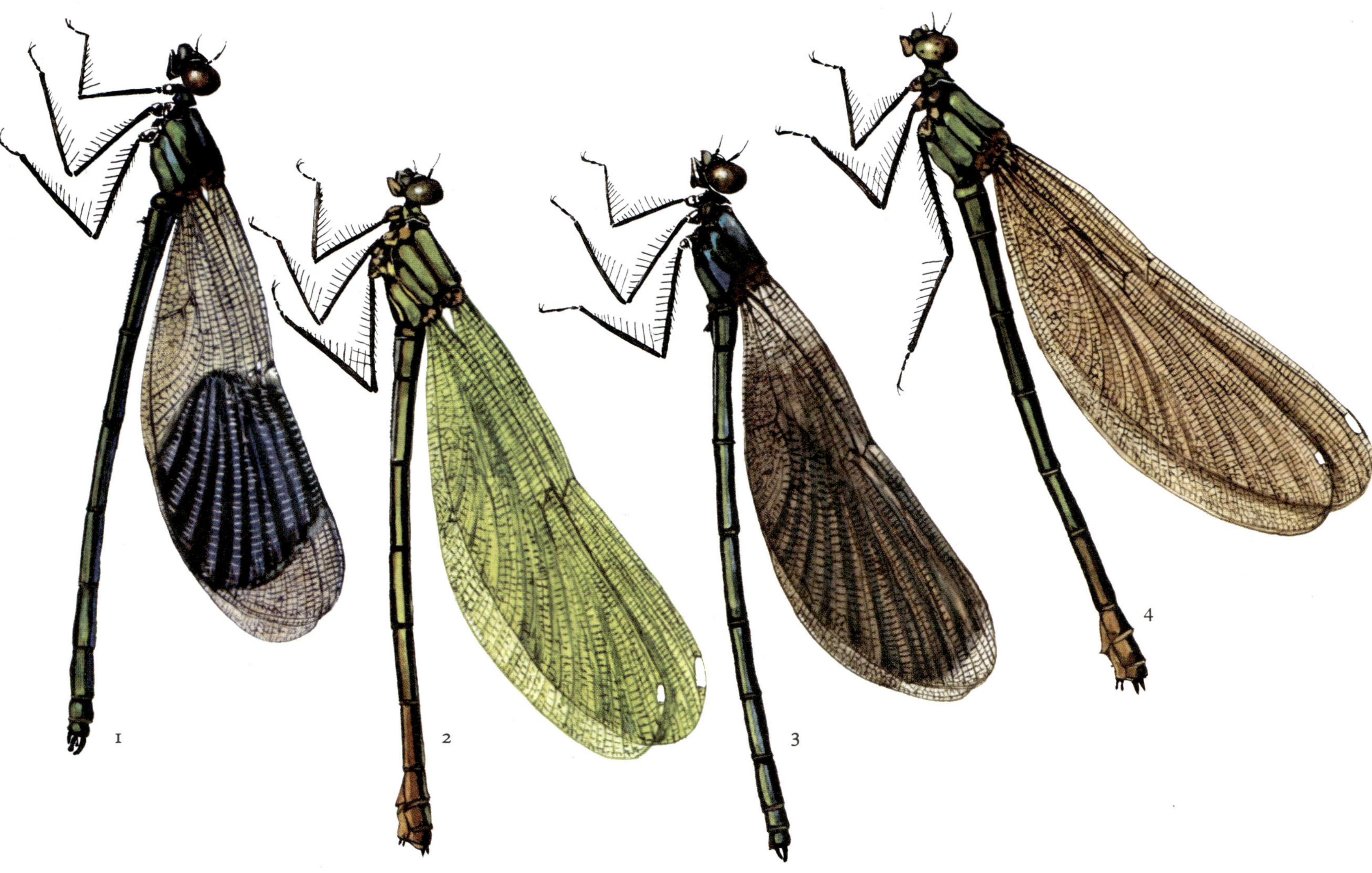

(× $2\frac{1}{2}$ *approx*) Plate 13

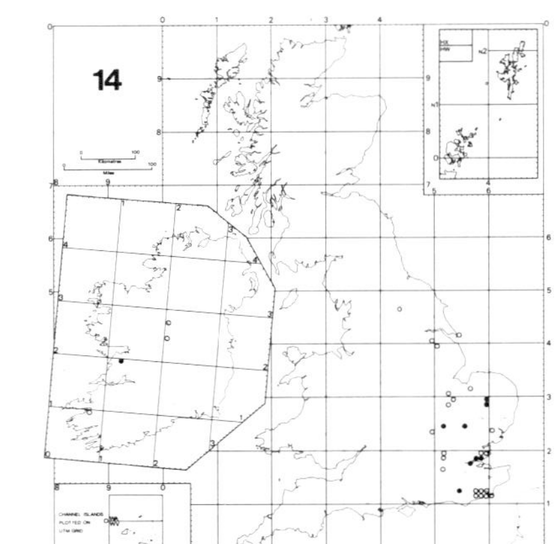

Lestes dryas

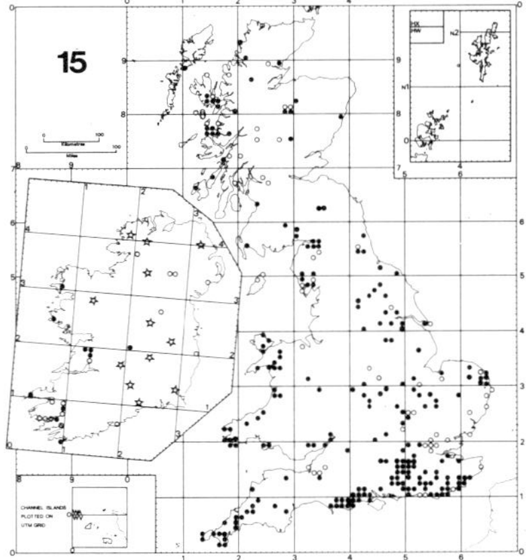

Lestes sponsa

Lestes dryas Kirby, 1890

The Scarce Green Lestes,
The Scarce Emerald Damselfly

1 ♂ A robust species. The powder-blue on the abdomen of the adult specimens usually occupies the basal two-thirds of segment 2.

2 ♂ Inferior (lower) anal appendages curved obliquely inwards at the tip.

3 ♂♀ Pterostigma about one-third as broad as long.

4 ♀ Body robust; shorter than the male.

5 ♀ Dark green markings on segment 1 of abdomen almost oblong.

6 ♀ Vulvar scale broad, extending beyond the tip of the abdomen – (red line).

Size. Wingspan 20–25mm; hindwing length 20–25mm. Average overall length ♂37mm, ♀34mm; abdomen length ♂28–33mm, ♀26–30mm.

Flight period. End of June to beginning of August.

Flight and habitat. This species prefers ditches almost filled with reeds or rushes. It settles well down in the vegetation and is best caught by sweeping. It must be a wanderer, for ditches which have dried up have been recolonised sporadically.

Status and distribution (Map 14, also page 99).
It is feared that this species, never really common, is now becoming very scarce. It has disappeared from several of its old localities near London through pollution of the habitat and has a precarious hold where it is still found.

Lestes sponsa (Hansemann, 1823)

The Green Lestes, The Emerald Damselfly

7 ♂ Slender species: the powder-blue on the abdomen of fully adult specimens covers all of segment 2.

8 ♂ Inferior anal appendages spatulate, directed straight backwards.

9 ♂♀ Pterostigma less than one-third as broad as long.

10 ♀ Slender species.

11 ♀ Dark green markings on segment 1 of abdomen rounded.

12 ♀ Vulvar scale slender, not extending beyond tip of abdomen.

Size. Wingspan 36mm; hindwing length ♂25–30mm, ♀20–24mm. Average overall length 38mm; abdomen length 26–33mm.

Flight period. Mid-June to end of September.

Flight and habitat. Unlike *L.dryas*, this species is quite at home in open ditches, as well as ponds and large lakes fringed with rushes. Boggy ground is also acceptable. On rainy or dull days rests in grass or heather. Both our lestes rest with wings half open (Fig.1d).

Status and distribution (Map 15, also page 100).
In many localities common and in some abundant. Found throughout the British Isles.

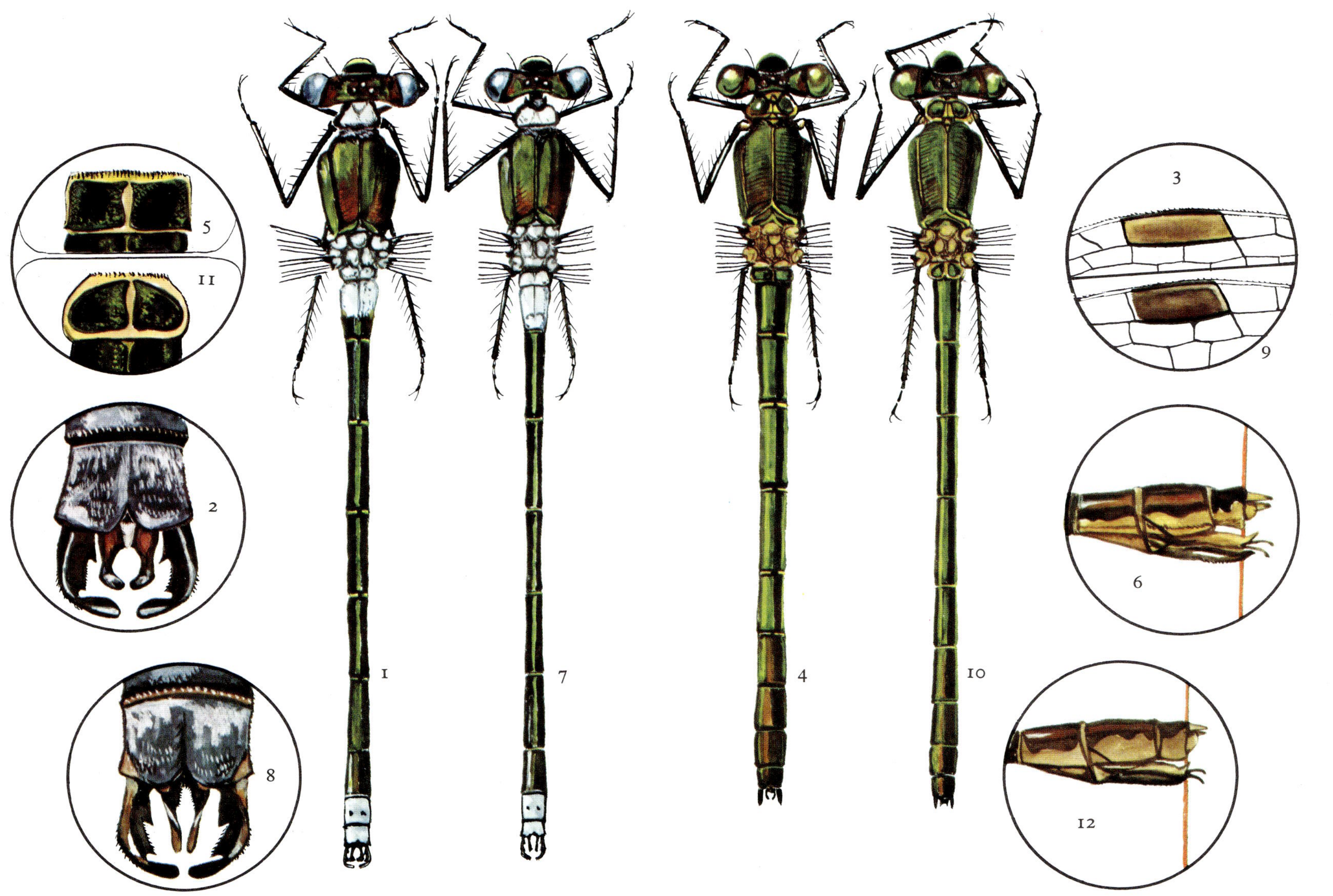

(×3½ *approx*) Plate 14

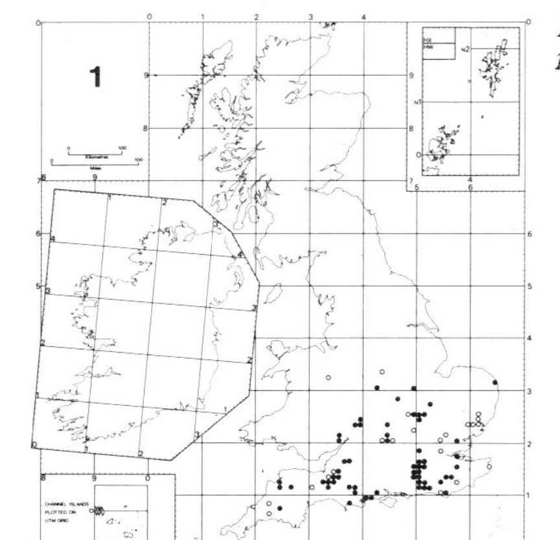

Platycnemis pennipes

Erythromma najas

Platycnemis pennipes (Pallas, 1771)

The White-legged Damselfly

1 ♂ In both sexes this damselfly is readily identified by the feather-like expansion of the hindtibia. The midtibia is also slightly expanded – not seen from above.
Both sexes are creamy white on emergence.
Males soon assume the palest blue.

2 ♂ Anal appendages.

3 ♀ Normal green form.

4 ♀ f.*lactea*. Note the few black markings.

5 ♂♀ The quadrilateral (discoidal cell) is almost rectangular and there are only two postquadrilateral cells before the subnodus.

6 ♂♀ All other damselflies, except the agrions, have the discoidal cell sharply angled.

Size. Wingspan 45mm; hindwing length 19–23mm. Average overall length 36mm; abdomen length 27–31mm.

Flight period. Mid-May to mid-August.

Flight and habitat. Has a preference for moving water with abundant vegetation typical of water meadows where it is frequently found flying in company with *Agrion splendens* (Pl.13, figs.1, 2). Specimens sometimes stray into nearby woodland. Flies with a fluttering flight and settles on floating or marginal vegetation.

Status and distribution (Map 1, also page 93).
A species which seems susceptible to even slight pollution, having disappeared from some of its localities in recent years. Still locally common where it occurs.

Erythromma najas (Hansemann, 1823)

The Red-eyed Damselfly

7 ♂ The robust appearance and outstanding red eyes make identification easy. Note also the black head with no postocular spots. Thorax entirely black.

8 ♀ Thorax with only short stripes. Eyes brown-red.

9 ♂♀ Two rows of cells between the costa and the radius distal to the pterostigma of the hindwing.

10 ♂♀ *Enallagma cyathigerum* usually has two rows of cells which may be broken as in the figure, but there are only three postquadrilateral cells before the subnodus.

11 ♂♀ *Ischnura*, *Ceriagrion*, *Pyrrhosoma* and *Coenagrion* have only one row of cells distal to the pterostigma.

Size. Wingspan ♂43mm, ♀46mm; hindwing length 19–24mm. Average overall length 35mm; abdomen length 25–30mm.

Flight period. Mid-May to end of August.

Flight and habitat. A powerful flier for a damselfly, keeping close to the water surface and well away from the margin of the lake or pond. Has a special preference for water lilies on which it rests for long periods, darting off in long sweeping circles to return to the same spot where many other males may be sharing the clump. Females prefer marginal vegetation.

Status and distribution (Map 3, also page 94).
Confined to midland and southern counties. In the Norfolk Broads it survives in slightly polluted water and, in some cases, where the once abundant water lily population has almost died out.

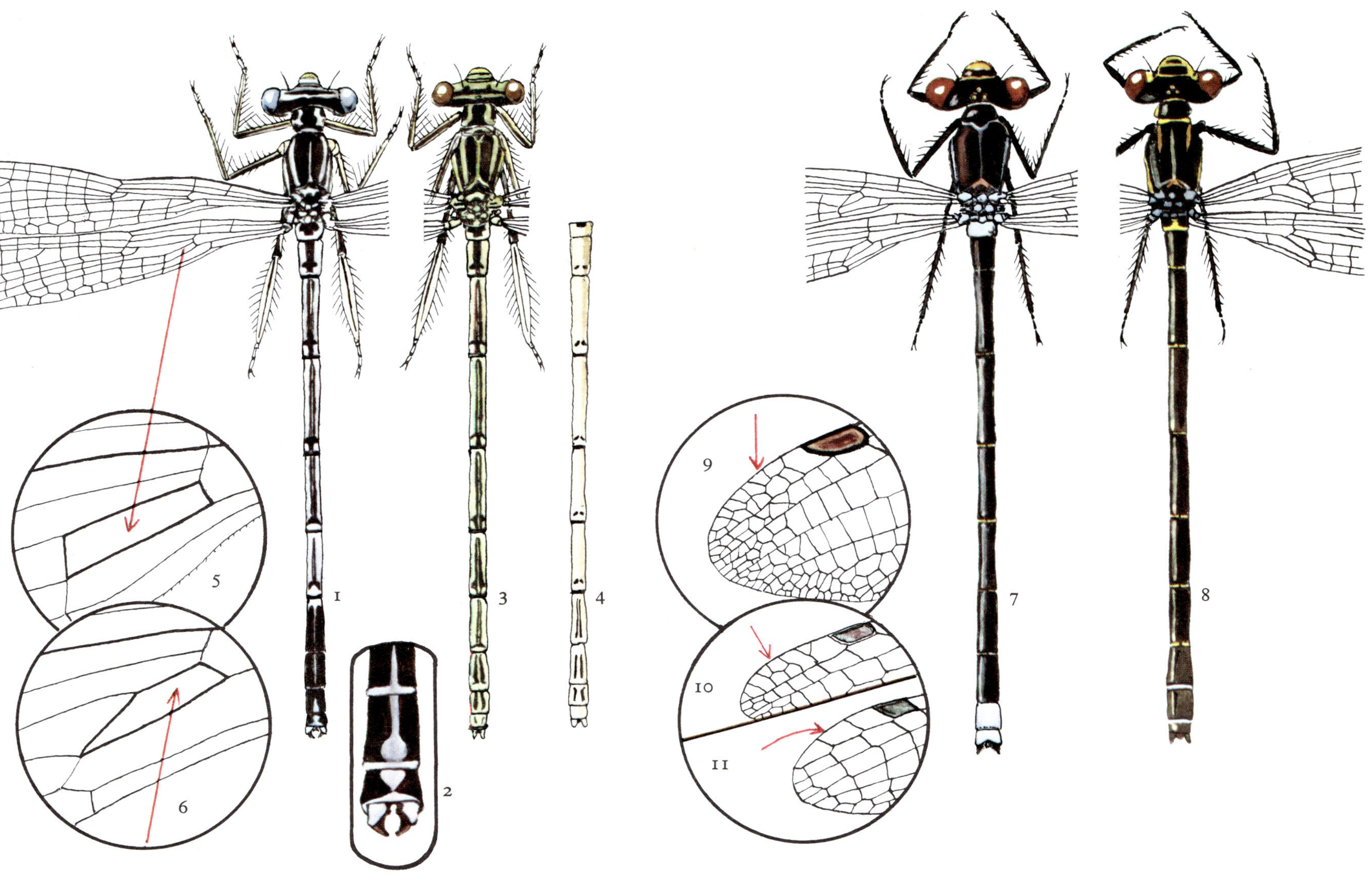

(×3 *approx*) Plate 15

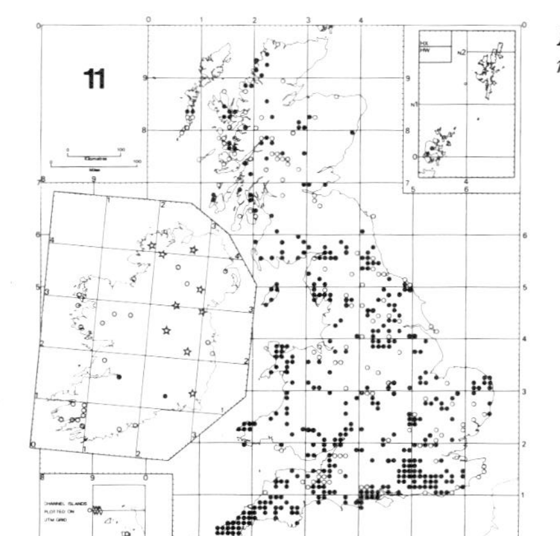

Pyrrhosoma nymphula

Ceriagrion tenellum

Pyrrhosoma nymphula (Sulzer, 1776)

The Large Red Damselfly

1 ♂ The antehumeral stripes vary from orange to deep crimson according to age. Forewing has 4 and hindwing 3 postquadrilateral cells before the subnodus.

2 ♀ Normal form.

3 ♀ Abdomen of female f.*fulvipes* Stephens. Black much reduced.

4 ♀ f.*melanotum* Selys. In this variety the thoracic stripes are always pale yellow even in fully adult specimens.
Intermediate forms occur between these extreme varieties.

Size. Wingspan ♂44mm, ♀48mm; hindwing length 19–24mm. Average overall length 36mm; abdomen length 25–29mm.

Flight period. Mid-May to mid-August.

Flight and habitat. The damselfly which has the reputation of being the first to appear in the spring and often the first entry in the recorder's notebook. Equally at home in slow-moving streams, canals, lakes, marshes and peat bogs and even in brackish water. Can easily be approached to photograph.

Status and distribution (Map 11, also page 98).
One of the commonest damselflies with a wide distribution over almost all of the British Isles.

Ceriagrion tenellum (de Villers, 1789)

The Small Red Damselfly

5 ♂ Note the pale red legs and the absence of antehumeral stripes.
Wings have 3 postquadrilateral cells before the subnodus.

6 ♀ Normal form.

7 ♀ f.*erythrogastrum* Selys in which the female resembles the male.

8 ♀ f.*melanogastrum* Selys. Thorax and abdomen entirely black.
The absence of antehumeral stripes, and the red legs will separate this form from the female *I.pumilio* (Pl.17, fig.12) which it closely resembles.

Size. Wingspan 36mm; hindwing length 25–28mm. Average overall length 31mm; abdomen length 23–26mm.

Flight period. Beginning of June to end of August.

Flight and habitat. A delicate species, breeding only in marshy localities or peat bogs, but usually common where it is found. Flight feeble and mainly from rush to rush, settling low on rushes or on heather near the breeding site.

Status and distribution (Map 2, also page 93).
Distribution, confined to the southern counties and very restricted by the choice of habitats so that it is essential to preserve these.

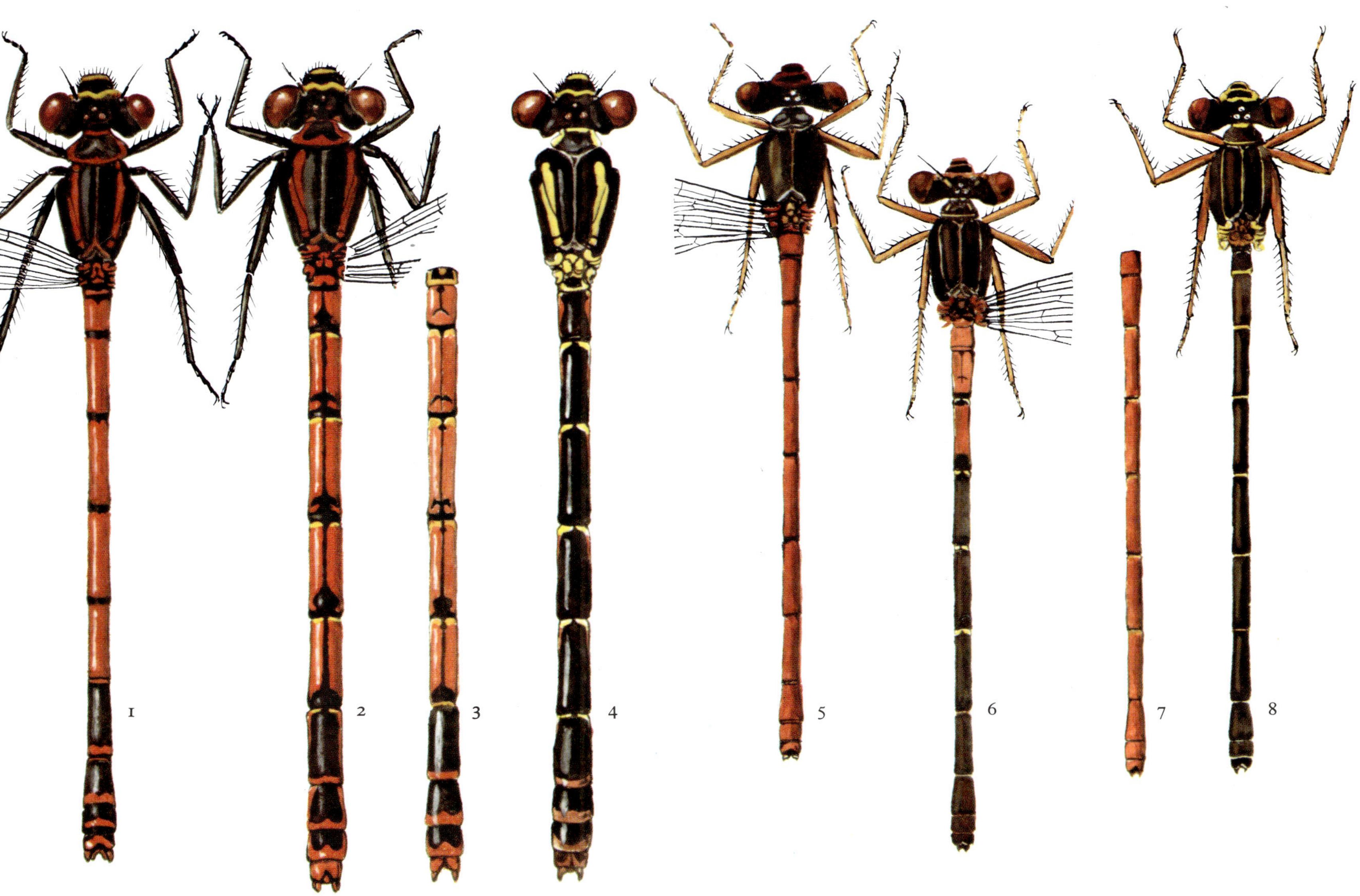

(×3½ *approx*) **Plate 16**

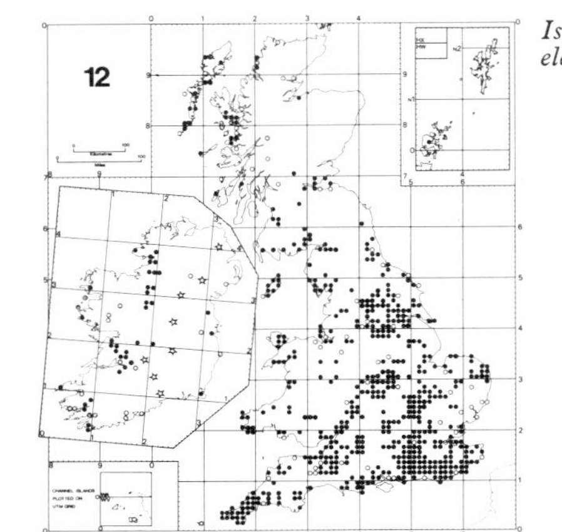

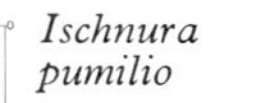

Ischnura elegans (van der Linden, 1820)

The Common Ischnura, The Blue-tailed Damselfly

1 ♂ Not subject to much colour variation.

2 ♂ Tip of abdomen showing segment 8 entirely blue. Anal appendages divaricate.

3 ♂♀ Pterostigma same size and shape in both fore- and hindwings; two coloured as shown.

4 ♀ Normal form.

5 ♂♀ Female f.*violacea* Selys, possibly a transitional colour form only.

6 ♂♀ Female f.*infuscans* Campion, with a dull brown band on segment 8 in place of blue.

7 ♂♀ Female f.*infuscans-obsoleta* Killington, with no thoracic stripes and segment 8 dull brown.

8 ♂♀ Female f.*rufescens* Stephens, with rose-pink thorax, segment 8 blue and light brown legs.

Size. Wingspan 35mm; hindwing length 14–20mm. Average overall length 31mm; abdomen length 22–29mm.

Flight period. End of May to beginning of September.

Flight and habitat. This species flies low amongst the herbage of sedgy ditches, canals, lakes and ponds and also slow-moving streams. In England it seems to have replaced *Pyrrhosoma nymphula* (Pl.16, figs.1,2) as the commonest damselfly.

Status and distribution (Map 12, also page 98).
One of the commonest of the damselflies distributed throughout the British Isles. Partially polluted ponds frequently have this species as the sole representative of the Odonata.

Ischnura pumilio (Charpentier, 1825)

The Scarce Ischnura,
The Scarce Blue-tailed Damselfly

9 ♂ Not subject to much colour variation.

10 ♂ Tip of abdomen showing segment 9 wholly blue, segment 8 only partly so.

11 ♂♀ Pterostigma of forewing of different shape and much larger than that of the hindwing; that of the forewing yellowish distally.

12 ♀ Normal form, best identified with reference to the pterostigma of both wings: that of the forewing is much larger.

13 ♂♀ Female f.*aurantiaca* Selys, with bright orange thorax and base of abdomen.
Note also the light brown legs and some wing veins orange.

Size. Wingspan 33mm; hindwing length 14–18mm. Average overall length 29mm; abdomen length 22–25mm.

Flight period. Mid-June to end of July.

Flight and habitat. A delicate species flying very low over boggy ground in the New Forest or elsewhere. Certainly a wanderer, ready to colonise any new patch of water. Has been seen ovipositing in a puddle by the roadside and in an almost dried up ditch, but the more boggy the situation, the more likely it is to be found.

Status and distribution (Map 13, also page 99).
In 1900 W. J. Lucas wrote, 'As a British insect this species seems to be lost at the present time'. However, the species has been recorded spasmodically many times in the New Forest since then and, being a wanderer, was most likely always present there as it was in 1975. Found in North Wales in July 1976.

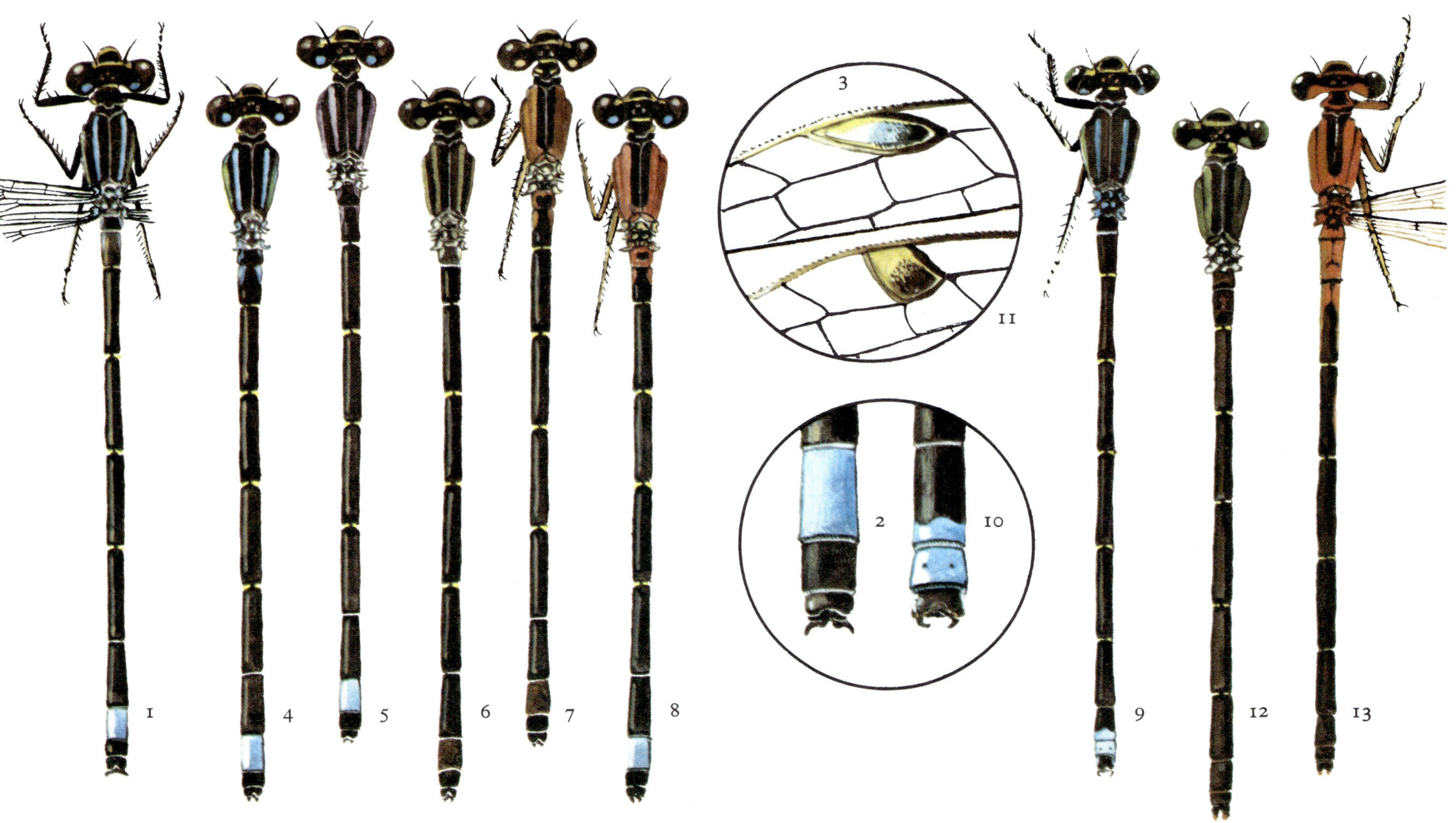

($\times 3\frac{1}{2}$ *approx*) Plate 17

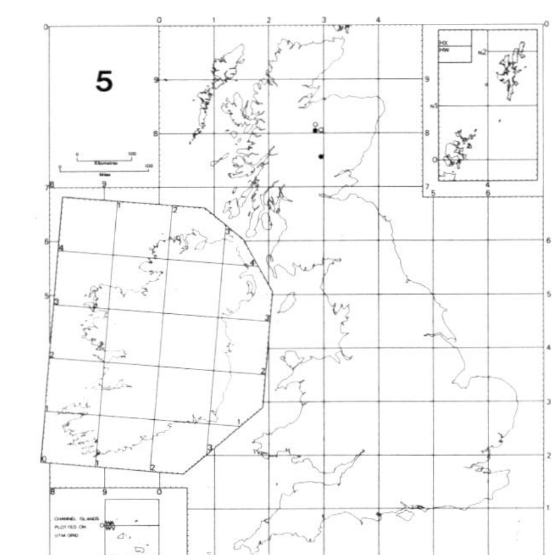

Coenagrion hastulatum

Enallagma cyathigerum

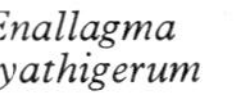

Coenagrion hastulatum (Charpentier, 1825)

The Northern Coenagrion, The Northern Damselfly

1 ♂ Segments 8–9 are blue as in *Enallagma*. Antehumeral stripes pale green to blue.

2 ♂ The black markings on segment 2 are not subject to much variation. Note particularly the black side markings above the spear-shaped central mark.

3 ♂ Anal appendages.

4 ♀ Best identified *in cop.*, but a close look at segments 1–2 of abdomen shows the thistle-marking with almost parallel sides. No ventral apical spine on segment 8.

5 ♀ Close-up of segments 1–2.

Size. Wingspan 40mm; hindwing length 17–22mm. Average overall length 31mm; abdomen length 24–26mm.

Flight period. Mid-June to beginning of August.

Flight and habitat. Frequents marshy spots and peat bogs in Scotland. Occasionally found on the margins of lochs in company with scores of *Enallagma cyathigerum* which it superficially resembles.

Status and distribution (Map 5, also page 95).
Restricted to Scotland but probably more widely distributed than present records indicate. Research is needed into both distribution and habits.

Enallagma cyathigerum (Charpentier, 1840)

The Common Blue Damselfly,
The Common Damselfly

6 ♂ Antehumeral stripes conspicuous and usually wider than in coenagrions.

7,8,9 ♂ Marking on segment 2 variable from an isolated spot (fig.7) to a spot with a stalk (fig.8) and, mostly in Scottish specimens, to a spear-shape (fig.9), leading to confusion with *C.hastulatum* so that careful attention should be paid to the shape of the anal appendages.

10 ♂ Anal appendages.

11 ♀ Normal form when fully adult.
Teneral specimens are straw-coloured.

12 ♀ Blue form with restricted black markings.

13 ♀ A robust ventral spine on segment 8 (side view). This serves to distinguish it from the coenagrions, and especially *C.hastulatum* whose haunts it shares in Scotland.

Size. Wingspan 38mm; hindwing length 18–20mm. Average overall length 32mm; abdomen length 24–28mm.

Flight period. Mid-May to mid-September.

Flight and habitat. An inhabitant of large open lakes, ponds, canals and streams where there is plenty of marginal vegetation. Usual flight is skimming low over large expanses of water, often facing the wind and being blown back by it. Sometimes flies low over surrounding land, especially among heather in Scotland.

Status and distribution (Map 10, also page 97).
It is very widely distributed in the British Isles and is usually plentiful where it occurs. Sometimes it is the only species at a Scottish loch and in this respect it may be compared with *Ischnura elegans* (Pl.17, figs.1–8) in England.

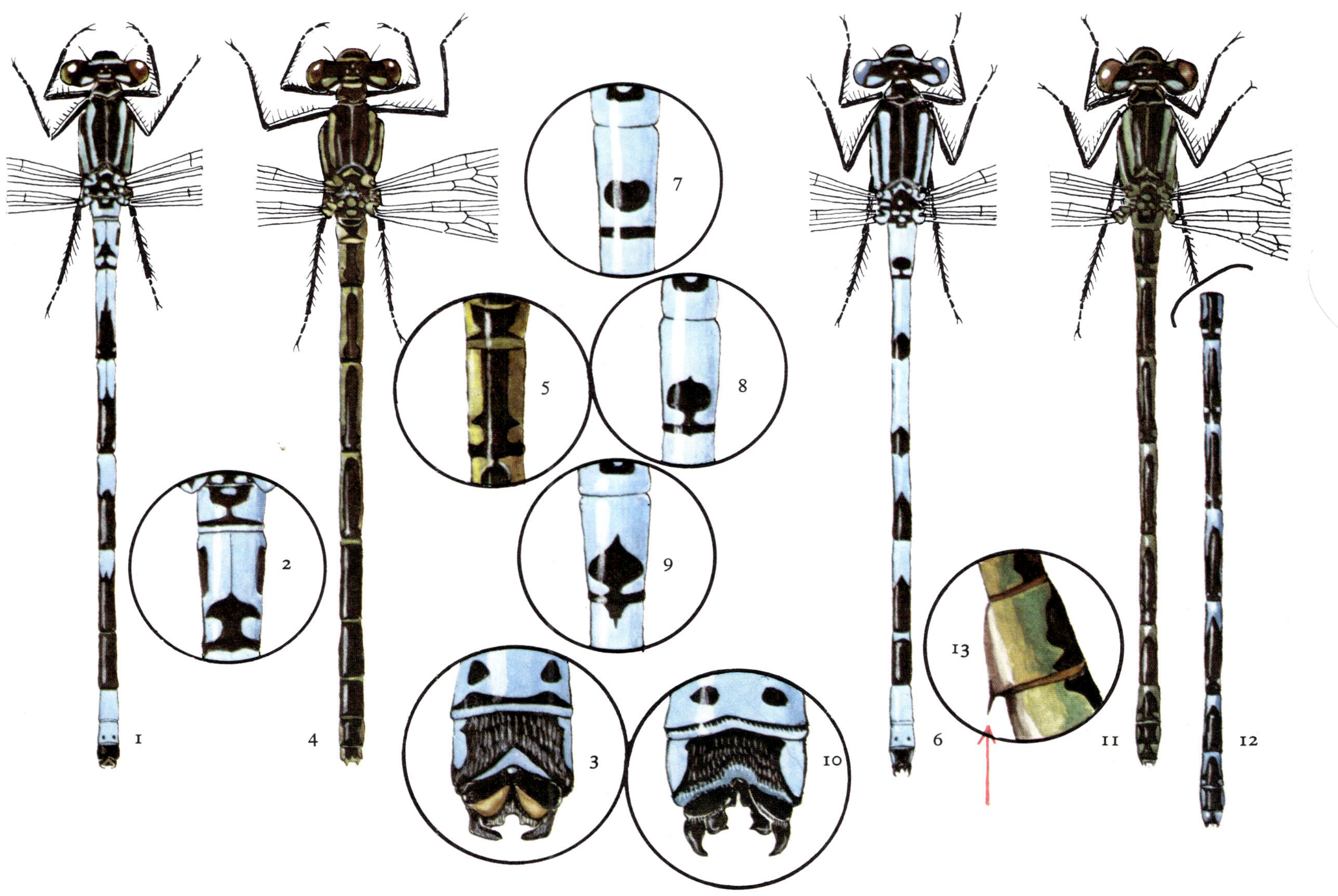

Plate 18 (×3½ approx)

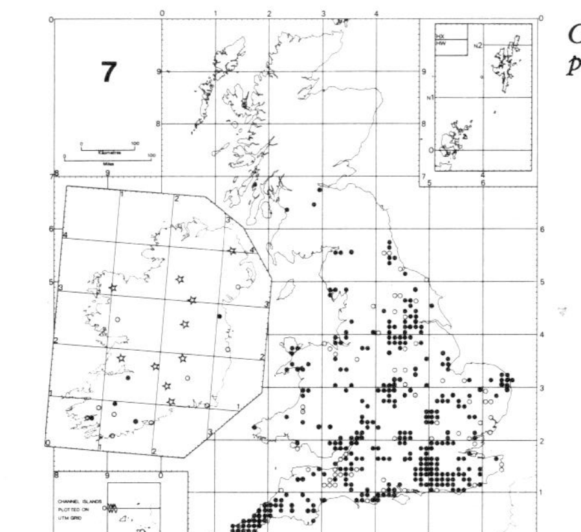

Coenagrion puella

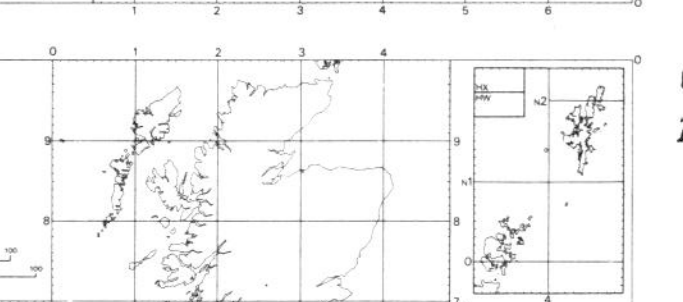

Coenagrion pulchellum

Coenagrion puella (Linnaeus, 1758)

The Common Coenagrion, The Azure Damselfly

1 ♂ Segment 8 all blue; 9 partly so. Antehumeral stripes complete.

2 ♂ Normal U-shaped mark on segment 2.

3 ♂ U-mark thickened and joined with a stalk to the apical band.

4 ♂ Prothorax, showing shape of hind margin from above.

5 ♂ Anal appendages.

6 ♀ Normal form.

7 ♀ Segments 1–2 of the normal form.

8 ♀ Blue form closely resembling the female of *C.pulchellum*, but note the thistle-shaped marking on segment 2 usually has a square top. Check prothorax.

Size. Wingspan 41mm; hindwing length 16–23mm. Average overall length 33mm; abdomen length 23–30mm.

Flight period. Mid-May to mid-August.

Flight and habitat. Frequents water meadows where there is luxuriant grass, or well reeded canals, ditches and ponds. Where *C.pulchellum* is present, careful examination is necessary to ensure correct determination as both species have variations which may overlap.

Status and distribution (Map 7, also page 96).
A common species in England and Ireland, but it is very local in Scotland.

Coenagrion pulchellum (van der Linden, 1825)

The Variable Coenagrion, The Variable Damselfly

9 ♂ Segment 8 all blue; 9 mostly black. Antehumeral stripes variable.

10 ♂ Normal marking on segment 2.

11 ♂ Abnormal form with antehumeral stripes absent and U-mark on segment 2 as in *C.puella*, from a specimen taken at Kings Lynn, Norfolk, 18.vii.1924 by the author.

12 ♂ Prothorax, showing shape of hind margin from above.

13 ♂ Anal appendages.

14 ♀ Normal form.

15 ♀ The mercury mark on segment 2 will help to identify this species. In this respect there may be confusion with the ♂ of *C.mercuriale*.

16 ♀ Usually the female has the thoracic stripes unbroken; the unique example shown was taken at Stalham, Norfolk, 5.vi.1958 by the author. Note also the very much reduced marking on segment 2.

Size. Wingspan 42mm; hindwing length 16–20mm. Average overall length 33mm; abdomen length 25–30mm.

Flight period. Mid-May to beginning of August.

Flight and habitat. Like *C.puella*, inhabits water meadows and dykes. Where there are lanes with high hedges and long grasses near the emergence sites, good use is made of them especially for shelter on windy days.

Status and distribution (Map 8, also page 96).
Becoming much less common than in the past, having disappeared from several well-known localities. Once teeming in the Norfolk Broads; only small numbers were present in 1975.

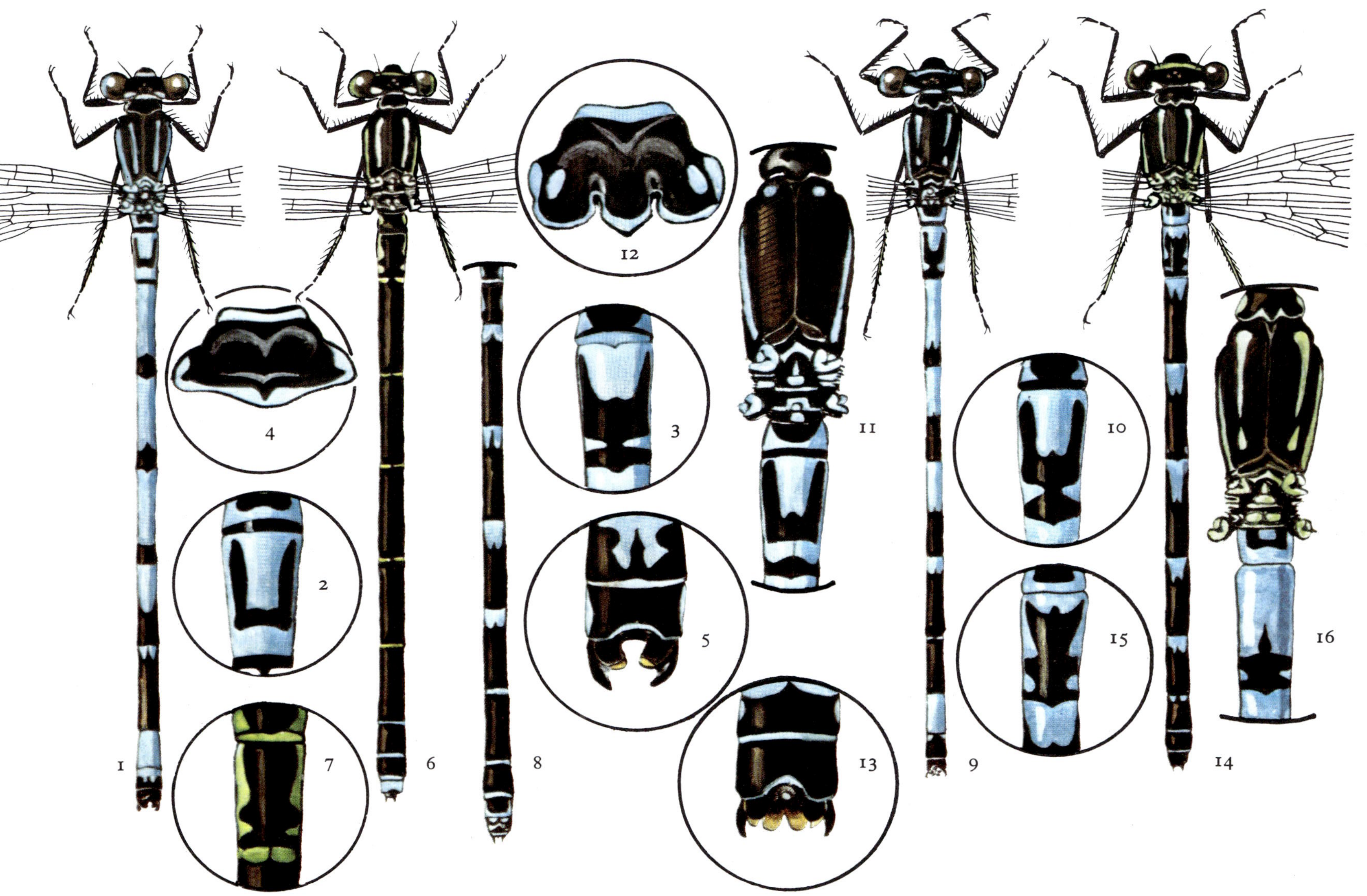

(×3½ *approx*) **Plate 19**

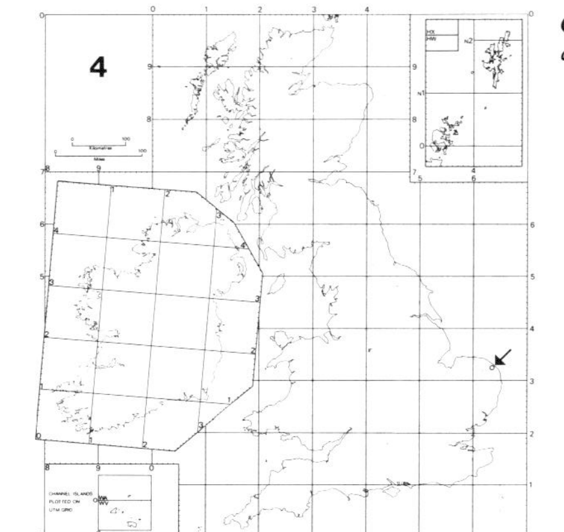

Coenagrion armatum

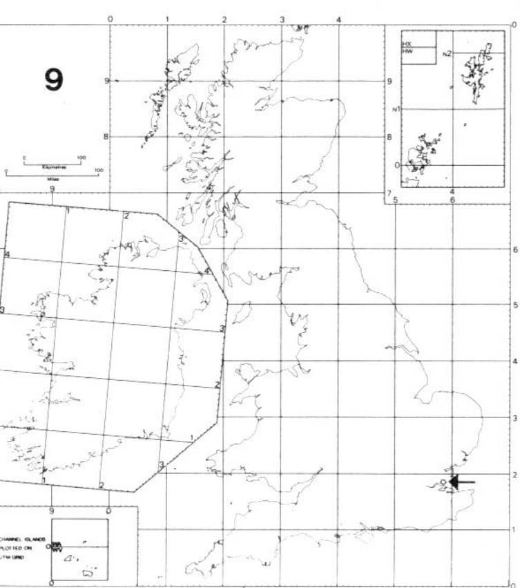

Coenagrion scitulum

6

Coenagrion mercuriale

Coenagrion armatum (Charpentier, 1840)

The Norfolk Coenagrion, The Norfolk Damselfly

1 ♂ Not likely to be confused with any other coenagrion by reason of the absence of thoracic stripes.

2 ♂ Note especially the enlarged anal appendages.

3 ♀ Easily identified by the bifid black markings on a background of blue or green on segment 8 and by the large amount of blue or green on segment 2.

Size. Wingspan 41mm; hindwing length 16–20mm. Average overall length 32mm; abdomen length 22–26mm.

Flight period. End of May to mid-June.

Flight and habitat. An elusive species which flies low between the reeds and is therefore difficult to follow. Chooses copiously reeded ponds or small boggy pools where it settles on water lilies or surrounding vegetation.

Status and distribution (Map 4, also page 94).
Last recorded in 1957. A Nature Conservancy Council survey in 1975 found the known sites near Stalham, Norfolk, badly polluted and quite unsuitable for the survival of the species. Only *Ischnura elegans* (Pl.17, figs.1–8) was seen, whereas 30 years ago this site had 16 species listed, including *Libellula fulva* (Pl.7, figs.6,8) and *Aeshna isosceles* (Pl.2, figs.4,6).

Coenagrion scitulum (Rambur, 1842)

The Dainty Coenagrion, The Dainty Damselfly

4 ♂ Normal form.

5 ♂ Anal appendages.

6 ♂ **7** ♂ Markings on segment 2 are extremely variable, two extremes being shown. Examination of the anal appendages is essential.

8 ♀ Closely resembles the ♀ of *Enallagma cyathigerum* but has no spine on segment 8. In the ♀ the underside of the head is white from below the eyes to the occiput which is black (Pl.18, fig.13).

Size. Wingspan 39mm; hindwing length 15–20mm. Average overall length 32mm; abdomen length 22–26mm.

Flight period. Mid-June to end of July.

Flight and habitat. Flying in much the same manner as *Enallagma cyathigerum* which it closely resembles, especially in the female. First discovered in 1946 by Miss C. Longfield and E. B. Pinniger at Benfleet, Essex, where it was flying along a ditch. In 1947 its headquarters were found by the author at a pond two miles farther east, near Hadleigh, where it was abundant for several years.

Status and distribution (Map 9, also page 97).
It is doubtful whether this small damselfly still occurs in Essex. The disastrous flooding of its habitat in 1953 wiped out the colony and destroyed all surrounding vegetation. It has been searched for annually since then without success.

Coenagrion mercuriale (Charpentier, 1840)

The Southern Coenagrion, The Southern Damselfly

9 ♂ The smallest coenagrion.

10 ♂ Mercury spot on segment 2, useful for identification.

11 ♂ Anal appendages.

12 ♀ Normal form. There is also a blue form.

13 ♀ The underside of the head is white.

Size. Wingspan 35mm; hindwing length 15–20mm. Average overall length 29mm; abdomen length 22–26mm.

Flight period. Mid-May to beginning of August.

Flight and habitat. This delicate species will seldom be found far away from the boggy ground where it breeds. Bog myrtle (*Myrica gale*) may help in prospecting a possible habitat. The species flies low over boggy parts and among grasses near by.

Status and distribution (Map 6, also page 95).
Restricted to the southern and south-western counties where it is locally common in favourable years. A New Forest species in need of protection.

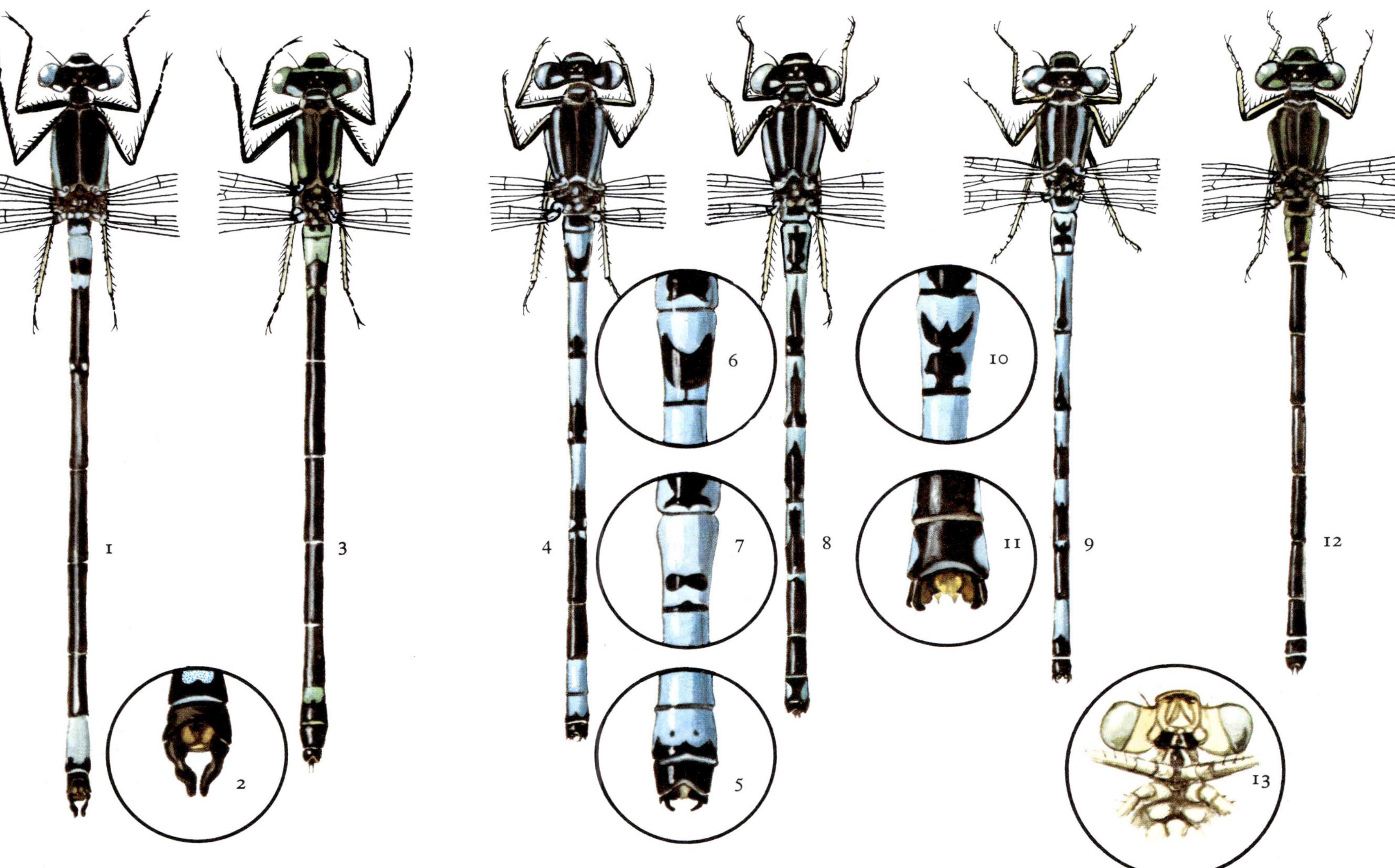

(×3½ *approx*) Plate 20

A KEY TO LARVAE*

A E Gardner

INTRODUCTION

The separation characters summarized in the following key have been based on those found in the mature larvae. In many species, however, the characters are sufficiently well developed to enable relatively immature specimens to be identified; these species have been indicated in the text.

Although thirty species of the British Odonata have been bred from the egg to the imaginal stage, it is considered necessary to breed the remaining thirteen species before any attempt is made to provide a key for the identification of the very early instars. Indeed, it may well prove impossible to provide a reliable key at specific level. However, some species have been found to exhibit distinctive characters at the second instar and these characters have been included in the keys to the mature larvae.

With most species a sufficient degree of maturity will have been reached for identification if it is found that the wing-sheaths reach beyond the third abdominal segment. It is considered inadvisable to name specimens prior to this stage unless special characters are evident; this applies especially to zygopterous larvae. The lengths of the mature larvae have been given and in many species will be seen to be very variable. Measurements are in millimetres from the front margin of the head, or forward protuberance of the labium, to the tip of the anal appendages. With spirit-preserved specimens a shrinkage of ten per cent may be expected. The exuvia of the zygopterous larvae may fall well below the minimum length indicated for a given species on account of the telescoping of the abdominal segments; whilst anisopterous exuviae may slightly exceed the maximum length indicated on account of the abdominal segments being fully distended. In order to facilitate identification, keys have been constructed for suborders, families, genera and finally for species, with the sole exception of the Corduliidae. In this family, the scheme adopted, namely the omission of a key to the genera, is considered easier for the student to follow. Wherever possible characters have been included which will assist the identification of living specimens. Unfortunately, however, this is not possible with all species and it may be found necessary to kill the subject in order to examine the labium or 'mask.' With exuviae, the labium may either be detached and made into a permanent slide mount, or merely attached to a slip of card and kept with the specimen. With the larger species it is usually sufficient to extend the labium by previously softening the base and labial suture in water for a short time.

Previous authors have relied on the number of premental and palpal setae to provide a sufficient means of identification for a number of species, but the examination of a long series of known larvae and exuviae has proved this character to be seldom reliable as the variation is often considerable. Although the full variation found in the number of premental and palpal setae is given, the character and disposition of small fields of setae have often been found to be more reliable guides. The shape of the labium and distal border of the labial palpi are also important separation characters. All drawings of the labium show the organ as flattened on a slide. The terminology used is that put forward by Corbet (1953).

In the Aeshnidae the supracoxal armature (Fig.6c) situated on the dorsal surface at the base of the forelegs, although slightly variable in outline, will help to confirm the identification. The shape of the head, both dorsal and frontal aspect, shape of the abdomen, mid-dorsal and lateral abdominal spines are important characters. Larvae breeding in muddy habitats frequently have the abdominal spines obscured by dirt; this may be cleaned off gently with a camel hair brush. Any dirt may be cleaned from exuviae by boiling in a weak solution of caustic potash for half-a-minute, followed by careful brushing.

With most zygopterous larvae the caudal lamellae provide a useful character for identification. A live larva may have a lamella removed without injury to the specimen by placing it in a dish of water and taking hold of the organ with a pair of tweezers, the points of which have been stoned to remove any excessive sharpness which may injure the lamella. When held by the tweezers the larva will cast the organ off. It is generally desirable to remove the median lamella as this is the most distinctive in outline. It may be examined in water as a temporary mount on a slide, or made into a permanent mount using glycerine jelly, a medium which shows up the tracheation well. The distorted lamellae of exuviae may be softened in water, straightened and mounted in a suitable medium. With those species of the Zygoptera in which the

Entomologist's Gaz.*, 1954, **5: 157–171, 193–213, with additions to *Sympetrum* Key, *Entomologist's Gaz.*, 1955, **6**: 94–95.

Figure 6

(a) *Aeshna juncea* (L.), labium

(b) *Coenagrion hastulatum* (Charp.), labium

1. Prementum
2. Median sulcus
3. Median lobe
4. Median cleft
5. Piliform setae
6. Distal margin of median lobe
7. Lateral margin of prementum
8. Spines
9. Spiniform setae
10. Labial palpus
11. End hook
12. Movable hook
13. Outer margin of palpus
14. Inner margin of palpus
15. Distal margin of palpus
16. Premental setae
17. Palpal setae
18. Intermediate hooks

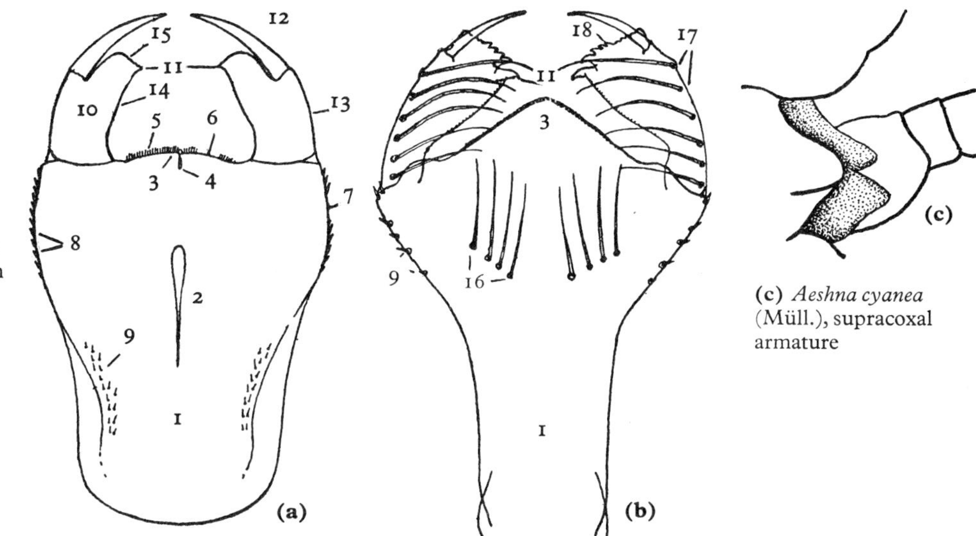

(c) *Aeshna cyanea* (Müll.), supracoxal armature

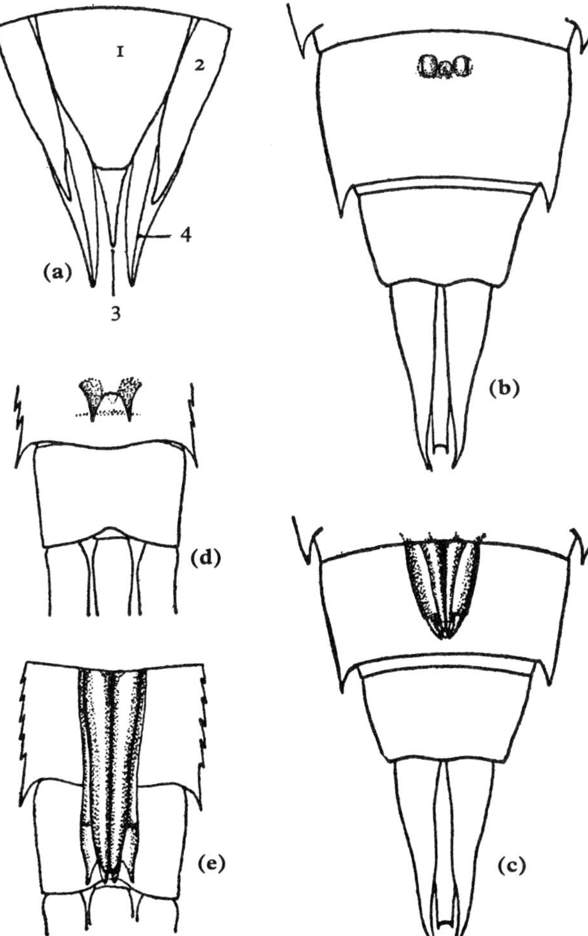

lamellae have the edge armature differentiated into stout ante- and fine postnodal setae, it must be remembered that the lateral lamellae generally have the greater number of antenodal setae on the dorsal edge, whereas with the median lamella the position is reversed. *Lamellae* are not infrequently lost and regrown; therefore care must be exercised when examining these organs otherwise confusion may result if a partly regrown organ is mistaken for the fully developed lamella.

Where single lamellae are illustrated they represent the median, the dorsal edge being shown uppermost in all examples excepting Figs.9d and 9g where the dorsal edge is towards the left.

In the Anisoptera the anal appendages (Fig.7a) also provide a useful character for identification of many species. The terminology adopted in my previous papers is that of Tillyard (1917) but this is held by some experts to be incorrect. It is considered that the appendix dorsalis should be known as the *epiproct*; the cerci as the *paraprocts*; whilst the cercoids developing late in the larval stage should be referred to as the true *cerci*. I have adopted this latter terminology in all cases where reference is made to the anal appendages.

Figure 7 *(left)*

(a) *Cordulia aenea* (L.), male anal appendages:
1. Male projection, 2. Cerci, 3. Epiproct, 4. Paraprocts

(b) *Aeshna juncea* (L.), male genitalia

(c) *A.juncea* (L.), female genitalia

(d) *Lestes sponsa* (Hans.), male genitalia

(e) *L.sponsa* (Hans.), female genitalia

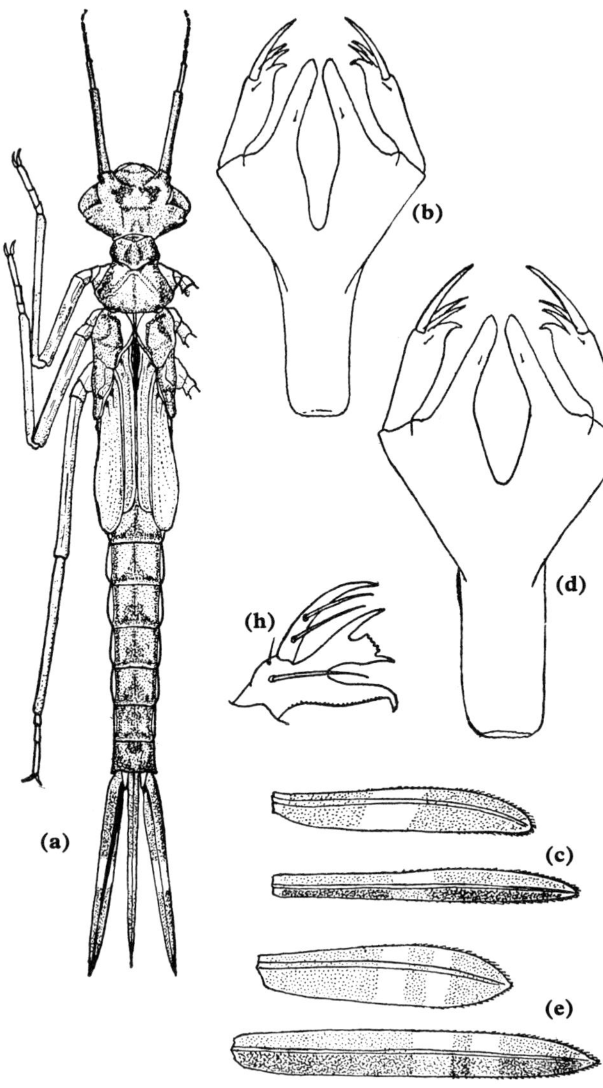

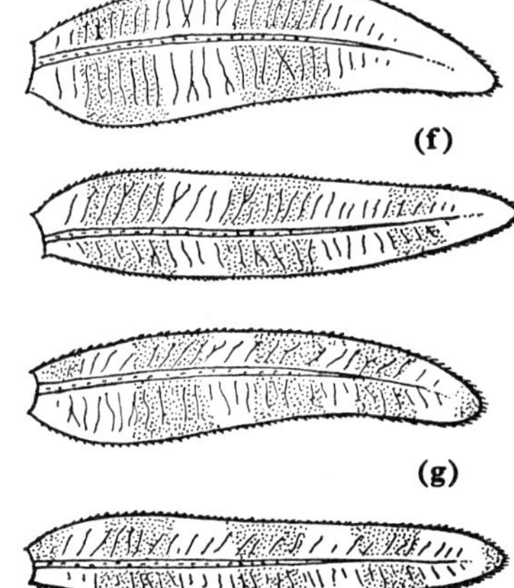

Figure 8

(a) *Agrion virgo* (L.), larva
(b) *A.virgo* (L.), labium
(c) *A.virgo* (L.), median and lateral caudal lamellae
(d) *A.splendens* (Harris), labium
(e) *A.splendens* (Harris), median and lateral lamellae
(f) *Lestes dryas* Kirby, median and lateral lamellae
(g) *L.sponsa* (Hans.), median and lateral lamellae
(h) *L.sponsa* (Hans.), labial palpus

The sex of even relatively immature larvae may be determined by the following characters:

In all the Zygoptera the male gonapophyses are relatively small and consist of two triangular processes (Fig.7d) on the ventral surface of the ninth abdominal segment. The female gonapophyses (Fig.7e) are conspicuous and generally extend over the ventral surface of the ninth and tenth segments. Within the Anisoptera, females of Cordulegasteridae and Aeshnidae may be determined by the conspicuous gonapophyses (Fig.7c) as in the Zygopterous species; in the remaining families the female gonapophyses are generally inconspicuous. All anisopterous males possess a male projection (Fig.7a:1) situated at the base of the epiproct on the dorsal surface; this is additional to the accessory genitalia which are indicated on the ventral surface of the second and third abdominal segments, and the genital pore on the ninth (Fig.7b).

The separation characters employed in the following key are based entirely on those found in the British species

Key to suborders

1 Larvae long and slender; abdominal pleurites infolded; abdomen terminating in three caudal lamellae .... **Zygoptera**

— Larvae comparatively shorter and more stoutly built; abdomen with ventral pleurites present; abdomen terminating in five spine-like appendages.......................... ....**Anisoptera** (p.79)

Suborder ZYGOPTERA

Key to Families

1 Antennae with scape as long as the remaining six segments taken together. Labium with median cleft wide, extending to nearly half the length of the prementum (Figs.8b,d). Caudal lamellae with laterals triquetral, median of the lamellar type (Figs.8c,e). (Apical combs of tibiae consisting of spinate setae) ....AGRIIDAE

— Antennae with scape considerably less than the total length of the remaining segments taken together. Labium with median cleft short, slit-like or with medium lobe entire. All caudal lamellae of the lamellar type..............2

2 Labium with prementum much contracted basally (ladle-shaped), not triangular in outline, median cleft slit-like (Fig.9c); labial palpi with movable hooks armed with setae. Caudal lamellae with secondary tracheae at right angles to main trunks, running nearly to edge of lamellae before branching. (Apical combs of tibiae consisting mainly of bidentate setae (Fig.9b))............LESTIDAE

— Labium not greatly contracted basally, triangular in outline, median lobe of prementum without median cleft; labial palpi with movable hooks not armed with setae.

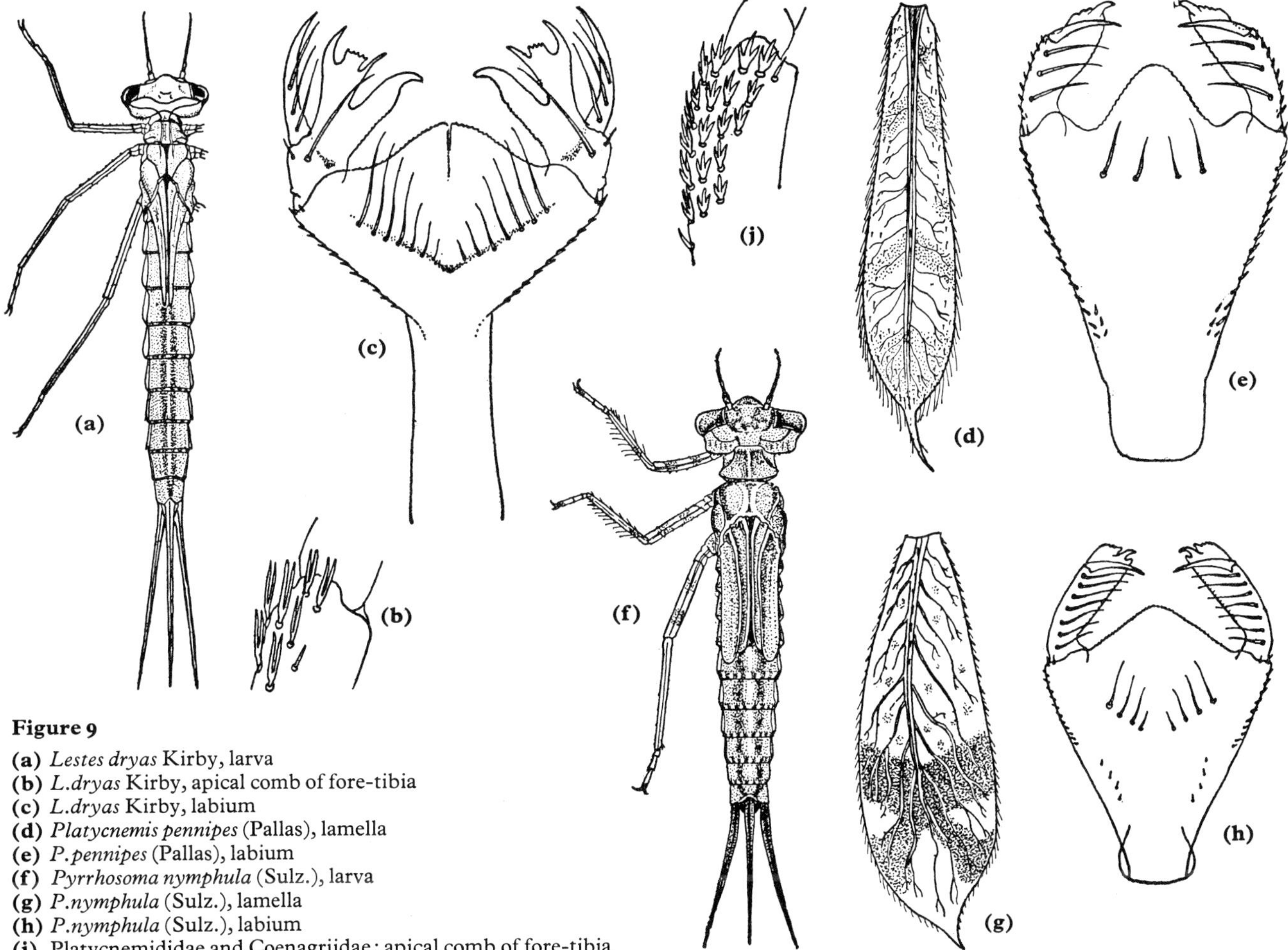

Figure 9

(a) *Lestes dryas* Kirby, larva
(b) *L.dryas* Kirby, apical comb of fore-tibia
(c) *L.dryas* Kirby, labium
(d) *Platycnemis pennipes* (Pallas), lamella
(e) *P.pennipes* (Pallas), labium
(f) *Pyrrhosoma nymphula* (Sulz.), larva
(g) *P.nymphula* (Sulz.), lamella
(h) *P.nymphula* (Sulz.), labium
(j) Platycnemididae and Coenagriidae: apical comb of fore-tibia

Caudal lamellae with secondary tracheae at an oblique angle to main trunks, much branched. (Apical combs of tibiae consisting mainly of tridentate setae (Fig.9j))........3

3 Antennae with first segment of flagellum shorter than pedicel. Labial palpi with outer margin armed with spinate setae (Fig.9e). Caudal lamellae denodate, with apices produced into long narrow points, marginal setae long, hair-like and of varying lengths, not differentiated into stout antenodal and fine postnodal setae (Fig.9d)...... .... PLATYCNEMIDIDAE

— Antennae with first segment of flagellum longer than pedicel. Labial palpi with outer margin not armed with spinate setae (except *Coenagrion mercuriale* (Charp.) which has them few in number and of piliform structure). Caudal lamellae denodate to nodate, not produced into long narrow points; marginal setae not relatively long, differentiated into stout antenodal and fine postnodal setae (except *Pyrrhosoma nymphula* (Sulzer))................... ....COENAGRIIDAE

Family AGRIIDAE

One genus *Agrion* Fabricius

Key to species

1 Labium with median cleft of prementum more than four times as long as broad (Fig.8b). Median caudal lamella narrow, nearly as long as laterals; lamellae dark in colour with a narrow pale band at about mid-length (Fig.8c). L. 30–35mm....................................*A.virgo* (Linnaeus)
Breeds in swift clear streams with clean sandy or gravelly bottoms.

— Labium with median cleft of prementum less than four times as long as broad (Fig.8d). Median caudal lamella broad, distinctly shorter than laterals (Fig.8e); lamellae dark, usually with two pale bands at about mid-length. L. 30–45mm...................................*A.splendens* (Harris)
Breeds in sluggish streams and occasionally ponds with muddy bottoms.

As these species occasionally breed in the same stream

if the conditions are suitable, and as the larvae are not infrequently found with one or more caudal lamellae missing, or regrown, care should be exercised when using the lamellae as a separation character. Immature specimens of both species may be readily determined by their characteristic appearance (Fig.8a).

Family LESTIDAE

One genus *Lestes* Leach

Key to species

1 Labial palpi with 2 setae on each movable hook (Fig.8h). Caudal lamellae narrower in proportion to length, of more even width from base to apex (Fig.8g). Female gonapophyses reaching to, or just beyond the tenth abdominal segment. L. 26·5–34·5mm...*L.sponsa* (Hansemann)
Breeds in ponds, canals and weedy ditches.

— Labial palpi with 3 or more setae on each movable hook (Fig.9c). Caudal lamellae broader in proportion to length, of a sharper apical taper and more pronounced curvature (all these characters most distinctive in the median lamella (Fig.8f)). Female gonapophyses reaching well beyond the tenth abdominal segment. L. 29–32mm ....*L.dryas* Kirby
Breeds in similar habitats to L.sponsa.
From the second instar onwards, the larvae of *Lestes* can be separated from other genera by the presence of the bidentate setae on the tibial combs.

Family PLATYCNEMIDIDAE

One genus *Platycnemis* Burmeister

One species recorded from Britain. Labium with premental setae 2+2, labial palpi with 3 setae (Fig.9e). Caudal lamellae (Fig.9d) distinctive in outline, with scattered setae on sides from base to apex; markings variable, sometimes confined to marginal spots. L. 18·5–22mm..*P.pennipes* (Pallas)
Breeds in weedy streams, rivers and seepages bordering streams.

Family COENAGRIIDAE

Key to genera

1 Caudal lamellae denodate, with distinctive dark pattern (Fig.9g) broad, of convex apical outline, apices acutely pointed; marginal setae not divided into stout antenodal and fine postnodal setae; strong setae few and widely spaced. (Head with postocular region somewhat rectangular in outline.).............*Pyrrhosoma* Charpentier

— Caudal lamellae subnodate or nodate, immaculate, blotched or with transverse bands of various outlines; marginal setae divided into stout antenodal and fine postnodal setae..2

Figure 10
(a) *Ceriagrion tenellum* (de Villers), head
(b) *C.tenellum* (de Villers), labium
(c) *C.tenellum* (de Villers), lamella
(d) *Ischnura elegans* (van der Linden), head
(e) *I.elegans* (van der Linden), labium
(f) *I.elegans* (van der Linden), lamella
(g) *Coenagrion puella* (L.), head
(h) *Enallagma cyathigerum* (Charp.), labium
(j) *E.cyathigerum* (Charp.), lamella

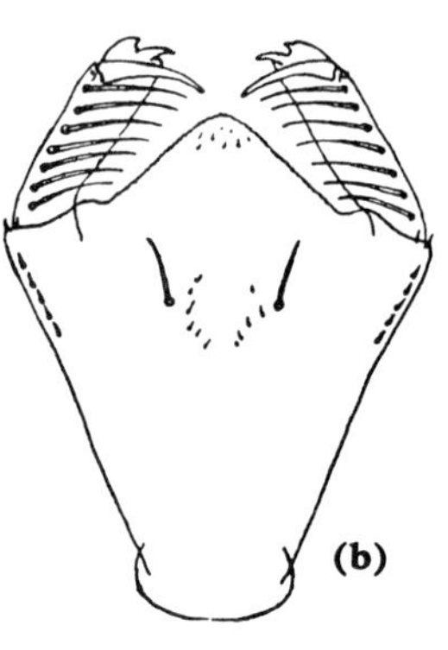

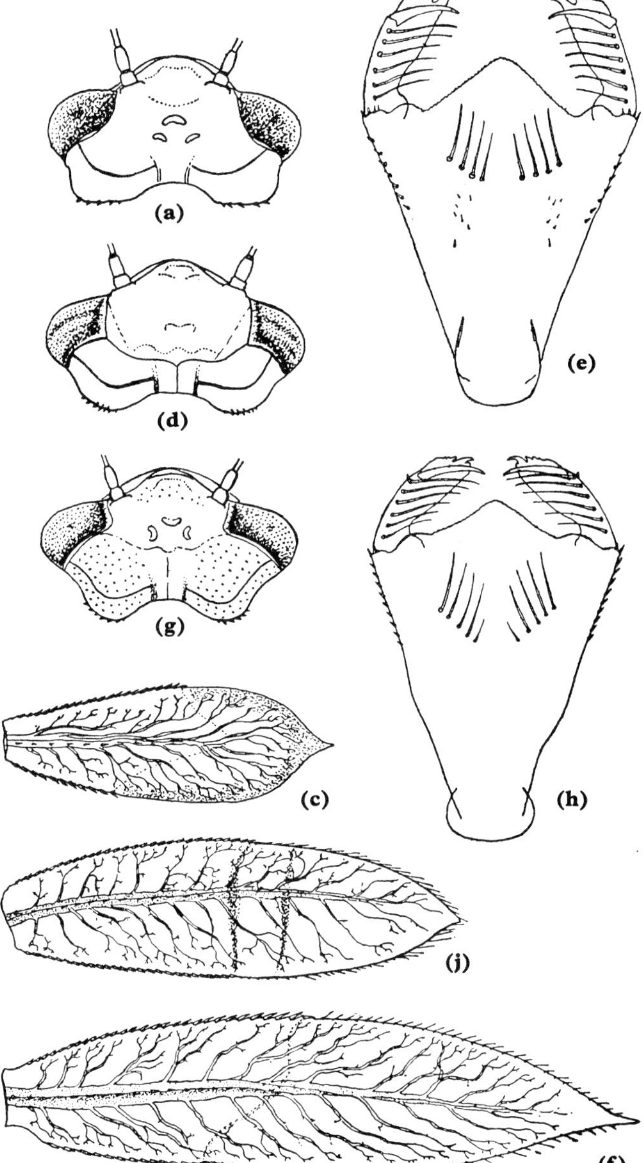

2 Caudal lamellae with marginal setae reaching to, or beyond mid-length on one of the two margins only........3

— Caudal lamellae with marginal setae reaching to, or beyond mid-length on both margins..............................5

3 Head with postocular region rectangular in outline (Fig. 10a). Caudal lamellae short, broad, obtusely pointed, marked with marginal blotches (Fig.10c). Labium with premental setae 1+1 (rarely 2+2); area between premental setae bearing a field of scattered short setae (Fig. 10b); distal margin of labial palpi nearly straight and armed with setae (Fig.11a).. ....*Ceriagrion tenellum* (de Villers)

— Head with postocular region of a sweeping curvilinear outline (Fig.10d). Labium with premental setae more than 2+2; area between premental setae not bearing a field of short scattered setae; distal margin of labial palpi bearing prominent intermediate hooks without setae (Fig.11b)..4

4 Caudal lamellae of medium length, broad, with apices acutely pointed (Fig.11h)...*Coenagrion scitulum* (Rambur)

— Caudal lamellae relatively long, narrow, with apices usually sharply pointed (Fig.10f).....*Ischnura* Charpentier

5 Larvae usually of more than 30mm in length. Caudal lamellae with apices obtusely rounded or convexo-angulate, postnodally marked with three distinctive dark bands and with tracheation prominently dark (Fig.12g)... ....*Erythromma* Charpentier

— Larvae of less than 30mm in length. Caudal lamellae not marked with three broad dark bands.............................6

6 Head without prominent spotting. Labial palpi bearing a short spine on the outer margin in line with the anterior palpal setae (Fig.11c). Caudal lamellae with antenodal and postnodal margins of approximately the same convexity in outline, usually with one to three narrow transverse bands (Fig.10j)...........................*Enallagma* Charpentier

— Head with or without prominent spotting (Fig.10g). Labial palpi without a short spine on the outer margin in line with the anterior palpal setae. Caudal lamellae with antenodal margins generally less convex than the postnodal, without pigmentation. (Sometimes showing a 'false' band from the lodgement of foreign matter along the nodal line.).....................................*Coenagrion* Kirby

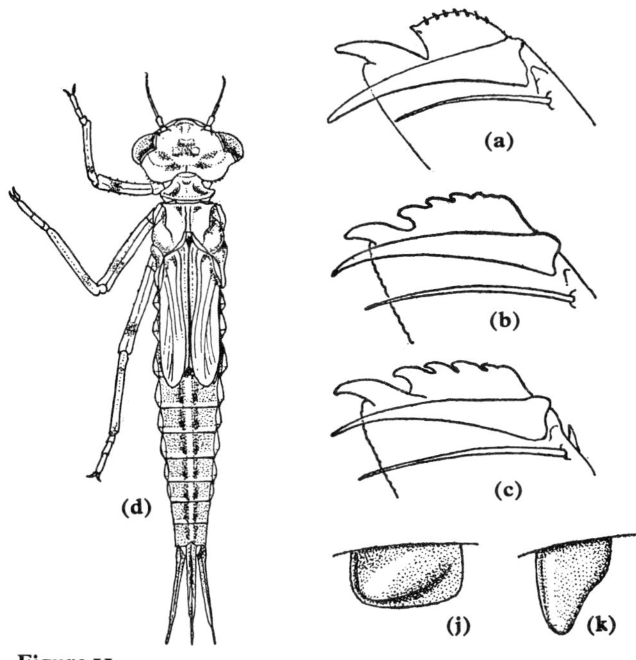

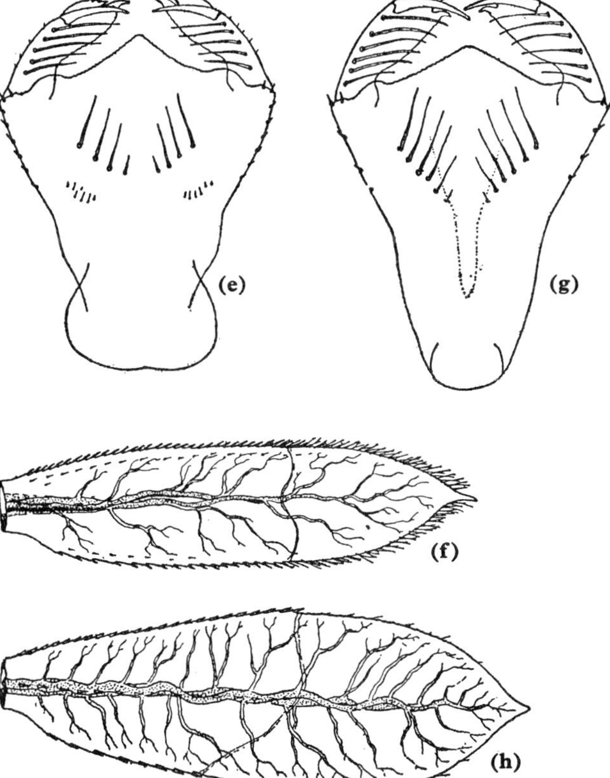

Figure 11

(a) *Ceriagrion tenellum* (de Villers), labial palpus
(b) *Ischnura elegans* (van der Linden), labial palpus
(c) *Enallagma cyathigerum* (Charp.), labial palpus
(d) *Coenagrion mercuriale* (Charp.), larva
(e) *C.mercuriale* (Charp.), labium
(f) *C.mercuriale* (Charp.), lamella
(g) *C.scitulum* (Ramb.), labium
(h) *C.scitulum* (Ramb.), lamella
(j) *C.hastulatum* (Charp.), left cercus, male
(k) *C.armatum* (Charp.), left cercus, male

Genus *Pyrrhosoma* Charpentier

One species recorded from Britain. Abdomen of rather stumpy appearance; mid-dorsal line pale, flanked by a dark suffusion, dark spots on each visible segment except tenth. Labium (Fig.9h) with premental setae 3+3 to 4+4; labial palpi with 6 to 7 setae. Caudal lamellae distinctive in shape and markings (Fig.9g). L. 19–22·5mm ....*P.nymphula* (Sulzer)
Breeds in ponds, lakes, canals, streams and marshes.
Small larvae of about 5·5mm (6th instar) can be identified by their stumpy appearance, square heads and the dark markings on the caudal lamellae.

Genus *Ischnura* Charpentier

Key to species

1 Labium (Fig.10e) with premental setae varying from 4+4 to 6+5; labial palpi with 6 to 7 setae. L. 21·5–25mm ....*I.elegans* (van der Linden)
Breeds in weedy ponds, lakes, slow moving and brackish waters.

— Labium with premental setae 6+6; labial palpi with 5 setae. L. 15–20mm......................*I.pumilio* (Charpentier)
Breeds in seepages, marshes and bogs.

Both these species have the labium with prementum bearing a field of short scattered setae proximal to the main premental setae (Fig.10e). This character is shared also by *Coenagrion mercuriale* (Charp.) but the larva (Fig.11d) is of such characteristic appearance that it cannot be confused with *Ischnura*.

Genus *Enallagma* Charpentier

One species found in Britain. Labium (Fig.10h) with premental setae 3+3 to 5+5; labial palpi with 6 to 7 setae. Caudal lamellae (Fig.10j) subnodate. Larvae generally of some tint of green; abdomen with pale mid-dorsal line flanked by V-shaped dark suffusions. L. 20–26·5mm.............................*E.cyathigerum* (Charpentier)
Breeds in ponds, lakes, canals, slow moving streams and in brackish water.

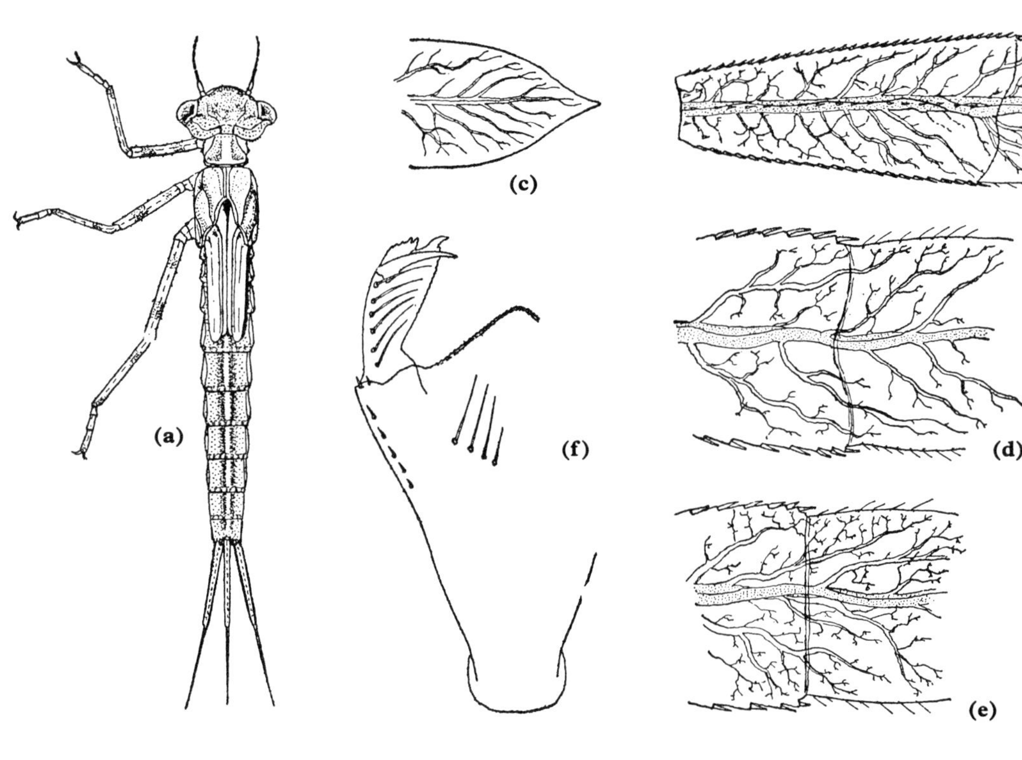

Figure 12

(a) *Coenagrion pulchellum* (van der Linden), larva
(b) *C.pulchellum* (van der Linden), lamella
(c) *C.puella* (L.), apex of lamella
(d) *C.armatum* (Charp.), nodal line of lamella
(e) *C.hastulatum* (Charp.), nodal line of lamella
(f) *Erythromma najas* (Hans.), labium
(g) *E.najas* (Hans.), lamella

Genus *Coenagrion* Kirby

Key to species

1 Head without prominent spotting; caudal lamellae subnodate 2

— Head with prominent spotting (Fig.10g); caudal lamellae nodate 3

2 Caudal lamellae short, boat-shaped (Fig.11f); antenodal marginal setae reaching beyond mid-length on both margins, becoming progressively longer and more slender towards node; a secondary series of setae on sides of lamellae reaching to, or beyond nodal line. Postnodal marginal setae relatively long, very numerous; secondary tracheae few in number, inclined at an angle of about 45 degrees to main trunks. Labium with prementum nearly as wide as long (Fig.11e), premental setae 3+3 to 4+4, a field of short setae proximal to these; labial palpi with 5 setae, outer margin bearing a few fine setae. L. 15–17mm .... *C.mercuriale* (Charpentier)
Breeds in clear weedy and boggy streams.

— Caudal lamellae of medium length, broad, with apices acutely pointed (Fig.11h); antenodal marginal setae reaching to mid-length on one margin only, not becoming markedly longer towards node, sides of lamellae bearing basal setae only. Postnodal marginal setae very fine, few in number; secondary tracheae numerous, inclined at an angle of more than 45 degrees to main trunks. Labium (Fig.11g) with prementum elongate, premental setae 4+4 to 5+5, no field of short setae on outer margin. L. 20–22mm .... *C.scitulum* (Rambur)
Recorded only from Essex where it has been found breeding in a small weedy pond near a salt marsh.

3 Antennae 6-segmented 4

— Antennae 7-segmented 5

4 Male cerci (Fig.11k) with inner margin concave. Caudal lamellae with nodal line not straight; secondary tracheae with sub-tracheae relatively few in number (Fig.12d). Labium with premental setae 4+4 to 5+5; labial palpi with 6 to 7 setae. L. 21–23mm .... *C.armatum* (Charpentier)
Breeds in shallow pools containing frogbit Hydrocharis morsusranae *in which the female places her eggs. Confined to the Norfolk Broads.*

— Male cerci (Fig.11j) with inner margin straight. Caudal lamellae with nodal line straight, secondary tracheae with sub-tracheae numerous (Fig.12e). Labium with premental setae 3+3 to 5+5; labial palpi with 5 to 7 setae. L. 21–23mm .... *C.hastulatum* (Charpentier)
Breeds in river shallows and bog-holes. Confined to a few counties in Scotland.

5 A high proportion of larvae with the narrowly-lanceolate caudal lamellae (Fig.12c) having bluntly-pointed apices. Labium with premental setae 5+5; labial palpi with 6 setae. May vary in having premental setae 4+4 and labial palpi with 5 to 7 setae. Larvae generally of some shade of green with wing-sheaths and lamellae brown. L. 22–25·75mm .... *C.puella* (*Linnaeus*)
Breeds in weedy ponds, lakes and canals.

— A high proportion of larvae with the caudal lamellae (Fig.12b) with rounded apices, this most obvious with the median lamella. Labium with premental setae 4+4; labial palpi with 6 setae. May vary in having the premental setae 5+5 and labial palpi with 5 setae. Larvae generally of some shade of brown to sepia, rarely green. L. 20–25·25mm .... *C.pulchellum* (van der Linden)
Breeds in similar habitats to C.puella.

Genus *Erythromma* Charpentier

One species found in Britain. Labium (Fig.12f) with premental setae 3+3, 4+4 to 3+5; labial palpi with 6 to 7 setae. Caudal lamellae (Fig.12g) nodate, with dark transverse apical bands and clearly defined tracheation distinctive. L. 29–32mm .... *E.najas* (Hansemann)
Breeds in clear weedy ponds, lakes and canals.

Genus *Ceriagrion* Selys

One species found in Britain. Labium distinctive (Fig. 10b); premental setae 1+1, rarely 2+2; labial palpi with 6 setae. Caudal lamellae (Fig.10c) subnodate. Small larvae generally of a brownish or olivaceous colour. L. 16–17mm .... *C.tenellum* (de Villers)
Breeds in boggy pools and peaty runnels.

Suborder ANISOPTERA

Key to Families

1 Labium with prementum flat, without major premental or palpal setae; distal margin of labial palpi without crenations 2

— Labium with prementum spoon-shaped, with major premental and palpal setae; distal margin of labial palpi with crenations 3

2 Antennae 4-segmented (Fig.13c). Front and middle tarsi with 2, hind with 3 segments .... GOMPHIDAE

— Antennae 7-segmented. All tarsi with 3 segments .... AESHNIDAE

3 Labium with median lobe of prementum bifid, the points ending in beak-like hooks; distal margin of labial palpi deeply serrated (Fig.16b) .... CORDULEGASTERIDAE

— Labium with median lobe of prementum not bifid; distal margin of labial palpi not deeply serrated 4

4 Cerci notably more than half the length of the paraprocts (Fig.18a). Distal margin of labial palpi with broad deep crenations (Fig.16d) .... CORDULIIDAE

— Cerci rarely half, generally less than half the length of the paraprocts (Fig.18f). Distal margin of labial palpi with crenations shallow or much flattened (Figs.18g,19c,f) .... LIBELLULIDAE

Family GOMPHIDAE

One genus *Gomphus* Leach

One species found in Britain. Larva (Fig.13a) distinctive in appearance. Head small and heart-shaped. Labium (Fig.13b) rectangular. Abdomen broad and flat, lateral spines on segments 6 to 9. L. 27–30mm........................... ....*G.vulgatissimus* (Linnaeus)
Breeds in swift streams with sandy bottoms, also the backwaters of some rivers. Burrows in the sand or silt.
Relatively immature specimens may be determined by the general outline and the segmentation of antennae and tarsi.

Family CORDULEGASTERIDAE

One genus *Cordulegaster* Leach

One species found in Britain. Larva (Fig.16a) large, hairy and distinctive in appearance. Labium (Fig.16b) with distal margin of labial palpi formed into deep asymmetrical dentations. Premental setae 4+4 to 5+5, a field of short setae proximal to these. Labial palpi with 4 to 5 major setae, 0 to 2 short anterior setae. Abdomen with lateral spines on segments 8 and 9. L. 35–42mm............. ....*C.boltonii* (Donovan)
Breeds in swift streams with sandy or muddy bottoms. The larvae lie in the detritus with only the fore-part of the head and the anal appendages protruding.
Immature specimens of 18mm, (and probably less) can be readily determined by their resemblance to the mature larva, also by the form of the labium.

Family AESHNIDAE

Key to genera

1 Eyes small, less than half the length of the lateral margin of the postocular lobes, the latter sloping markedly inwards (Fig.13e). Dorsal surface of abdomen with an obtuse spine-like process on the distal margin of the ninth tergite and a vestigial process on eighth (Fig.13f). Length

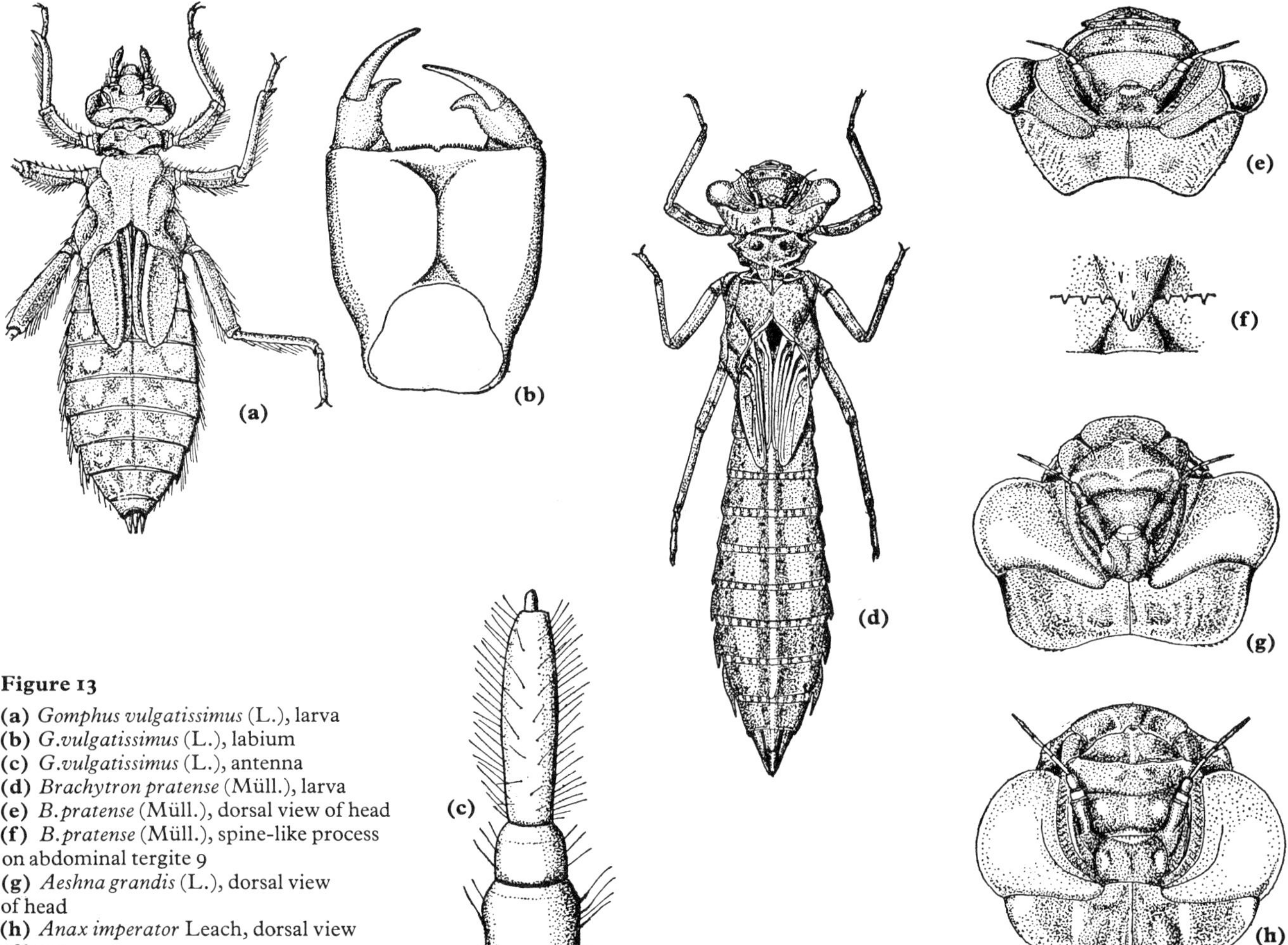

Figure 13
(a) *Gomphus vulgatissimus* (L.), larva
(b) *G.vulgatissimus* (L.), labium
(c) *G.vulgatissimus* (L.), antenna
(d) *Brachytron pratense* (Müll.), larva
(e) *B.pratense* (Müll.), dorsal view of head
(f) *B.pratense* (Müll.), spine-like process on abdominal tergite 9
(g) *Aeshna grandis* (L.), dorsal view of head
(h) *Anax imperator* Leach, dorsal view of head

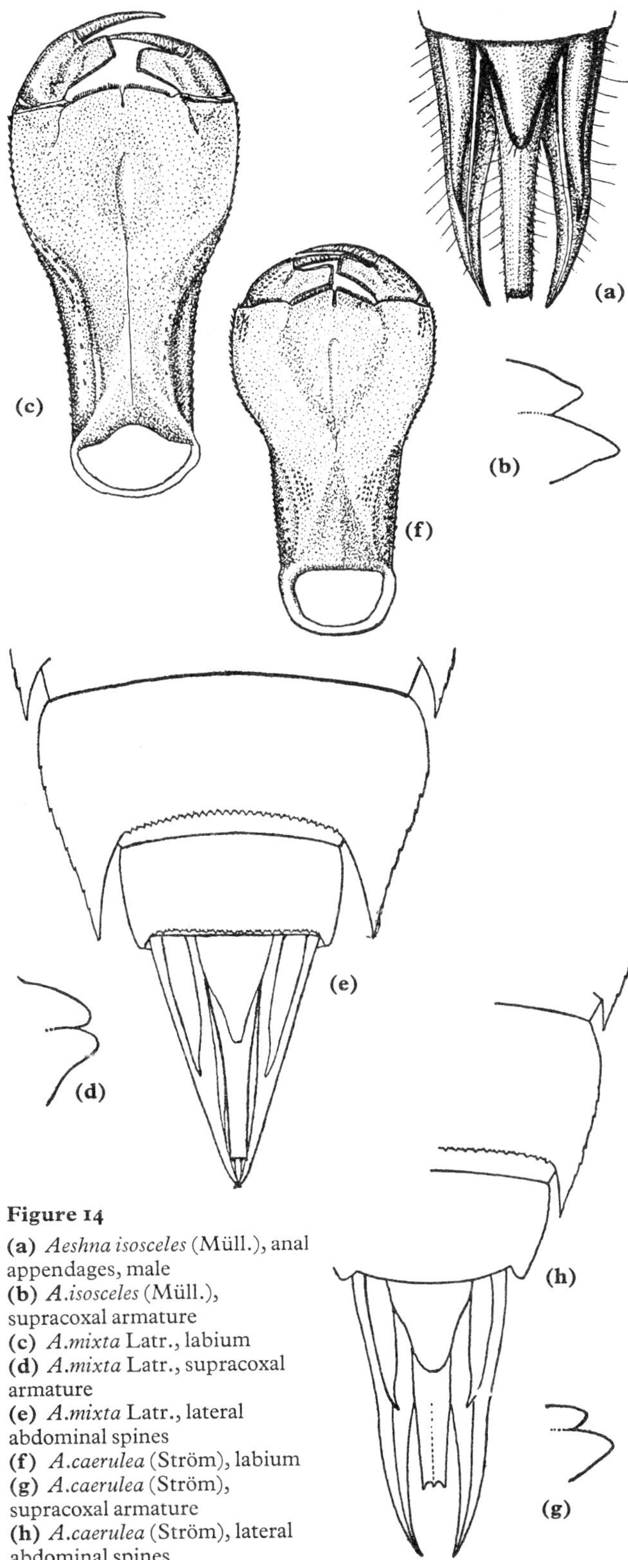

Figure 14
(a) *Aeshna isosceles* (Müll.), anal appendages, male
(b) *A.isosceles* (Müll.), supracoxal armature
(c) *A.mixta* Latr., labium
(d) *A.mixta* Latr., supracoxal armature
(e) *A.mixta* Latr., lateral abdominal spines
(f) *A.caerulea* (Ström), labium
(g) *A.caerulea* (Ström), supracoxal armature
(h) *A.caerulea* (Ström), lateral abdominal spines

of the anal appendages less than the combined lengths of the ninth and tenth segments................*Brachytron* Selys

— Eyes large, half, or more than half the length of the lateral margin of the postocular lobes, the latter not sloping markedly inwards. Dorsal surface of abdomen immaculate. Length of the anal appendages as long as, or longer than the combined lengths of the ninth and tenth segments...2

2 Eyes markedly flattened dorsally, posterior margins forming a transverse straight line; outline of head of a rounded appearance (Fig.13h). Larvae rarely of less than 49mm in length..*Anax* Leach

— Eyes not markedly flattened dorsally, posterior margins not forming a transverse straight line; outline of head not of a rounded appearance (Fig.13g). Larvae rarely exceeding 49mm in length....................*Aeshna* Fabricius

Genus *Brachytron* Selys

One species found in Britain. Head distinctive in appearance (Fig.13e). Abdomen with lateral spines on segments 5 to 9. L. 35–40mm (Fig.13d).......................... ....*B.pratense* (Müller)
Breeds in dykes, ponds, lakes and canals. Often found clinging to submerged sticks, roots and broken sedges.

The second instar larva (length about 2·5mm) can be identified by means of a spine-like process on the lateral margin of the postocular lobes. These are not absorbed until the seventh instar (length about 8mm). From *Aeshna grandis* (Linnaeus), which also exhibits this character in the early instars, separation can be effected by noting the absence of the mid-dorsal abdominal protruberance on the ninth tergite, which is conspicuous in immature specimens of *B.pratense*.

Genus *Aeshna* Fabricius

Key to species

1 Cerci two-thirds the length of the paraprocts, slender and incurved (Fig.14a). Supracoxal armature as Fig.14b. (Abdomen with lateral spines on segments 6 to 9, those on 9 reaching a little beyond the middle of the tenth segment. Distal margin of epiproct nearly straight.) L. 38–44mm....................................*A.isosceles* (Müller)
Breeds in weedy dykes and broads. Confined to the area of the Norfolk Broads.

— Cerci less than two-thirds the length of the paraprocts...2

2 Larvae of not more than 38mm, in length.......................3

— Larvae of more than 38mm, in length...........................4

3 Lateral abdominal spine on segment 9 reaching nearly to the distal margin of the tenth segment (Fig.14e). Distal margin of epiproct nearly straight. Supracoxal armature as Fig.14d. (Labium as Fig.14c; lateral abdominal spines on segments 6 to 9.) L. 30–38mm..........*A.mixta* Latreille

— Lateral abdominal spine on segment 9 only reaching to about one-third over the tenth segment (Fig.14h). Distal

margin of epiproct bifid. Supracoxal armature as Fig.14g. (Labium as Fig.14f; lateral abdominal spines on segments 7 to 9, perhaps sometimes a vestigial one on 6.) L. about 35mm..*A.caerulea* (Ström)*
Confined to a few districts in Scotland where it breeds in sphagnum bogs.

4 Distal margin of epiproct concave (Fig.15m). Labium (Fig.15j) with length of prementum nearly twice the width of the front margin. Supracoxal armature as Fig.15k. (Lateral abdominal spines on segments 6 to 9.) L. 38–48mm......................................*A.cyanea* (Müller)
Breeds in ponds, lakes and canals.

— Distal margin of epiproct bifid (Figs.15d,h). Labium (Figs.15a,e) with length of prementum markedly less than twice the width of the front margin..............................5

5 Labium (Fig.15a) somewhat rectangular in outline. Supracoxal armature as Fig.15b. Lateral abdominal spines on segments 7 to 9 (sometimes a vestigial one on 6), that on 9 not reaching more than one-third over the tenth segment (Fig.15c). L. 40–51mm............................ ....*A.juncea* (Linnaeus)
Breeds in weedy ponds, lakes and peat pools.

— Labium (Fig.15e) less rectangular in outline. Supracoxal armature as Fig.15f. Lateral abdominal spines on segments 6 to 9 (sometimes a vestigial one on 5), that on 9 reaching to the middle of the tenth segment (Fig.15g). L. 40–46mm..................................*A.grandis* (Linnaeus)
Breeds in ponds, lakes and canals.
For the identification of the very immature larvae of *A. grandis* see separation characters given for this species and *Brachytron pratense*.

*Has 6-segmented antennae. See *Entomologist's Gaz.*, 1955, **6**:85.

Genus *Anax* Leach

One species found in Britain. Larvae of robust appearance, head distinctive in outline (Fig.13h). Abdomen with lateral spines on segments 7 to 9. L. 45–56mm......... ....*A.imperator* Leach
Breeds in weedy ponds, lakes and canals. It is one of the first species to colonise a partly filled pond or gravel pit.

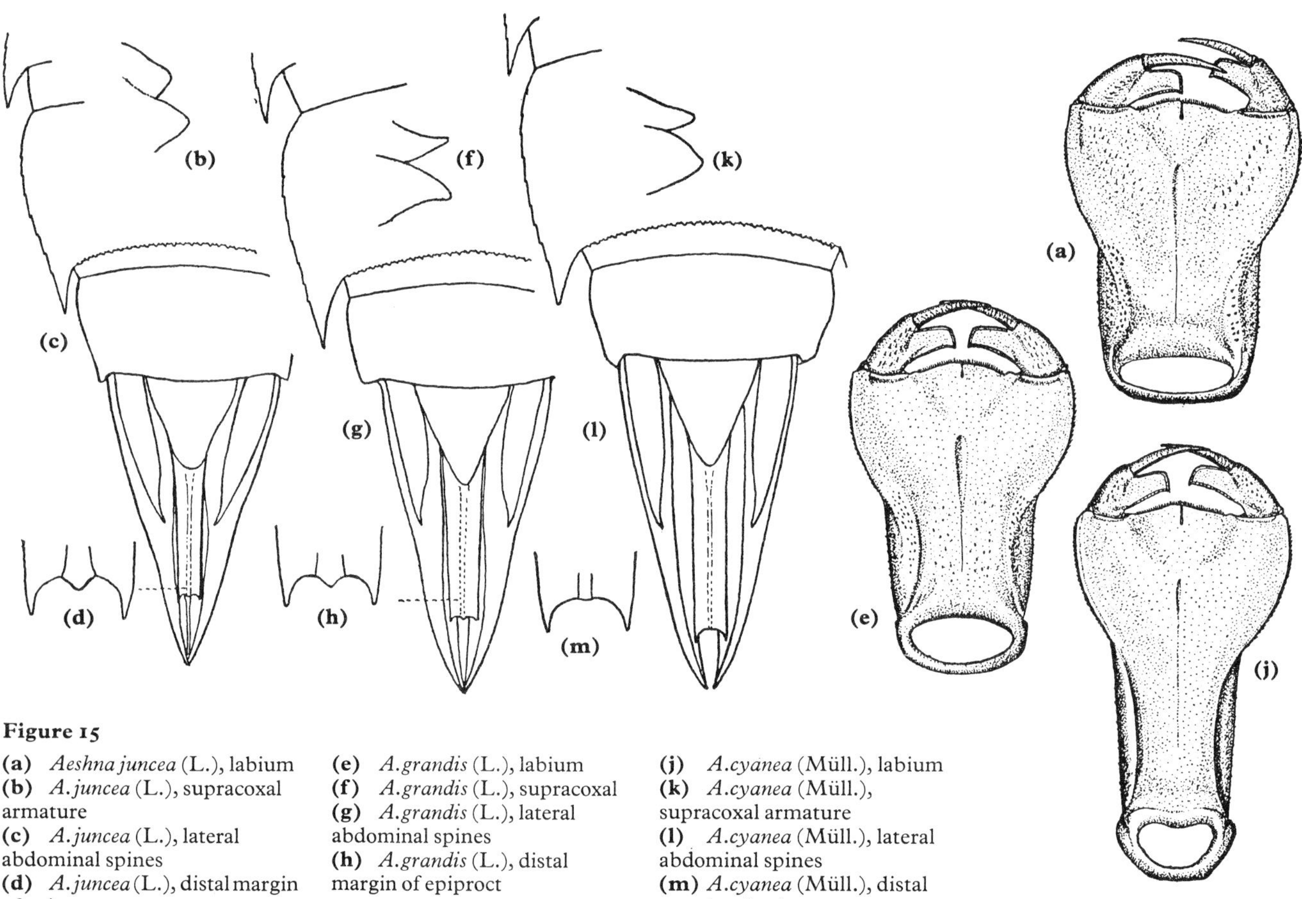

Figure 15
(a) *Aeshna juncea* (L.), labium
(b) *A.juncea* (L.), supracoxal armature
(c) *A.juncea* (L.), lateral abdominal spines
(d) *A.juncea* (L.), distal margin of epiproct
(e) *A.grandis* (L.), labium
(f) *A.grandis* (L.), supracoxal
(g) *A.grandis* (L.), lateral abdominal spines
(h) *A.grandis* (L.), distal margin of epiproct
(j) *A.cyanea* (Müll.), labium
(k) *A.cyanea* (Müll.), supracoxal armature
(l) *A.cyanea* (Müll.), lateral abdominal spines
(m) *A.cyanea* (Müll.), distal margin of epiproct

Family CORDULIIDAE

Key to species

1 Abdomen armed with prominent mid-dorsal spines, dorsal surface sparsely covered with hair-like setae........2

— Abdomen not armed with prominent mid-dorsal spines; dorsal surface with hair-like or pectinate setae numerous 3

2 Abdomen with mid-dorsal spine on segment 9 small (sometimes only vestigial) (Fig.17b). Abdomen when viewed dorsally appearing somewhat truncate (Fig.17a). Head viewed from the front as Fig.17c; occiput not bearing short obtuse spine-like processes. Labium with outer margin of prementum immaculate; labial palpi with outer margins armed with short setae, their length being less than the distance between individual setae (Fig.16c); distal margin with crenations armed with 3 to 4 setae (Fig.16d). (Labium with premental setae 12+12 to 15+15; labial palpi with 8 to 9 setae. Abdomen with recurved mid-dorsal spines on segments 4 to 9, lateral spines on 8 and 9.) L. 22·5–25mm...*Cordulia aenea* (Linnaeus)
Breeds in weedy ponds, lakes and canals.

— Abdomen with mid-dorsal spine on segment 9 of medium length (Fig.17d). Abdomen viewed dorsally of fusiform outline. Head when viewed from the front as Fig.17e; occiput bearing a pair of obtuse spine-like processes in line with the base of the antennae. Labium with outer margin of prementum armed with setae; labial palpi with setae on outer margins long, shorter setae interspersed, the former as long as the distance between individual setae (Fig.16e); distal margin with crenations armed with 6 to 9 setae (Fig.16f). (Labium with premental setae 11+11 to 12+12; labial palpi with 6 to 7 setae. Abdomen with recurved mid-dorsal spines on segments 4 to 9 (sometimes a vestigial one on 3), lateral spines on 8 and 9.) L. 24–25mm...*Somatochlora metallica* (van der Linden)
Breeds in ponds, canals and moorland bog-holes.

Second instar larvae of *C.aenea* and *S.metallica* have obtuse spine-like processes on the occiput, these persisting in *S.metallica* and becoming progressively shorter. In *C.aenea* they become absorbed at about the sixth instar (length about 6mm).

3 Abdomen not armed with lateral spines, sides more parallel, posterior segments obtuse (Fig.18b); abdominal setae spinate or piliform. Male projection with distal margin obtuse. Labial palpi with distal margin consisting of 8 to 11 crenations, each armed with 3 to 5 setae (Figs. 17f,g). (Premental setae 9+9 to 14+14; labial palpi with 7 to 9 setae.) L. 17–22·5mm...........*S.arctica* (Zetterstedt)
Breeds in sheltered runnels and seepages on moorlands. Confined to a few counties in Scotland, and in Kerry.

— Abdomen bearing lateral spines on segments 8 and 9, fusiform in outline, posterior segments more acutely tapered to anal appendages (Fig.18c). Setae on dorsal

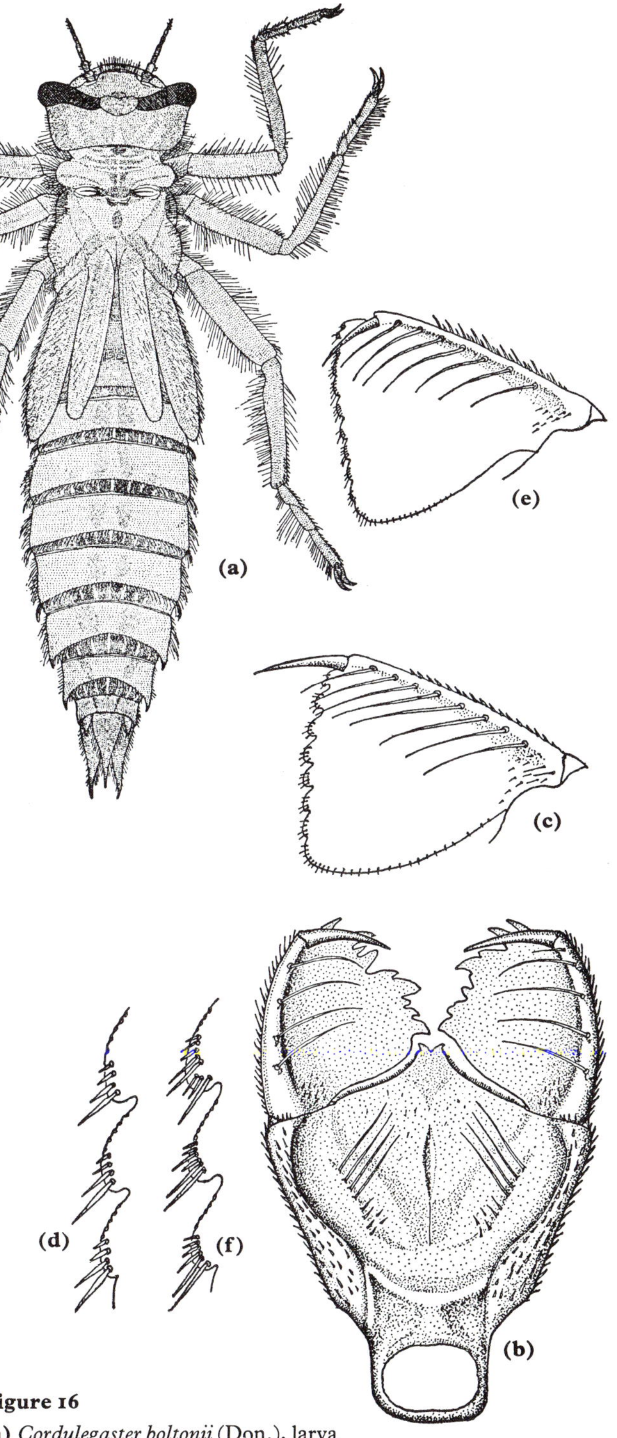

Figure 16
(a) *Cordulegaster boltonii* (Don.), larva
(b) *C.boltonii* (Don.), labium
(c) *Cordulia aenea* (L.), labial palpus
(d) *C.aenea* (L.), distal margin of palpus
(e) *Somatochlora metallica* (van der Linden), labial palpus
(f) *S.metallica* (van der Linden), distal margin of palpus

surface of head, thorax and abdomen consisting mainly of scale-like pectinate setae (Fig.18d). Male projection with distal margin truncate. Labial palpi with distal margin consisting of 6 to 8 crenations, each armed with 5 to 9 setae (Figs.17h,j). (Premental setae 11+11 to 12+12; labial palpi with 7 to 8 setae.) L. 19–22mm................ ....*Oxygastra curtisii* (Dale)
Breeds in one, possibly two sluggish but well oxygenated streams in the S. of England.
From the sixth instar (6mm) larvae may be determined by the scale-like setae on the dorsal surface of the abdomen.

Family LIBELLULIDAE

Key to genera

1 Larvae of distinctive appearance (Figs.21a,b,c and Fig. 23a). Head with outer margin of postocular lobes of a sweeping curvilinear outline. Legs long and slender, hind when fully extended reaching to well beyond the apex of abdomen. Abdomen with lateral spines on segments 8 and 9 generally prominent..2

— Head with outer margin of postocular lobes not of a sweeping curvilinear outline (Fig.18e). Legs of moderate length, stout, hind when fully extended barely reaching beyond apex of abdomen. Abdomen with lateral spines on segments 8 and 9 not prominent..............................3

2 Ventral surface of abdomen with distinctive markings (Fig.23b)...................................*Leucorrhinia* Brittinger

— Ventral surface of abdomen immaculate......................... .... *Sympetrum* Newman

3 Abdomen without mid-dorsal spine on segment 8. Labium with premental armature consisting of 2 to 4 long setae inserted near each lateral margin and two medial fields of short spiniform setae, these latter flanked by 4 to 7 setae of medium length (Fig.18g). (*Libellula*

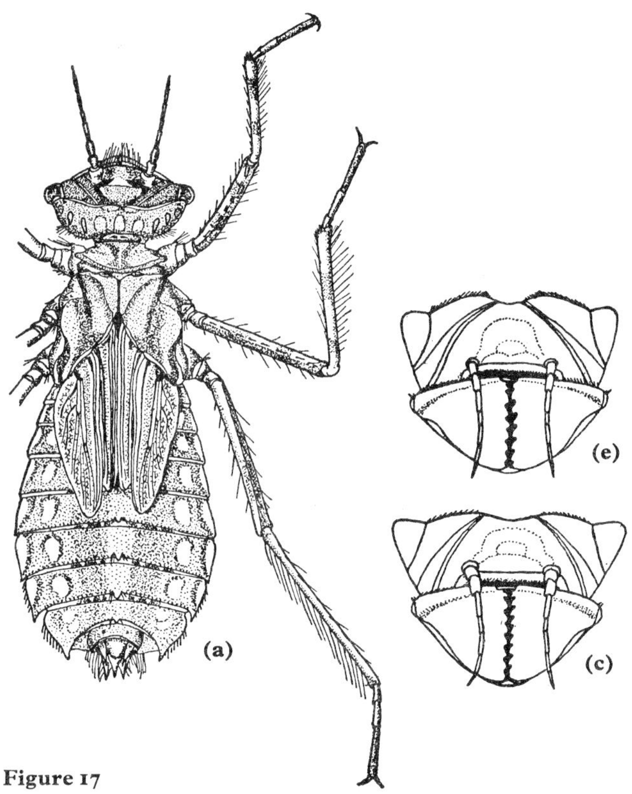

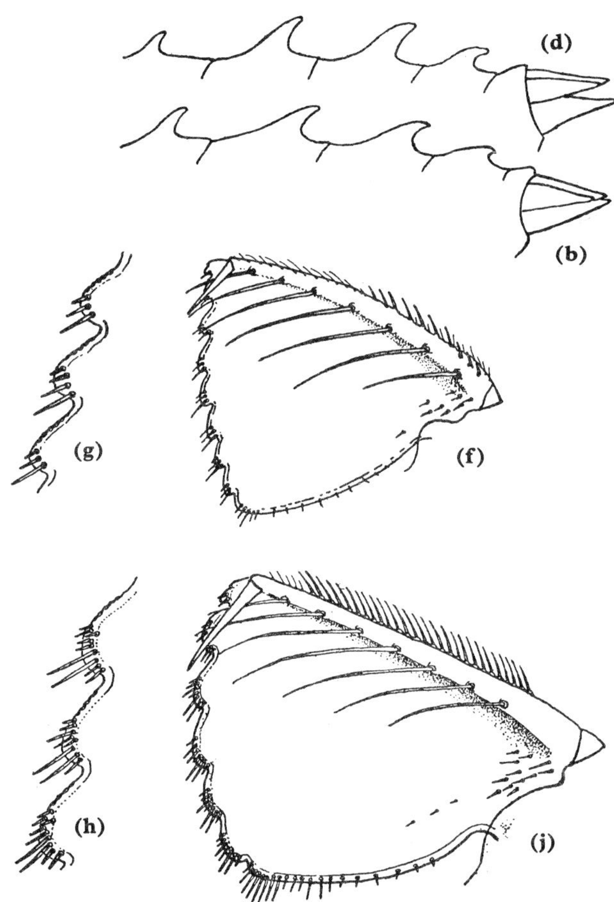

Figure 17
(a) *Cordulia aenea* (L.), larva
(b) *C.aenea* (L.), mid-dorsal abdominal spines
(c) *C.aenea* (L.), head from in front
(d) *Somatochlora metallica* (van der Linden), mid-dorsal abdominal spines
(e) *S.metallica* (van der Linden), head from in front
(f) *S.arctica* (Zett.), labial palpus
(g) *S.arctica* (Zett.), distal margin of palpus
(h) *Oxygastra curtisii* (Dale), distal margin of palpus
(j) *O.curtisii* (Dale), labial palpus

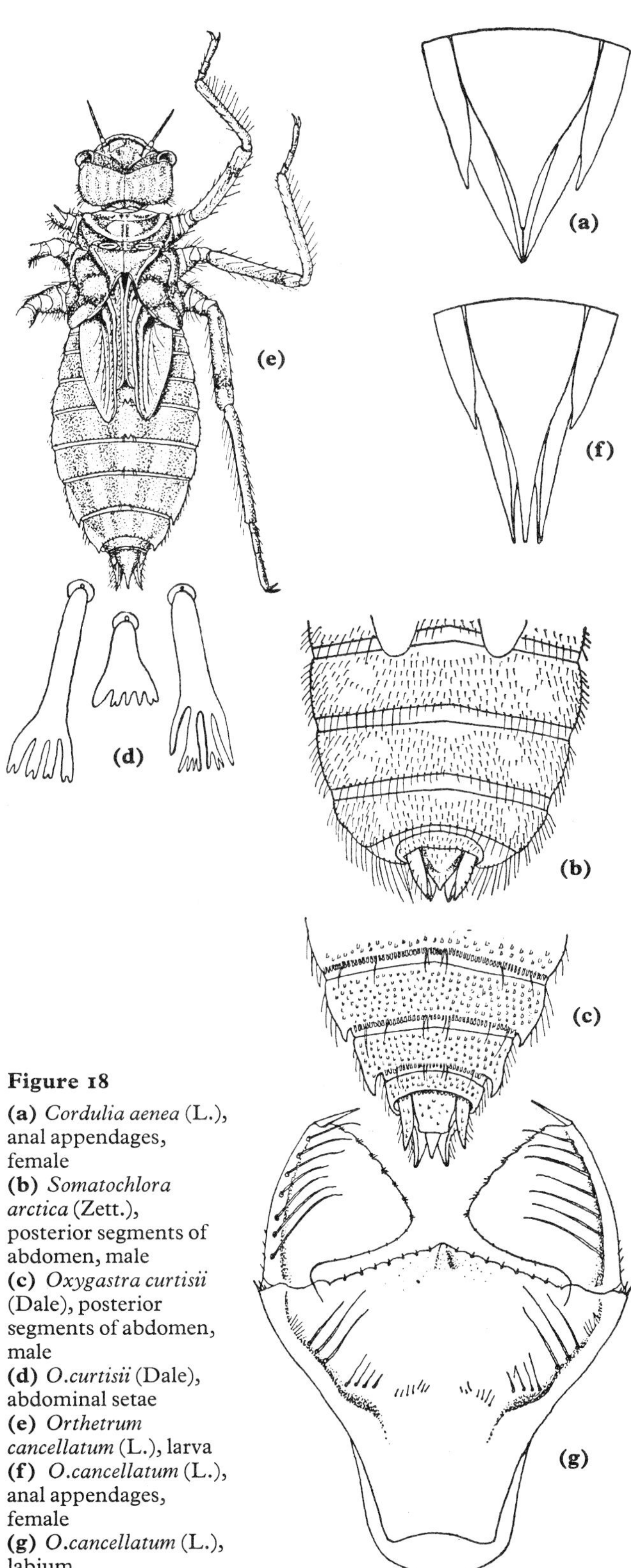

Figure 18

(a) *Cordulia aenea* (L.), anal appendages, female
(b) *Somatochlora arctica* (Zett.), posterior segments of abdomen, male
(c) *Oxygastra curtisii* (Dale), posterior segments of abdomen, male
(d) *O.curtisii* (Dale), abdominal setae
(e) *Orthetrum cancellatum* (L.), larva
(f) *O.cancellatum* (L.), anal appendages, female
(g) *O.cancellatum* (L.), labium

fulva Müller, which has the premental setae disposed in a somewhat similar manner, may be readily identified by the prominent mid-dorsal abdominal spines on segments 4 to 9)..*Orthetrum* Newman

— Abdomen with mid-dorsal spine on segment 8. Premental setae arranged as Figs.20b,d,f.......*Libellula* Linnaeus

Genus *Orthetrum* Newman

Key to species

1 Abdomen with mid-dorsal spines on segments 4 to 7 and a smooth and slightly raised mid-dorsal area on segments 8 and 9. Labium with premental setae consisting of 2 long setae inserted near each lateral margin and two medial fields of from 10 to 12 short spiniform setae, these latter flanked by from 4 to 7 setae of medium length. Labial palpi with 3 setae (rarely 4 to 5). Male projection with distal margin obtuse. (Short lateral spines on segments 8 and 9). L. 17–23mm...............*O.coerulescens* (Fabricius)
Breeds in streams, weedy ponds, bogs and marshes.

— Abdomen with mid-dorsal spines on segments 3 to 6, without a smooth and slightly raised mid-dorsal area on segments 8 and 9. Labium with premental setae consisting of 3 (rarely 2 or 4) long setae inserted near each lateral margin and two medial fields of from 7 to 8 short spiniform setae, these latter flanked by 4 setae of medium length (Fig.18g). Labial palpi with 7 (rarely 6) setae. Male projection with distal margin acute. (Short lateral spines on segments 8 and 9.) L. 23–25·5mm (Fig.18e).....
....*O.cancellatum* (Linnaeus)
Breeds in ponds and lakes, shows a marked liking for clay and gravel pits.

Genus *Libellula* Linnaeus

Key to species

1 Abdomen with long recurved mid-dorsal spines on segments 4 to 9 (Fig.19h). Labium (Fig.20f) with premental setae consisting of 3 long setae inserted near each lateral margin, slightly anterior to these a chain of from 2 to 5 short spiniform setae extending forwards to two medial fields of about 10 short spiniform setae. Labial palpi with 4 (rarely 5) setae. (Abdomen with short lateral spines on segments 8 and 9.) L. 22–25mm......................
....*L.fulva* Müller
Breeds in slow-moving muddy streams, canals, dykes and bog-pools.
From the sixth instar (5mm), larvae may be determined by the disposition of the premental setae and the mid-dorsal abdominal spines on segments 4 to 9.

— Abdomen with obtuse mid-dorsal spines on segments 4 to 8. Labium with premental setae not arranged in six distinct fields...2

2 Head when viewed dorsally appearing somewhat rectangular in outline, labium with only a slight forward protrusion, prolongation of eyes directed diagonally

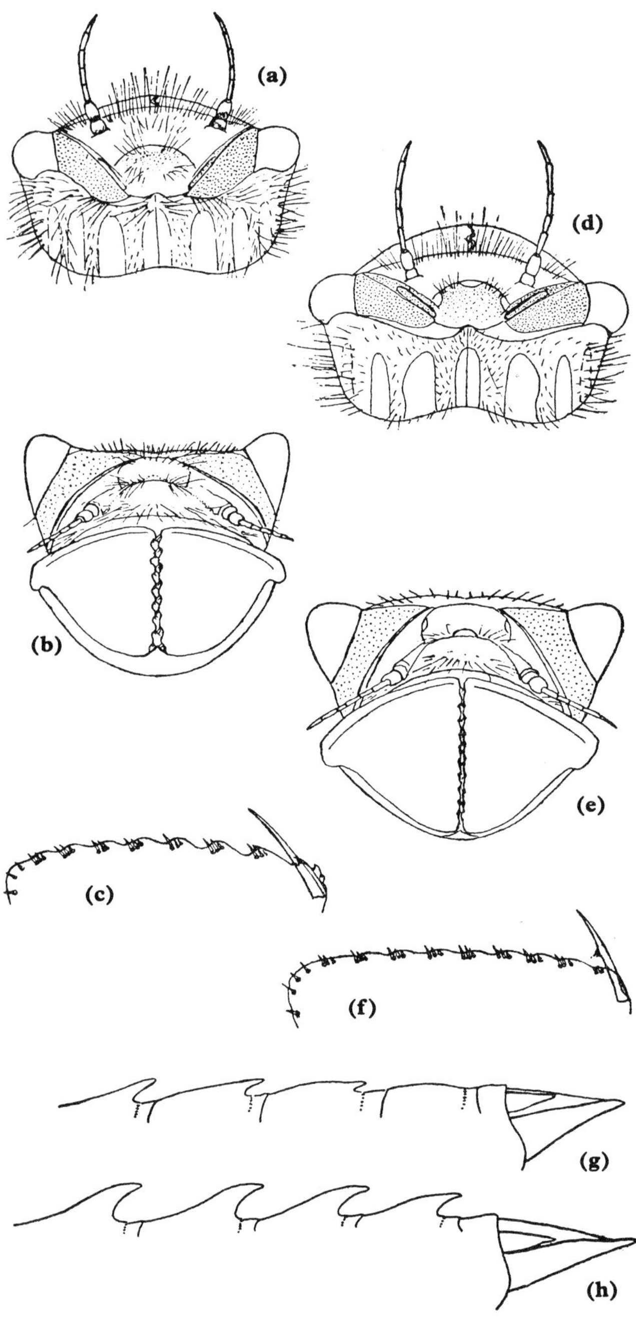

Figure 19

(a) *Libellula depressa* L., head dorsal view
(b) *L.depressa* L., head from in front
(c) *L.depressa* L., distal margin of labial palpus
(d) *L.quadrimaculata* L., head dorsal view
(e) *L.quadrimaculata* L., head from in front
(f) *L.quadrimaculata* L., distal margin of labial palpus
(g) *L.quadrimaculata* L., mid-dorsal abdominal spines
(h) *L.fulva* Müll., mid-dorsal abdominal spines

backwards (Fig.19a). Head when viewed from in front with eyes strongly upraised, epicranium markedly below a line taken across the top of the eyes (Fig.19b). Antennae with segments 6 and 7 of almost equal length (Fig.20c). Labial palpi with crenations of distal margin moderately deep and rounded in outline (Fig.19c). Premental setae 9+9 to 11+11, slightly anterior to these two medial fields of 3 to 5 short setae (Fig.20b). Abdomen marked with alternate light and dark suffusions (Fig.20a), apical segments truncate. (Labial palpi with 9 to 11 setae. Abdomen with obtuse mid-dorsal spines on segments 4 to 8 (sometimes a vestigial one on 3), short lateral spines on 8 and 9.) L. 22·5–25mm...............*L.depressa* Linnaeus
Breeds in ponds, lakes and canals.

— Head when viewed dorsally appearing pentagonal in outline, labium with a strong forward protrusion, prolongation of eyes more transverse (Fig.19d). Head when viewed from in front with eyes less strongly upraised, epicranium in line with, or slightly above the level of the top of the eyes (Fig.19e). Antennae with segment 7 markedly shorter than 6 (Fig.20e). Labial palpi with crenations of distal margin shallow and flattened in outline (Fig.19f). Premental setae 10+10 to 13+13, in alignment (Fig.20d). Abdomen of a uniform sepia tint, apical segments not truncate. (Labial palpi with 7 to 11 setae, usually 7 to 8. Abdomen with mid-dorsal spines on segments 4 to 8 (Fig.19g), short lateral spines on 8 and 9.) L. 22–26mm. ....*L.quadrimaculata* Linnaeus
Breeds in ponds, lakes, canals, brackish water, bog-holes and occasionally slow-moving streams.

Genus *Sympetrum* Newman

Key to species

1 Abdomen without mid-dorsal spines (Fig.21a). (Labium with premental setae 18+18; labial palpi with 14 setae (both premental and palpal setae may be found to vary in number). Abdomen with short lateral spines on segments 8 and 9.) L. about 18mm................*S.fonscolombei* (Selys)
An infrequent immigrant which has been recorded as breeding in S. England. Weedy ponds and lakes would be suitable habitats.
Immature specimens of over 6mm in length may be determined by the lack of mid-dorsal spines.

— Abdomen with mid-dorsal spines.................................2

2 Lateral spine on segment 9 of abdomen with inner margin half, or nearly half the length of the outside margin of spine and segment taken together (Figs.21b,c and 22d)...3

— Lateral spine on segment 9 of abdomen with inner margin markedly less than half the length of the outside margin of spine and segment taken together (Figs.22c,f) 5

3 Abdomen with mid-dorsal spines on segments 3 to 8, that on 3 small. Labium with premental setae 14+14 to 15+15; labial palpi with 10 to 12 setae (usually 11). L. 17–18mm................................*S.vulgatum* (Linnaeus)

A rare immigrant. Would breed in similar habitats to S. striolatum *(Charp.). The larva has not been found in Britain.*

— Abdomen without a mid-dorsal spine on segment 3.......4

4 Abdomen with almost straight mid-dorsal spines on segments 4 to 8. Lateral spines straight or only slightly incurved. Labium with premental setae 15+16 to 16+16; labial palpi with 11 setae. L. 16·5–17·5mm.............. ....*S.nigrescens* Lucas

Appears to favour waters close to, or not far removed from the coast. Generally of a more northern distribution than the succeeding species.

— Abdomen with mid-dorsal spines on segments 5 to 8 (rarely a vestigial one on 4).......................................4(a)

4(a) Abdomen with recurved mid-dorsal spines on segments 4 to 8 (rarely a vestigial one on 4). Lateral spines generally incurved. Head viewed dorsally as Fig.21b; viewed from in front as Fig.22a. (Larvae approaching metamorphosis with head pattern (Fig.21b) having 'bulges' posterior to the lateral branches of the epicranial suture with a linear posterior margin.) Labium with premental setae 14+14 to 15+15 (more rarely 13 to 18); labial palpi with 11 to 12 setae. L. 15·5–18mm..............*S.striolatum* (Charpentier)

Breeds in ponds, lakes and canals.

— Head viewed dorsally as Fig.21c; viewed from in front as Fig.22b. (Larvae approaching metamorphosis with head pattern (Fig.21c) with 'bulges' posterior to the lateral branches of the epicranial suture inevident or vaguely defined by a diffuse border.) Labium with premental

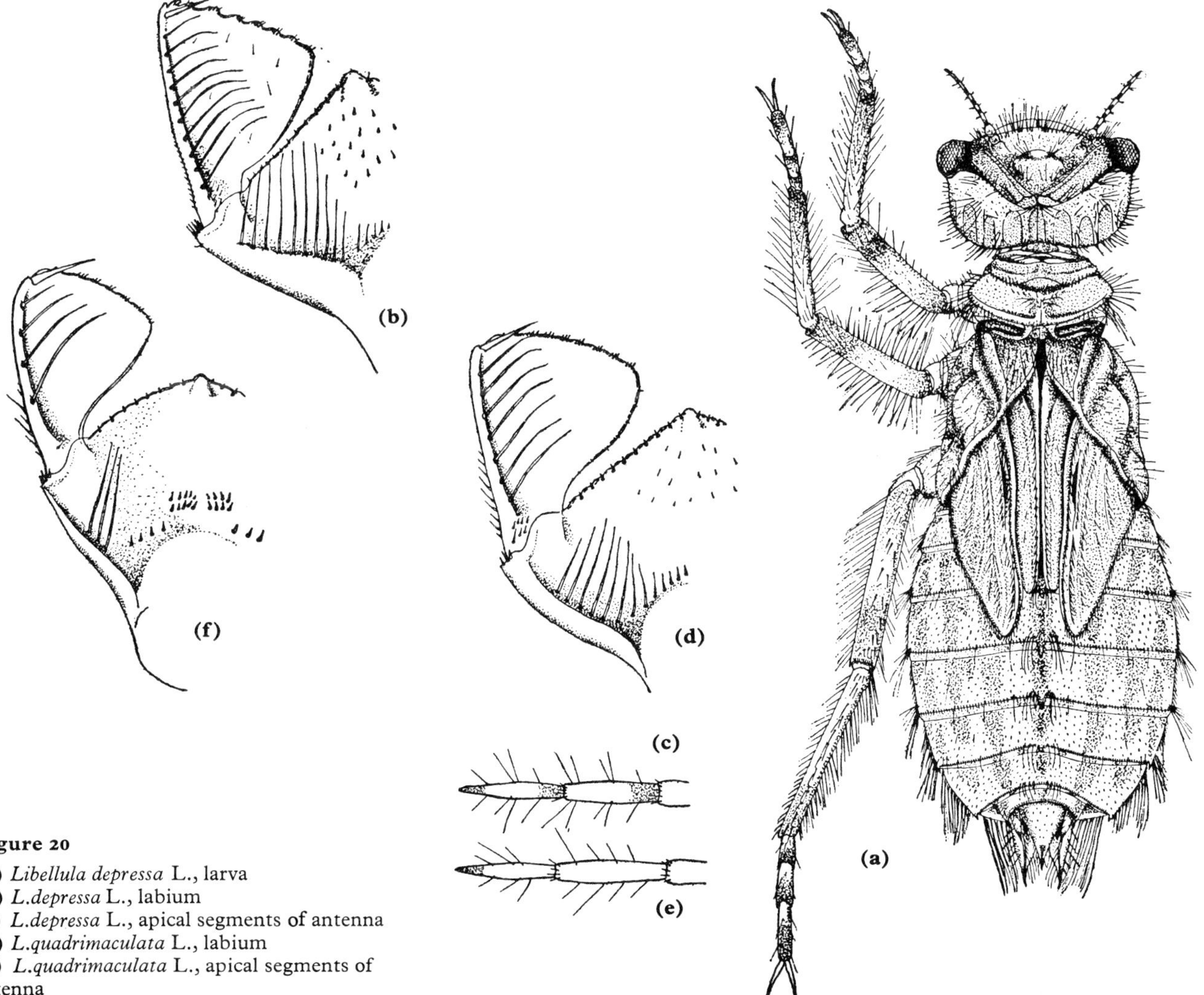

Figure 20

(a) *Libellula depressa* L., larva
(b) *L.depressa* L., labium
(c) *L.depressa* L., apical segments of antenna
(d) *L.quadrimaculata* L., labium
(e) *L.quadrimaculata* L., apical segments of antenna
(f) *L.fulva* Müll., labium

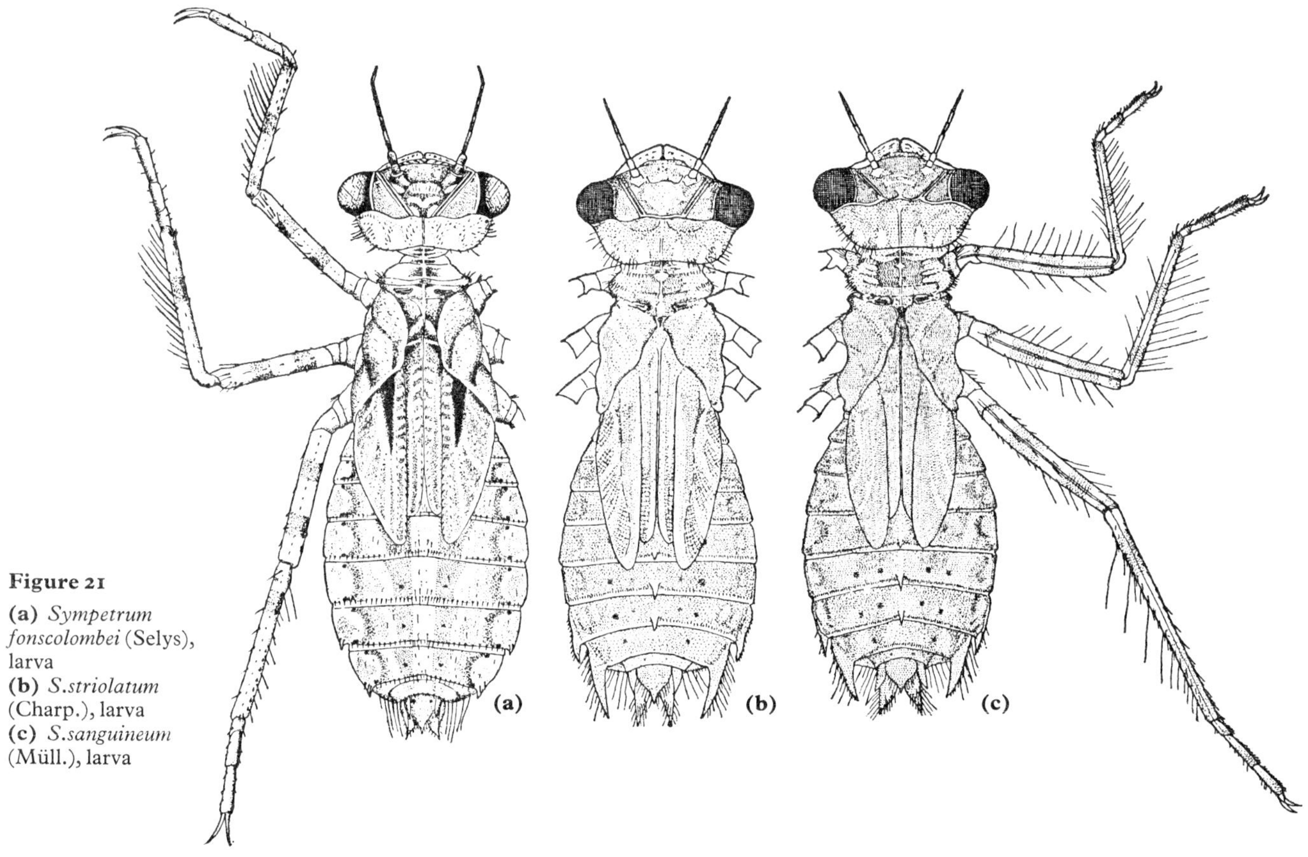

Figure 21
(a) *Sympetrum fonscolombei* (Selys), larva
(b) *S.striolatum* (Charp.), larva
(c) *S.sanguineum* (Müll.), larva

setae 12+12 to 14+14; labial palpi with 9 to 11 setae. L. 15–17mm...............................*S.sanguineum* (Müller)
Breeds in ponds and lakes, favouring sites occupied by bulrush (Typha latifolia *L.*) *and horsetails* (Equisetum *spp.*), *where the larvae lurk under the tangle of roots.*
On an average the nymphs of *S.striolatum* are larger and the lateral abdominal spine on segment 9 longer than that of *S.sanguineum*, but as these characters are subject to variation they cannot be completely relied upon.

5 Abdomen with mid-dorsal spines on segments 5 to 7 (sometimes a vestigial one on 8). (Labium with premental setae 10+10 to 15+15 (usually 13+13 to 14+14); labial palpi with 10 to 12 setae (usually 11).) Abdomen with short lateral spines on segments 8 and 9 (Fig.22f). L. 14–16mm................................*S.scoticum* (Donovan)
Breeds in rushy pools and moorland bog-holes.

— Abdomen with mid-dorsal spines on segments 6 to 8. (Labium with premental setae 10+10 to 15+15 (usually 13+13 to 14+14)); labial palpi with 11 setae. Abdomen with short lateral spines on segments 8 and 9 (Fig.22c). L. about 16·5mm.........*S.flaveolum* (Linnaeus)
A more frequent immigrant than S.fonscolombei *and would breed in similar habitats.*

Genus *Leucorrhinia* Brittinger

One species found in Britain (Fig.23a). Abdomen with mid-dorsal spines on segments 4 to 6 (sometimes a vestigial one on 7); lateral spines on 8 and 9. Ventral surface marked with distinctive dark bands (Fig.23b). Labium with premental setae 12+12 to 15+15; labial palpi with 10 to 11 setae. L. 18–20mm.................... ....*L.dubia* (van der Linden)
Breeds in sphagnum pools and marshes.
Immature larvae of 11mm, may be determined by the dark markings on the ventral surface of the abdomen.

References

Corbet, P. S., 1953. A terminology for the labium of larval Odonata. *Entomologist* **86**: 191–196.

Tillyard, R. J., 1917. *The Biology of Dragonflies.* Cambridge.

Figs.9a,16a,21b and 21c have been reproduced from drawings by Colonel Niall MacNeill, MRIA, FRES.

Figure 22

(a) *Sympetrum striolatum* (Charp.), head from in front
(b) *S.sanguineum* (Müll.), head from in front
(c) *S.flaveolum* (L.), lateral abdominal spines
(d) *S.vulgatum* (L.), lateral abdominal spines

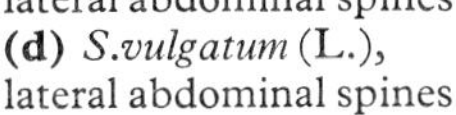

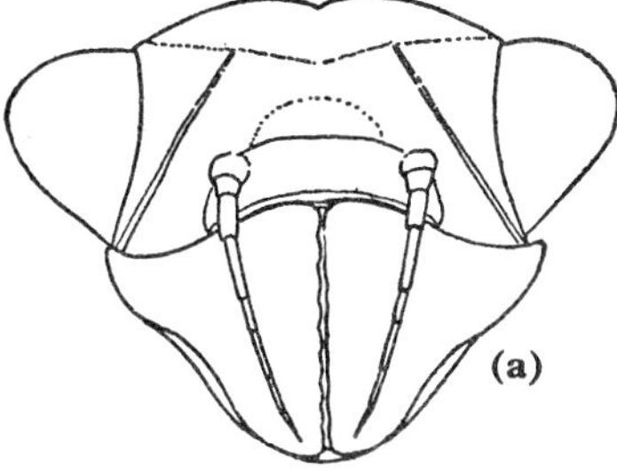

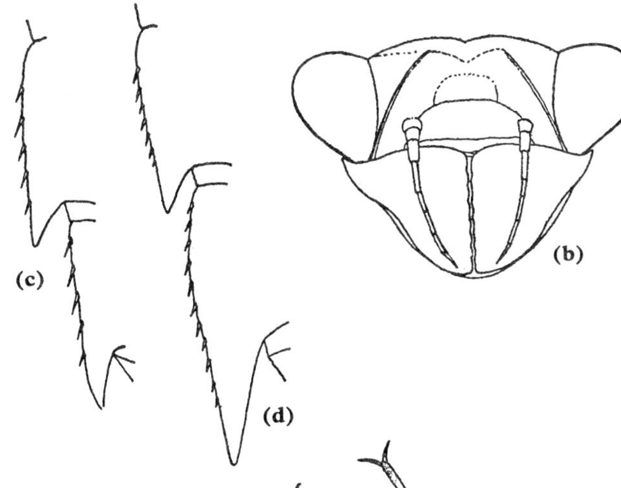

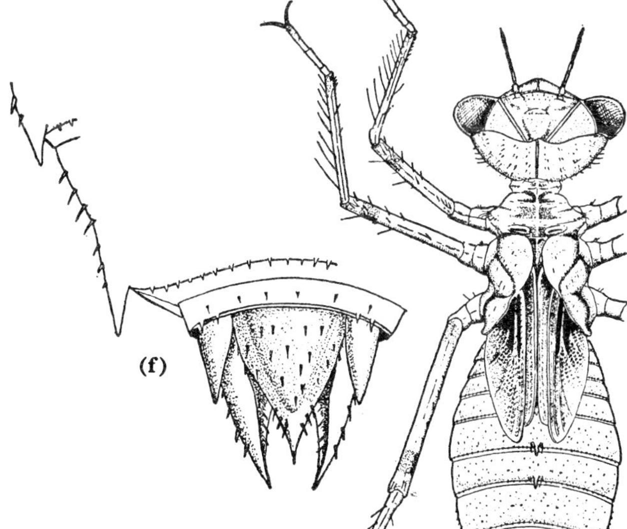

(e) *S.scoticum* (Don.), larva
(f) *S.scoticum* (Don.), anal appendages and lateral spines, male

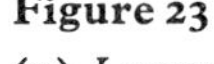

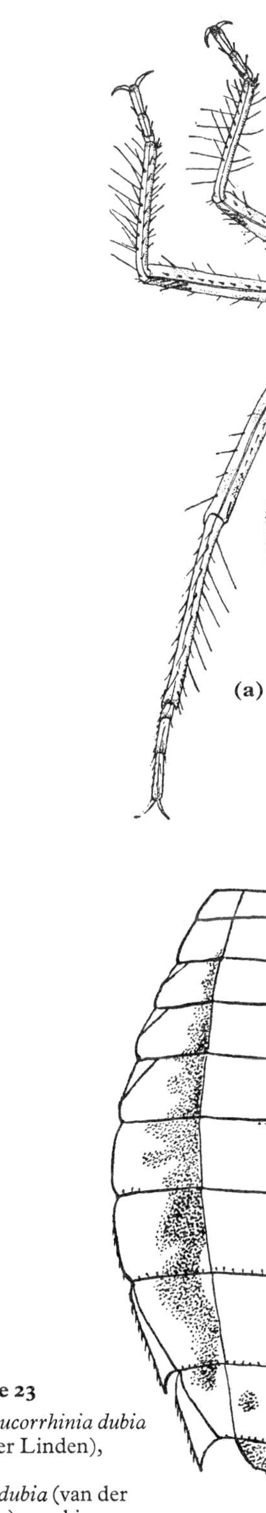

Figure 23

(a) *Leucorrhinia dubia* (van der Linden), larva
(b) *L.dubia* (van der Linden), markings on ventral surface of abdomen

England and Wales

1 West Cornwall (with Scilly)
2 East Cornwall
3 South Devon
4 North Devon
5 South Somerset
6 North Somerset
7 North Wiltshire
8 South Wiltshire
9 Dorset
10 Isle of Wight
11 South Hampshire
12 North Hampshire
13 West Sussex
14 East Sussex
15 East Kent
16 West Kent
17 Surrey
18 South Essex
19 North Essex
20 Hertfordshire
21 Middlesex
22 Berkshire
23 Oxfordshire
24 Buckinghamshire
25 East Suffolk
26 West Suffolk
27 East Norfolk
28 West Norfolk
29 Cambridgeshire
30 Bedfordshire
31 Huntingdonshire
32 Northamptonshire
33 East Gloucestershire
34 West Gloucestershire
35 Monmouthshire
36 Herefordshire
37 Worcestershire
38 Warwickshire
39 Staffordshire
40 Shropshire (Salop)
41 Glamorgan
42 Breconshire
43 Radnorshire
44 Carmarthenshire
45 Pembrokeshire
46 Cardiganshire
47 Montgomeryshire
48 Merionethshire
49 Caernarvonshire
50 Denbighshire
51 Flintshire
52 Anglesey
53 South Lincolnshire
54 North Lincolnshire
55 Leicestershire (with Rutland)
56 Nottinghamshire
57 Derbyshire
58 Cheshire
59 South Lancashire
60 West Lancashire
61 South-east Yorkshire
62 North-east Yorkshire
63 South-west Yorkshire
64 Mid-west Yorkshire
65 North-west Yorkshire
66 Durham
67 South Northumberland
68 North Northumberland (Cheviot)
69 Westmorland with North Lancashire
70 Cumberland
71 Isle of Man
113 Channel Isles

Scotland

72 Dumfries-shire
73 Kirkcudbrightshire
74 Wigtownshire
75 Ayrshire
76 Renfrewshire
77 Lanarkshire
78 Peebleshire
79 Selkirkshire
80 Roxburghshire
81 Berwickshire
82 East Lothian (Haddington)
83 Midlothian (Edinburgh)
84 West Lothian (Linlithgow)
85 Fifeshire (with Kinross)
86 Stirlingshire
87 West Perthshire (with Clackmannan)
88 Mid Perthshire
89 East Perthshire
90 Angus (Forfar)
91 Kincardineshire
92 South Aberdeenshire
93 North Aberdeenshire
94 Banffshire
95 Moray (Elgin)
96 East Inverness-shire (with Nairn)
97 West Inverness-shire
98 Argyll Main
99 Dunbartonshire
100 Clyde Isles
101 Kintyre
102 South Ebudes
103 Mid Ebudes
104 North Ebudes
105 West Ross
106 East Ross
107 East Sutherland
108 West Sutherland
109 Caithness
110 Outer Hebrides
111 Orkney Islands
112 Shetland Islands (Zetland)

Ireland

H.1 South Kerry
H.2 North Kerry
H.3 West Cork
H.4 Mid Cork
H.5 East Cork
H.6 Waterford
H.7 South Tipperary
H.8 Limerick
H.9 Clare
H.10 North Tipperary
H.11 Kilkenny
H.12 Wexford
H.13 Carlow
H.14 Leix (Queen's County)
H.15 South-east Galway
H.16 West Galway
H.17 North-east Galway
H.18 Offaly (King's County)
H.19 Kildare
H.20 Wicklow
H.21 Dublin
H.22 Meath
H.23 West Meath
H.24 Longford
H.25 Roscommon
H.26 East Mayo
H.27 West Mayo
H.28 Sligo
H.29 Leitrim
H.30 Cavan
H.31 Louth
H.32 Monaghan
H.33 Fermanagh
H.34 East Donegal
H.35 West Donegal
H.36 Tyrone
H.37 Armagh
H.38 Down
H.39 Antrim
H.40 Londonderry

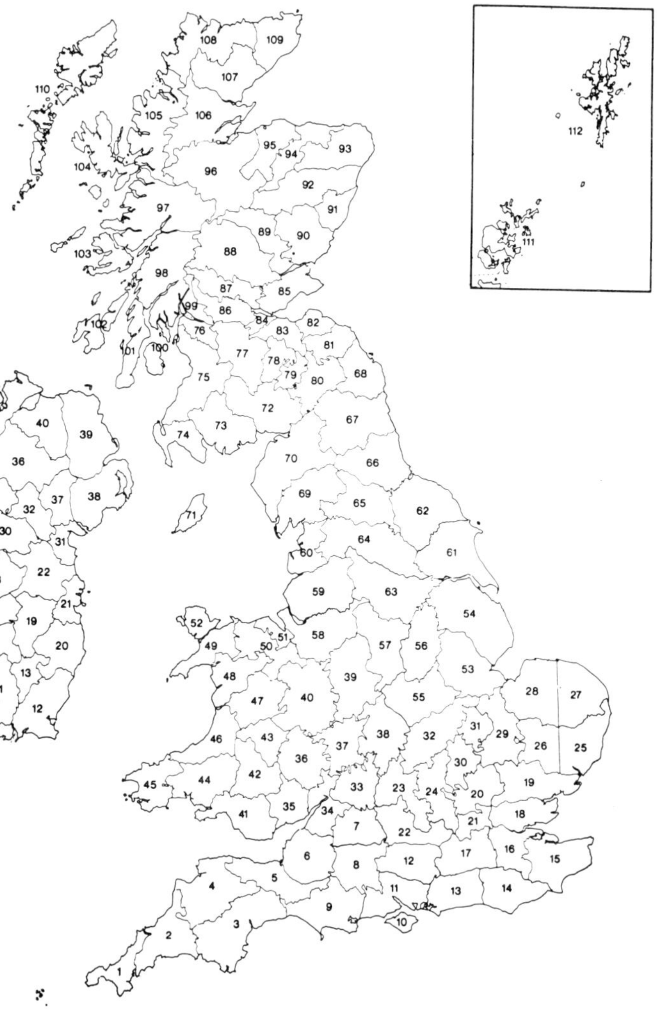

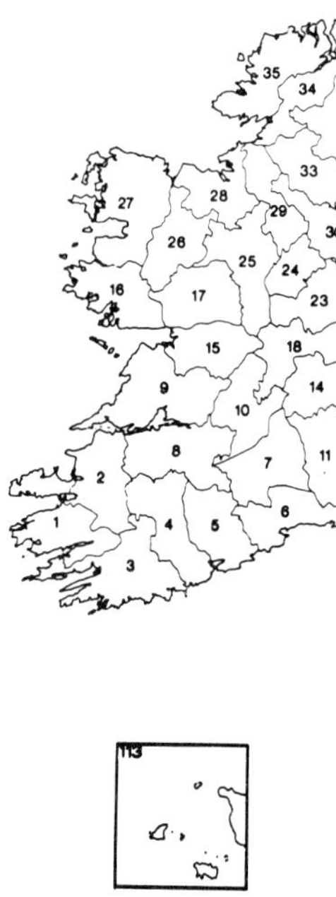

Vice-counties

THE MAPS

In order to facilitate the location by vice-counties of records indicated on the 10km square dot distribution maps, the Watsonian vice-county division of Great Britain and Ireland is printed on the facing page.

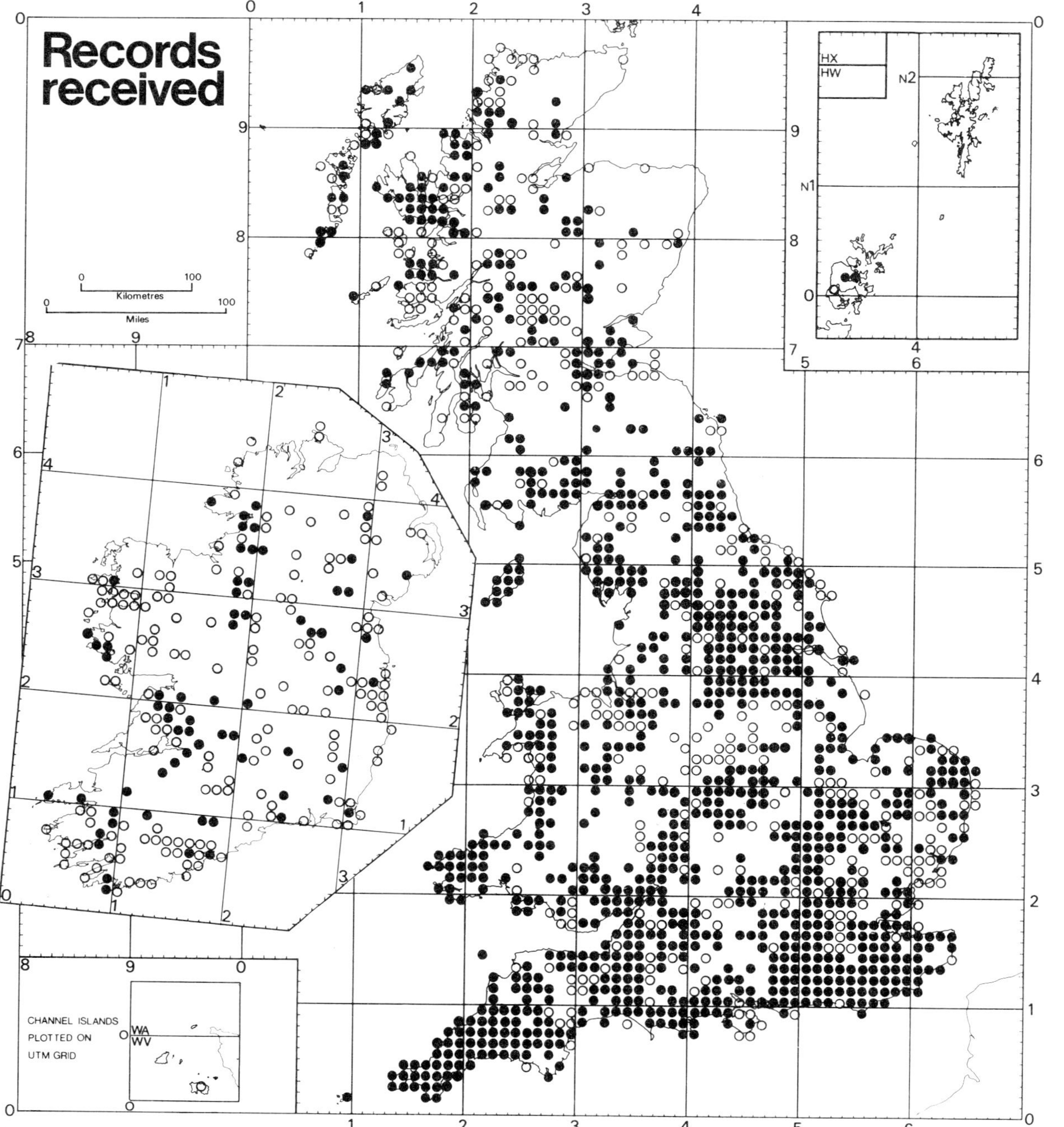

The Distribution Maps

The distribution maps show from which 10km square of the National Grid each species has been recorded. Solid dots represent post-1960 records; open circles earlier records. In the case of Ireland some records can only be localised to vice-county level. Where these are the only records from the vice-county they have been indicated on the maps with a star: they are all old records made before 1960.

All records received at the Biological Records Centre up to the end of January 1977 have been incorporated on the maps, as well as data abstracted from museum material and the literature. Without the help of a great many entomologists, which cannot be acknowledged individually, this work could not have been accomplished.

The provisional nature and incompleteness of the maps will, it is hoped, stimulate readers to send additional records to the national biological records centres (Biological Records Centre, Monks Wood Experimental Station, Abbots Ripton, Huntingdon, Cambs, PE17 2LS, for Great Britain and the Irish Biological Records Centre, An Foras Forbartha, St. Martin's House, Waterloo Road, Dublin 4, for Ireland).

The map of records received shows the coverage so far achieved.

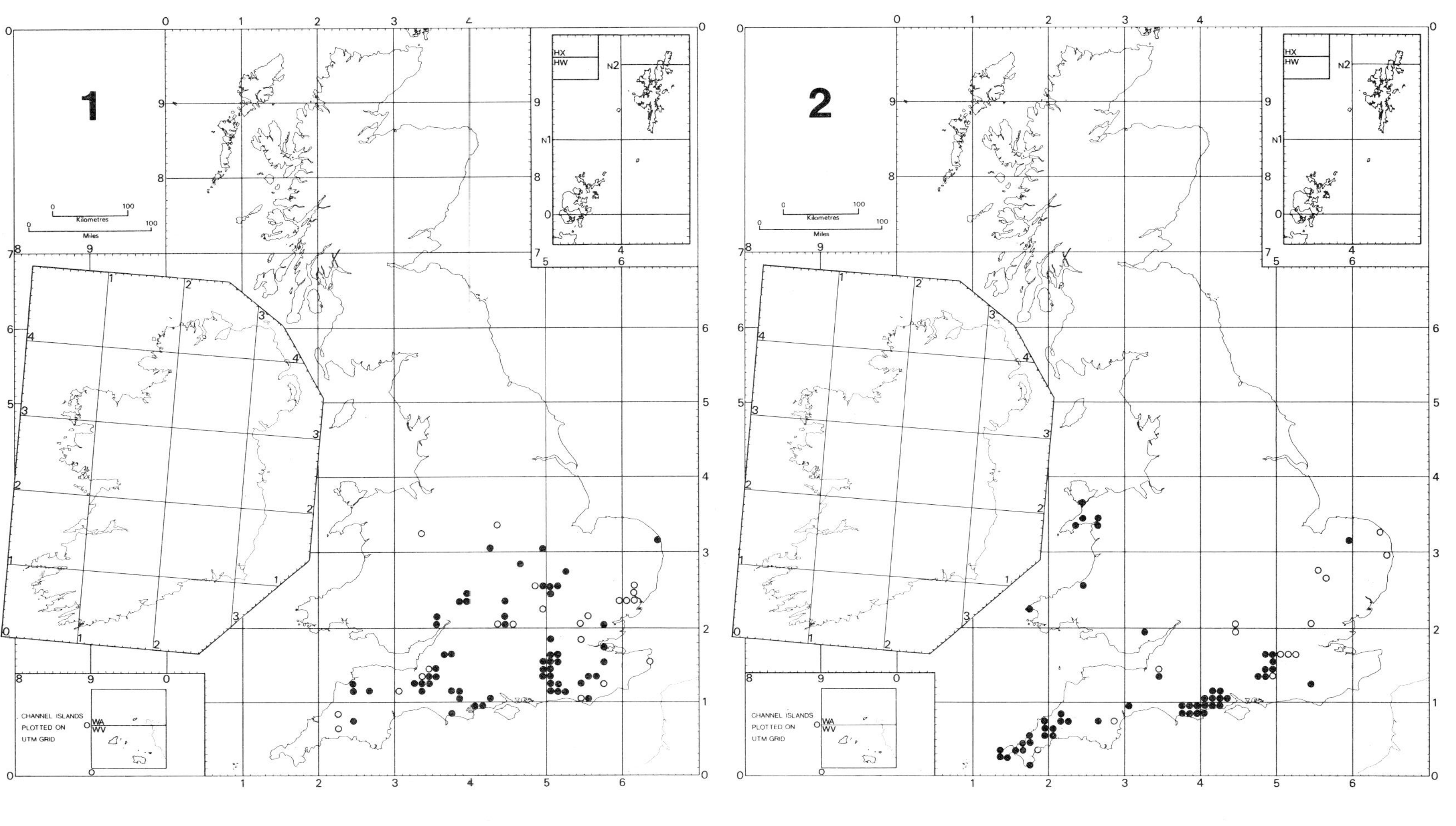

Platycnemis pennipes

Ceriagrion tenellum

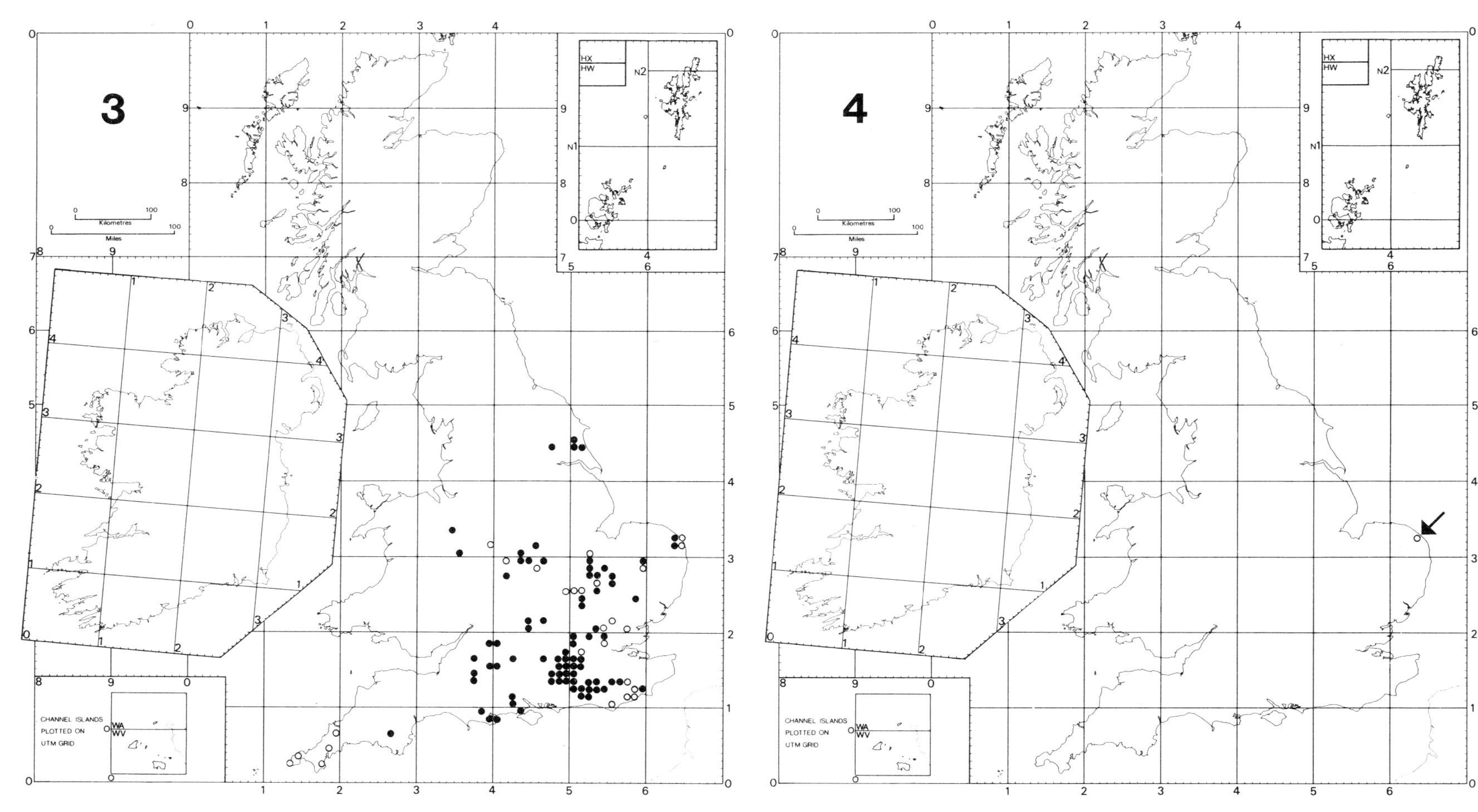

Erythromma najas

Coenagrion armatum

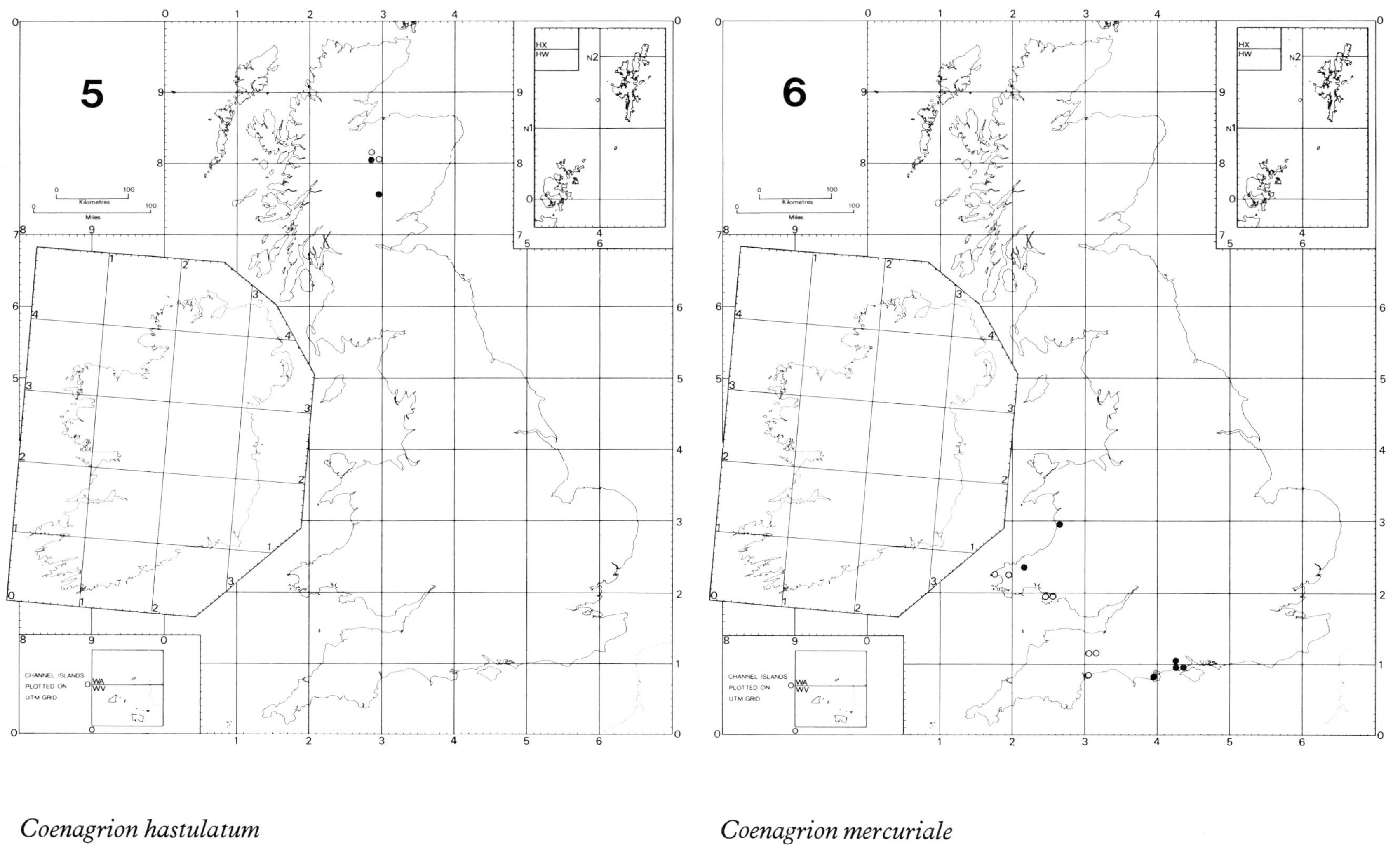

Coenagrion hastulatum

Coenagrion mercuriale

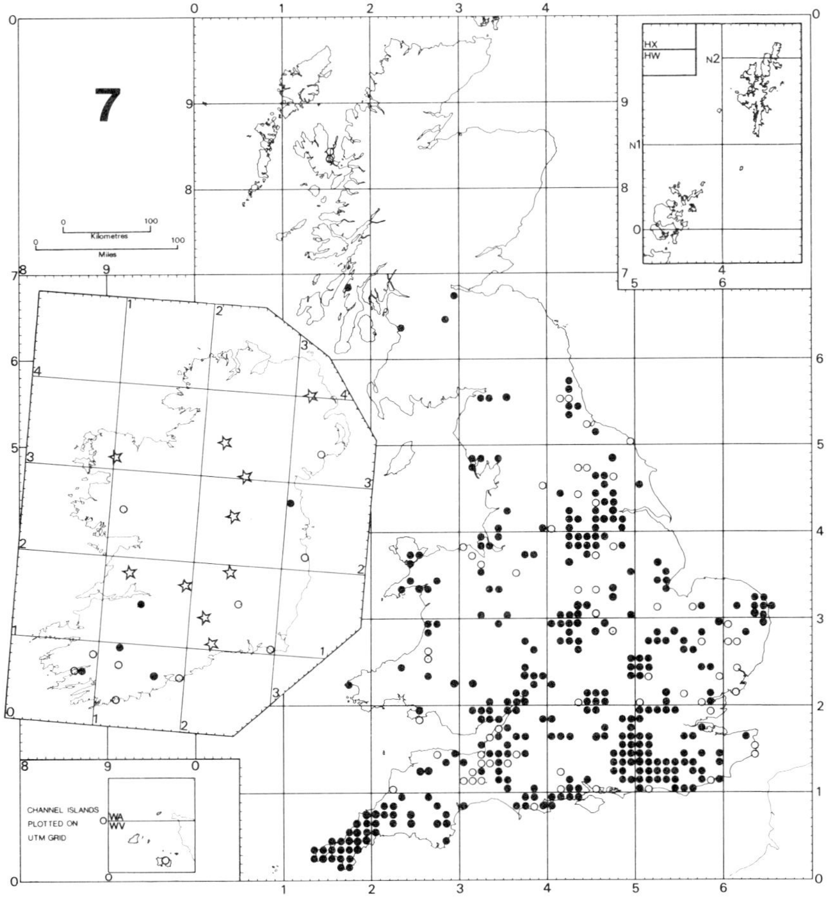

7

Coenagrion puella

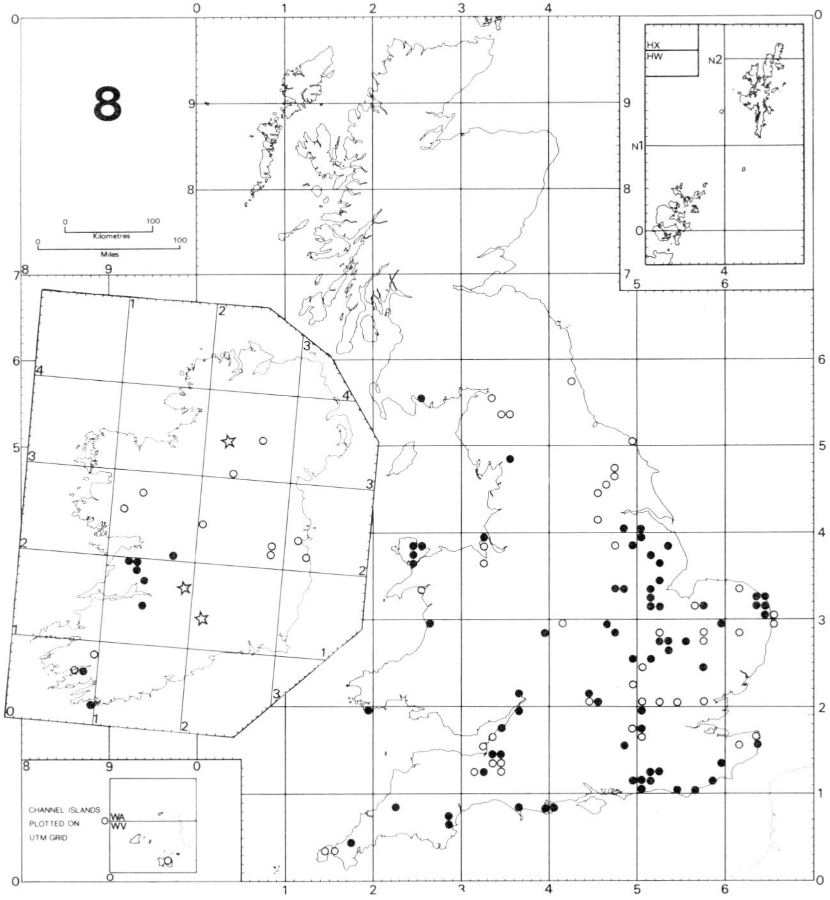

8

Coenagrion pulchellum

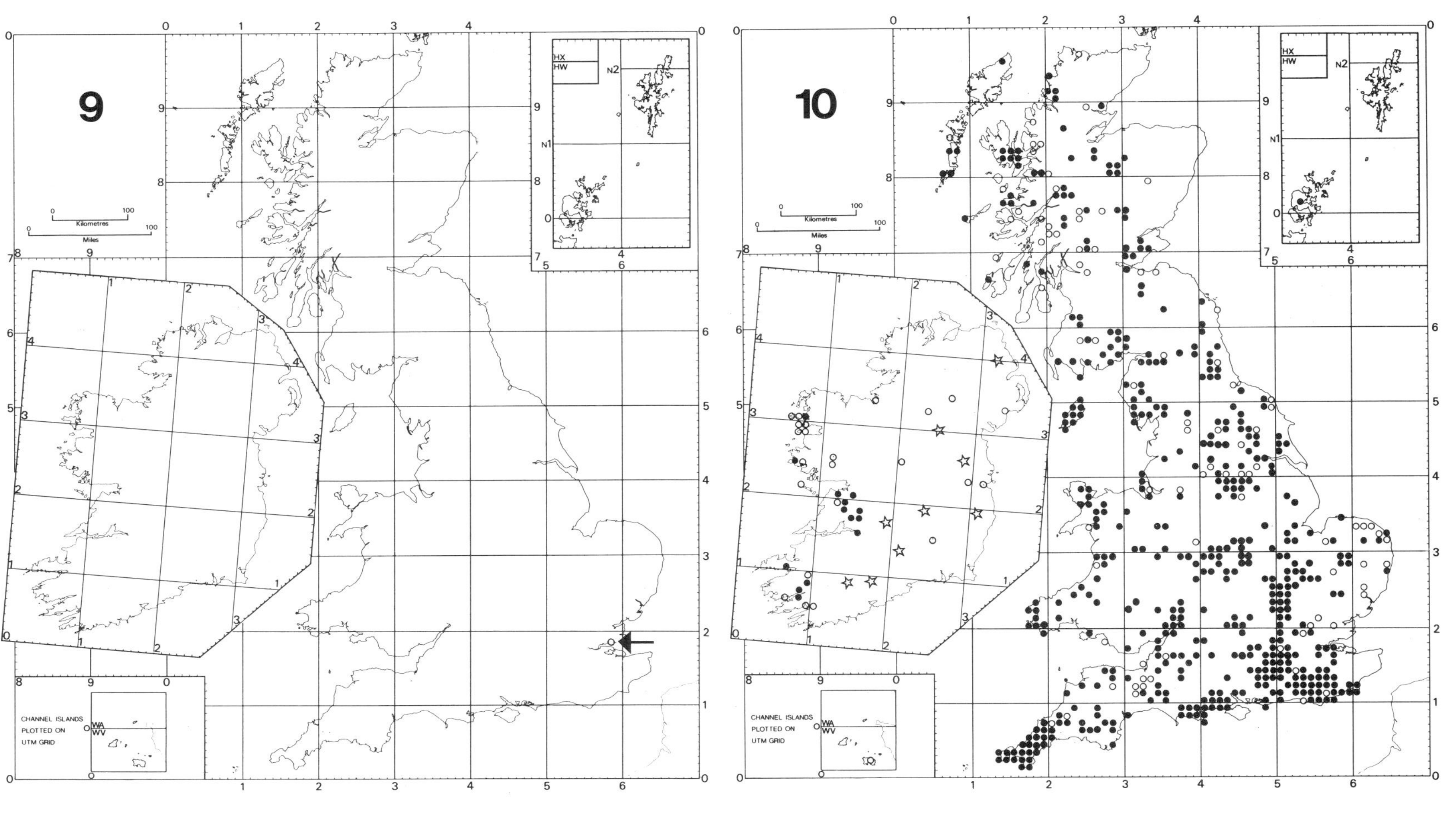

Coenagrion scitulum

Enallagma cyathigerum

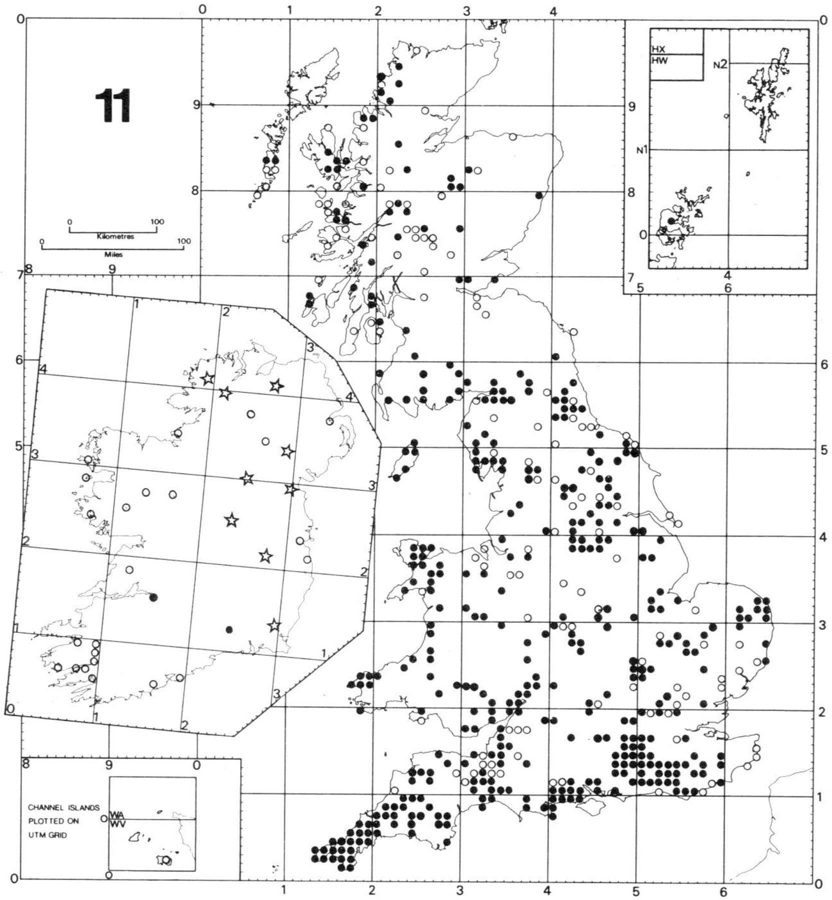

11

0 100 Kilometres

0 100 Miles

CHANNEL ISLANDS PLOTTED ON UTM GRID

Pyrrhosoma nymphula

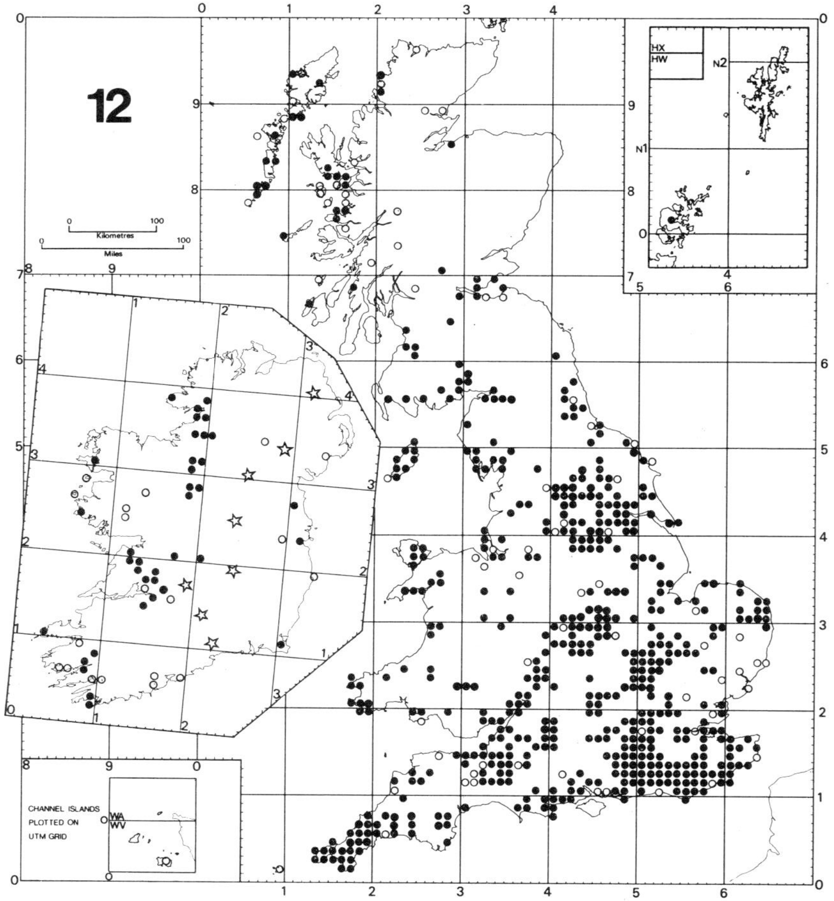

12

0 100 Kilometres

0 100 Miles

CHANNEL ISLANDS PLOTTED ON UTM GRID

Ischnura elegans

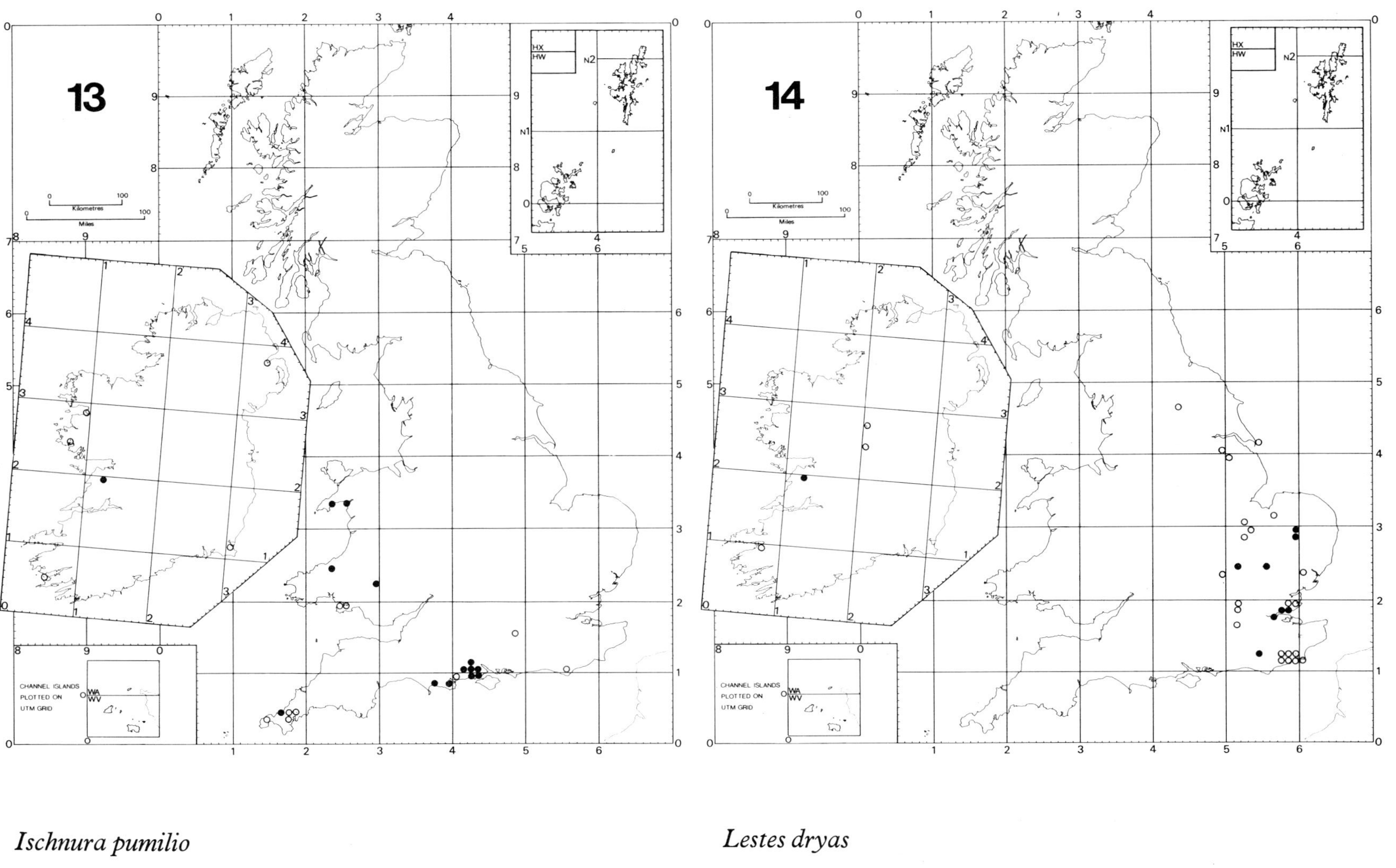

Ischnura pumilio

Lestes dryas

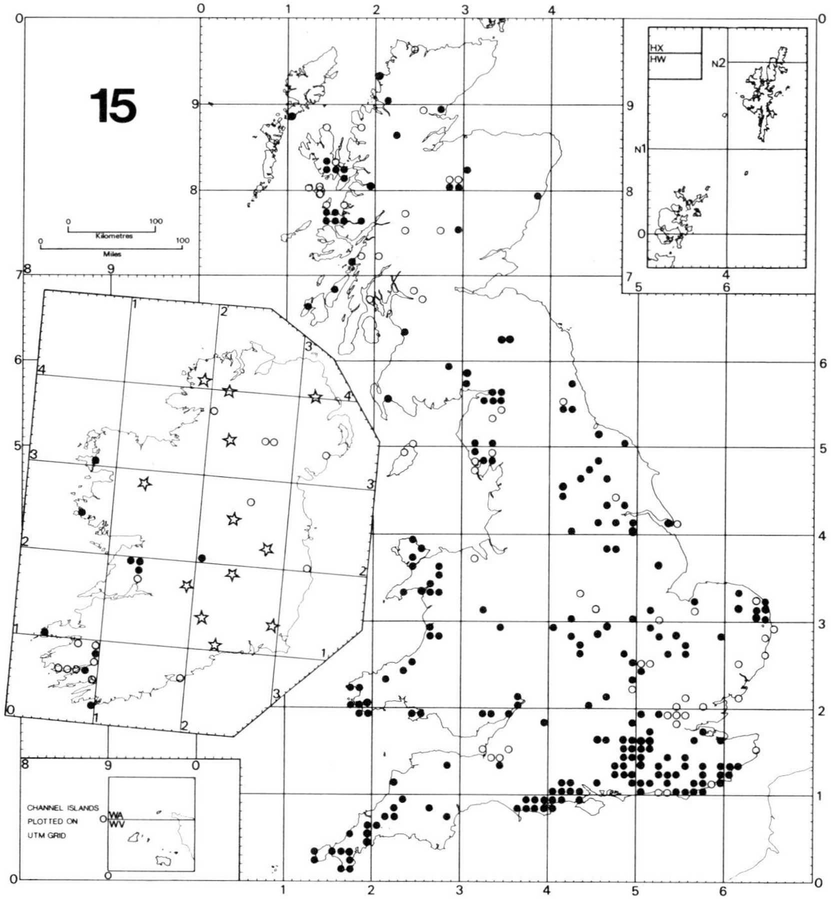

15

Kilometres 0 100
Miles 0 100

CHANNEL ISLANDS PLOTTED ON UTM GRID

Lestes sponsa

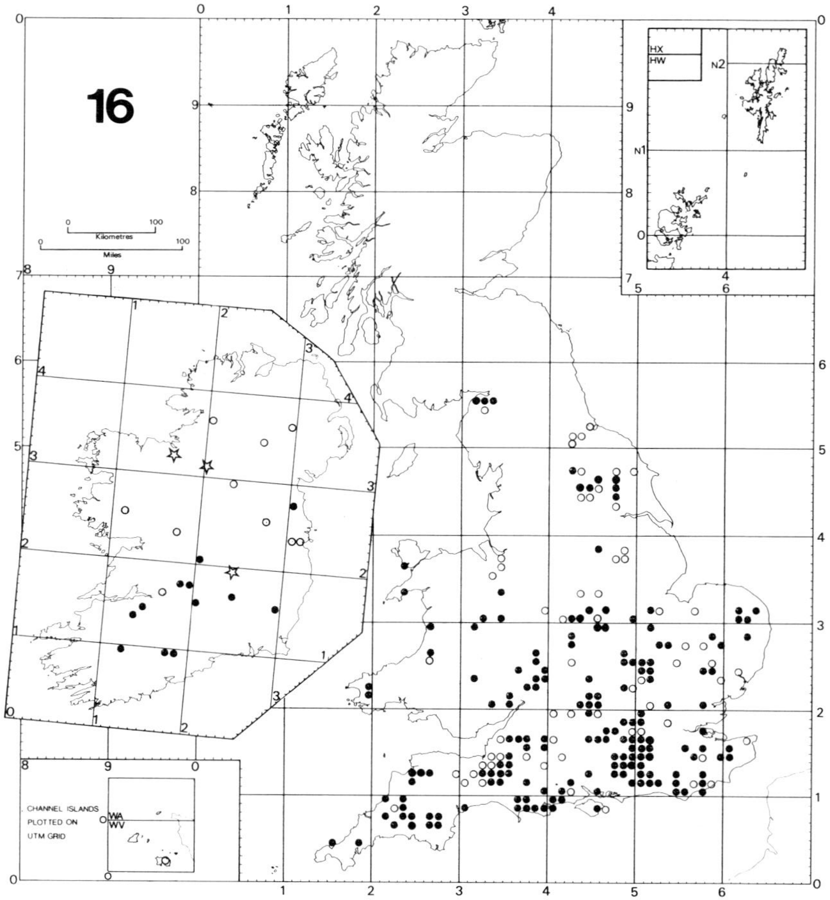

16

Kilometres 0 100
Miles 0 100

CHANNEL ISLANDS PLOTTED ON UTM GRID

Agrion splendens

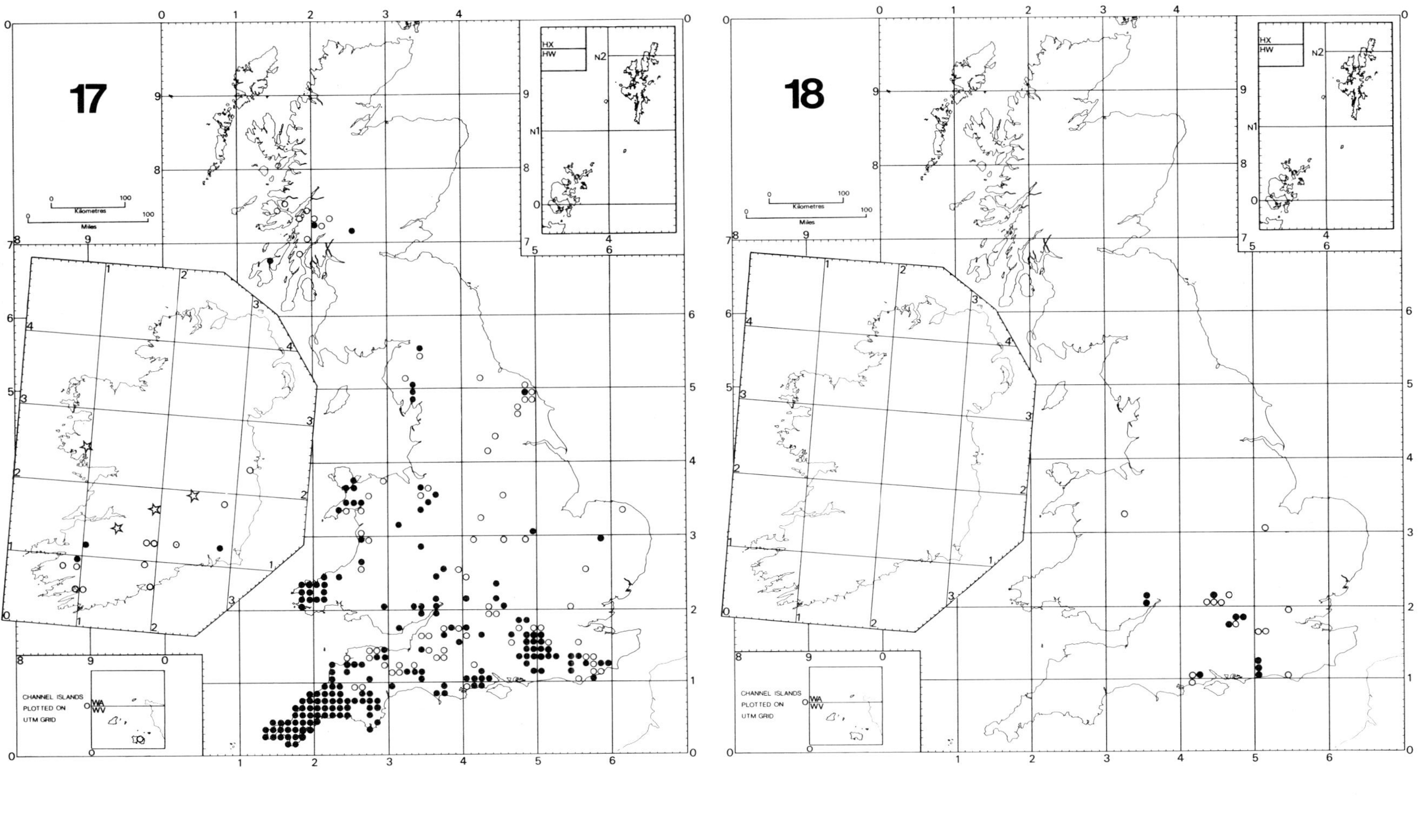

Agrion virgo

Gomphus vulgatissimus

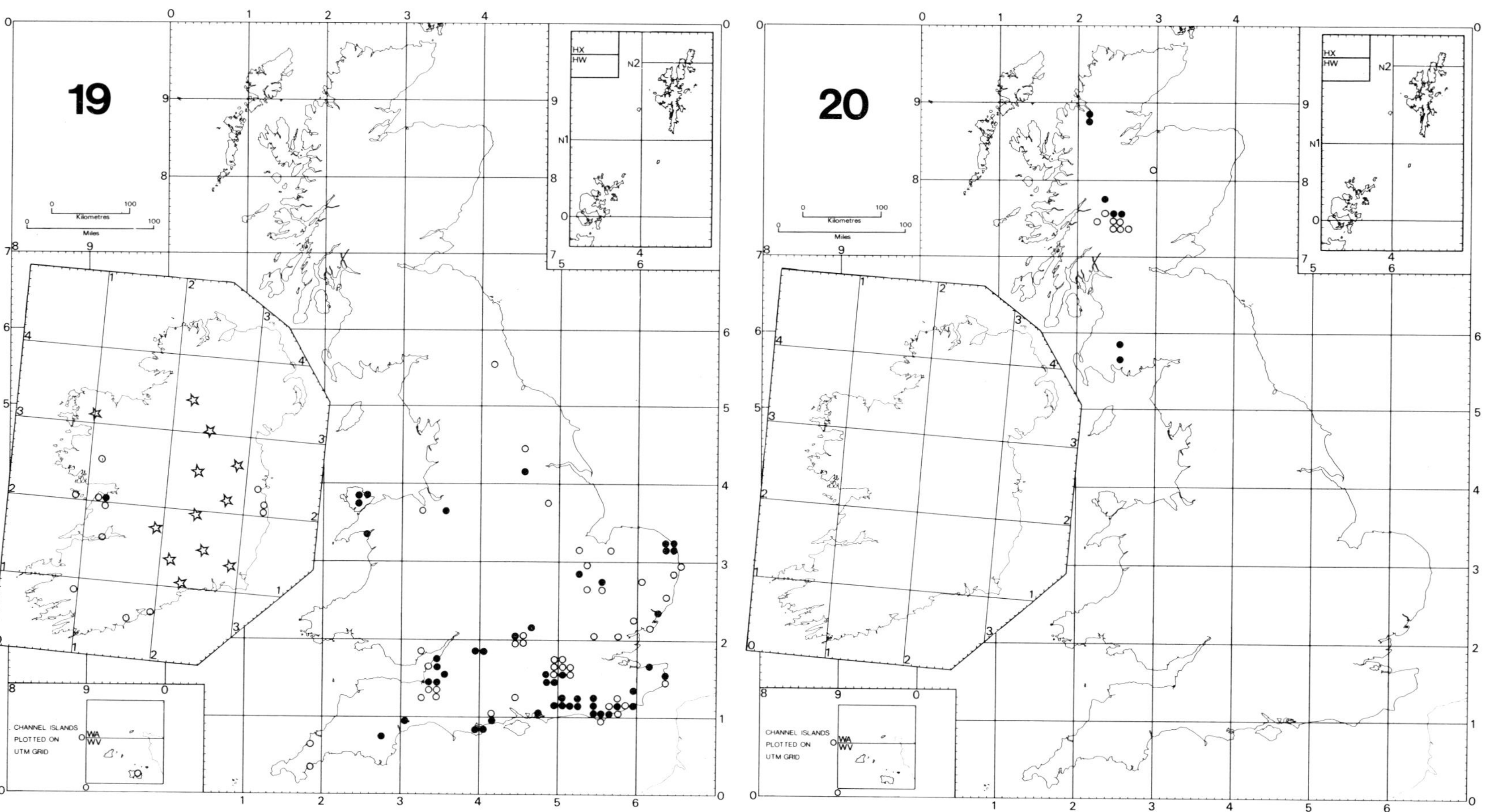

Brachytron pratense

Aeshna caerulea

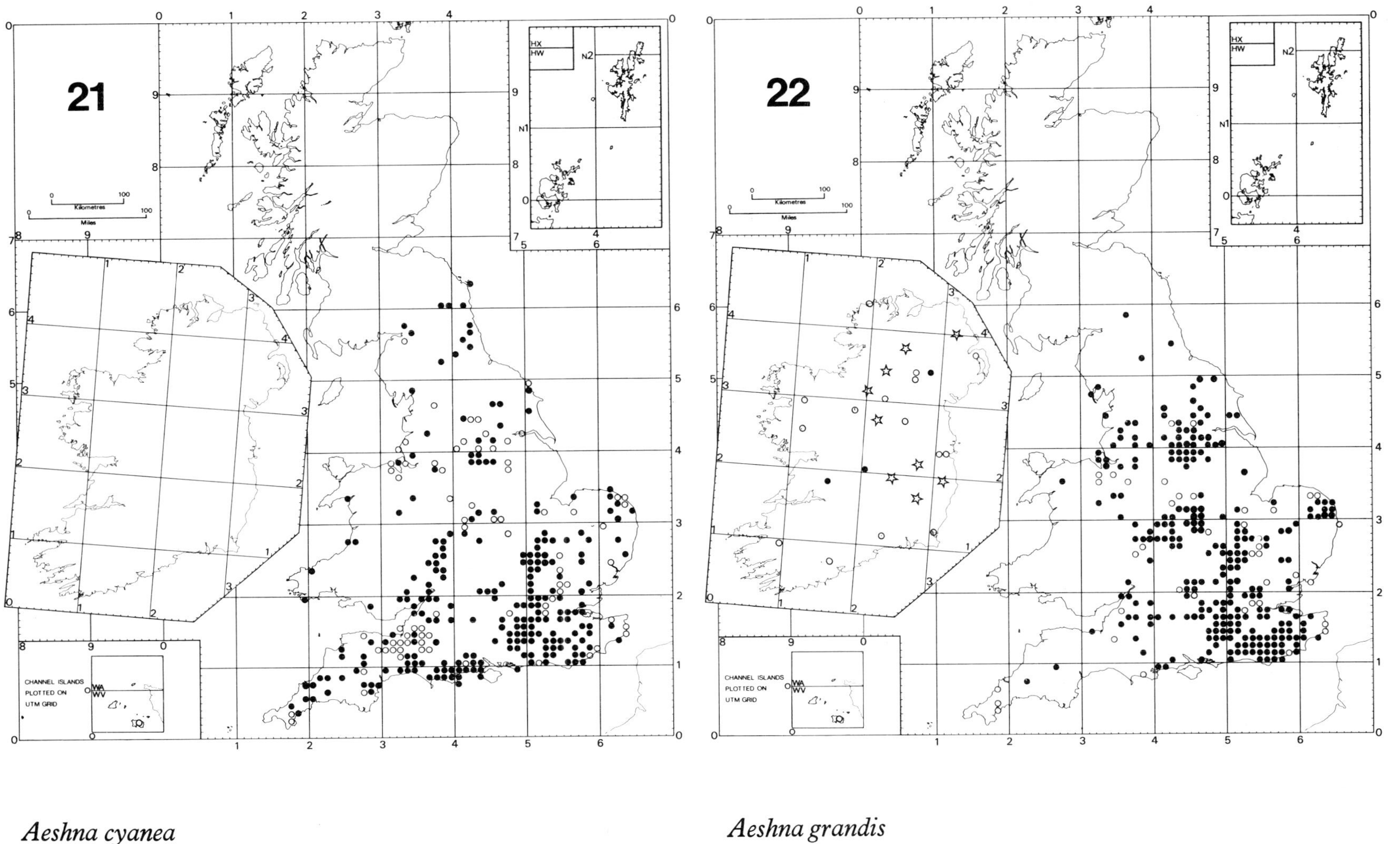

Aeshna cyanea

Aeshna grandis

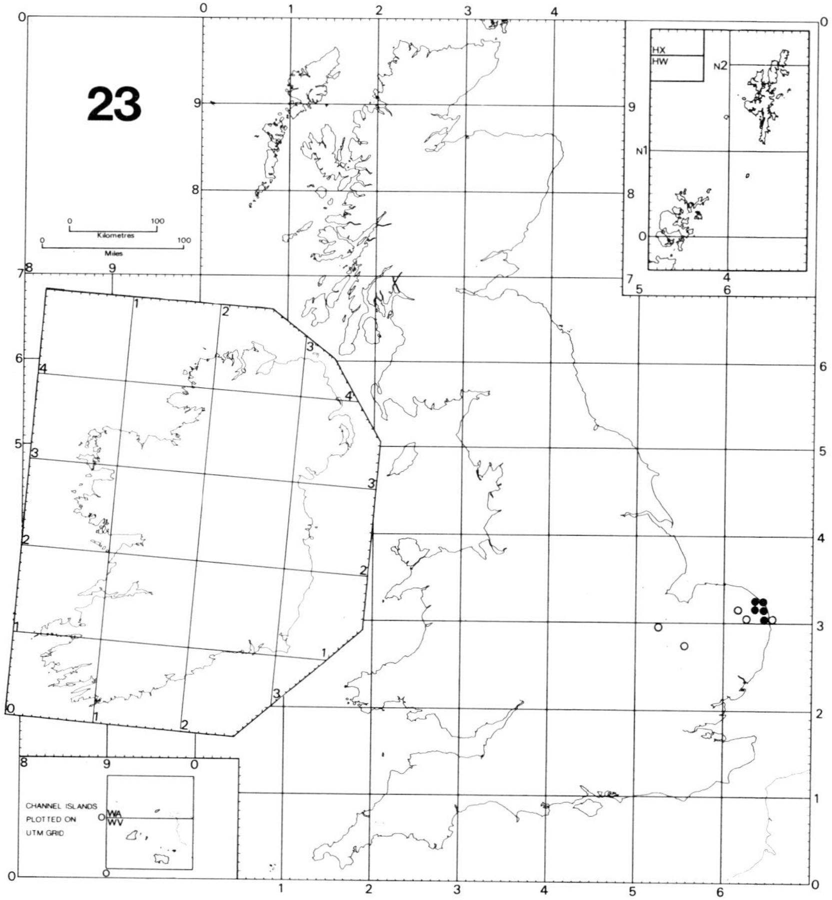
23
Kilometres
Miles
CHANNEL ISLANDS
PLOTTED ON
UTM GRID
HX
HW
N2
N1
WA
WV

Aeshna isosceles

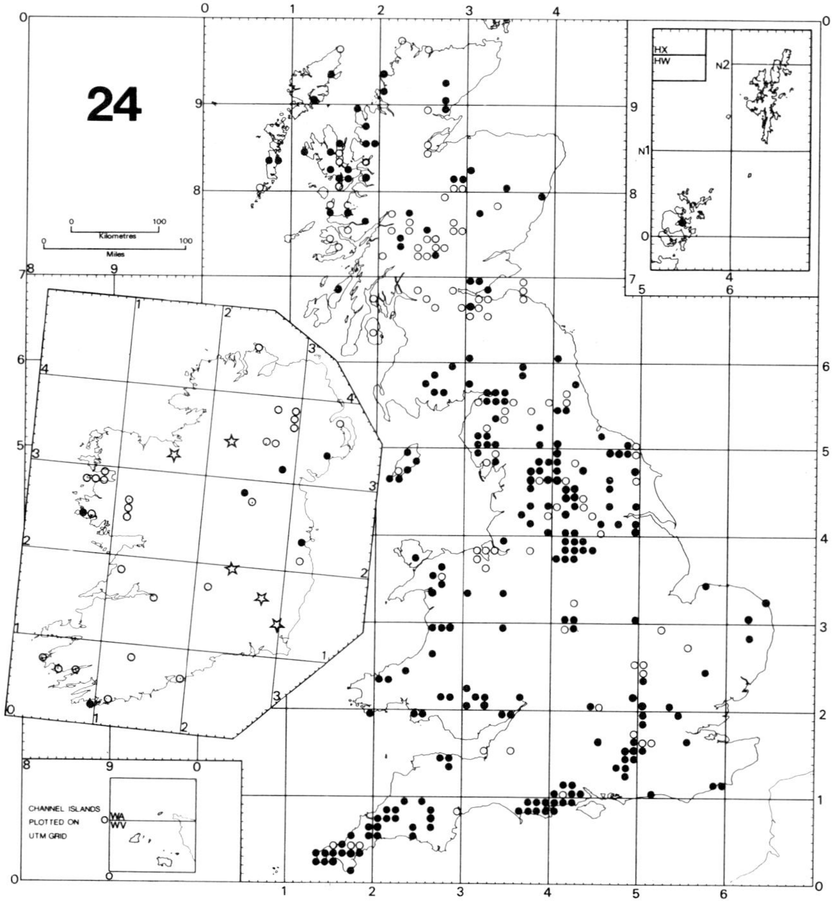
24
Kilometres
Miles
CHANNEL ISLANDS
PLOTTED ON
UTM GRID
HX
HW
N2
N1
WA
WV

Aeshna juncea

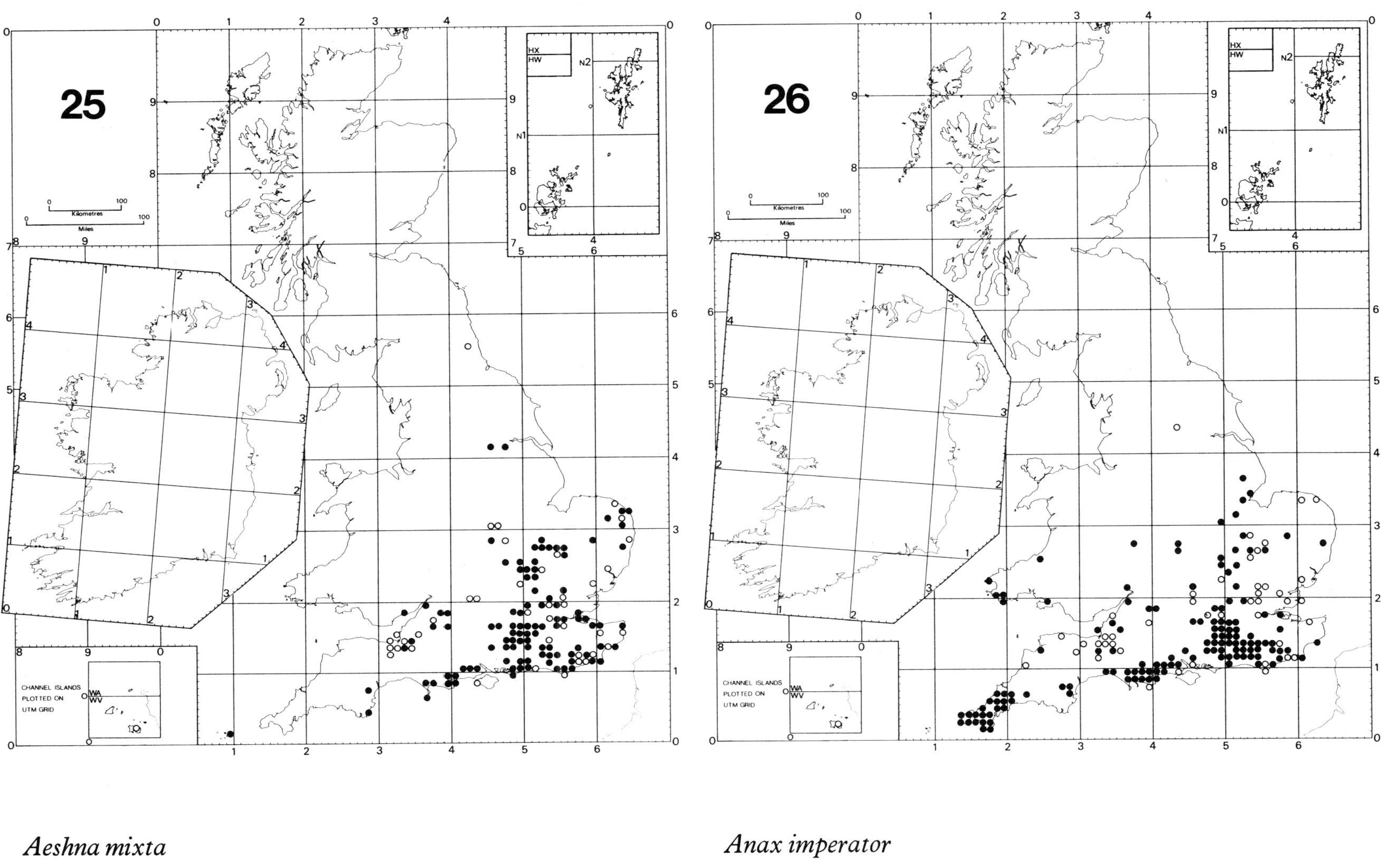

Aeshna mixta

Anax imperator

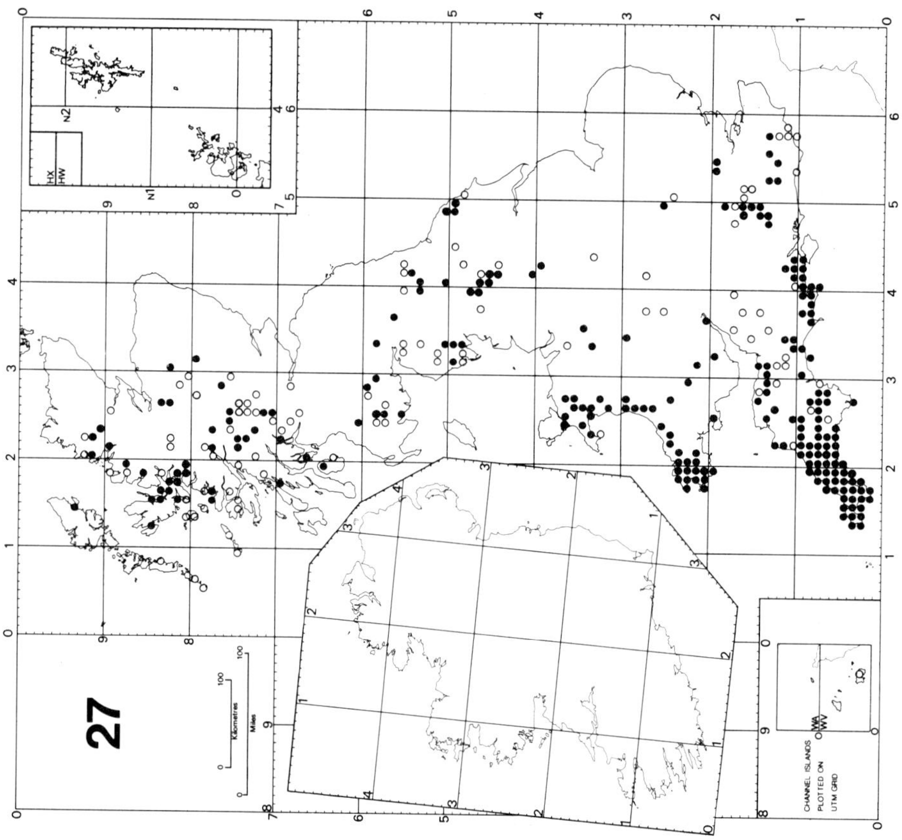

27

Kilometres

Miles

CHANNEL ISLANDS PLOTTED ON UTM GRID

Cordulegaster boltonii

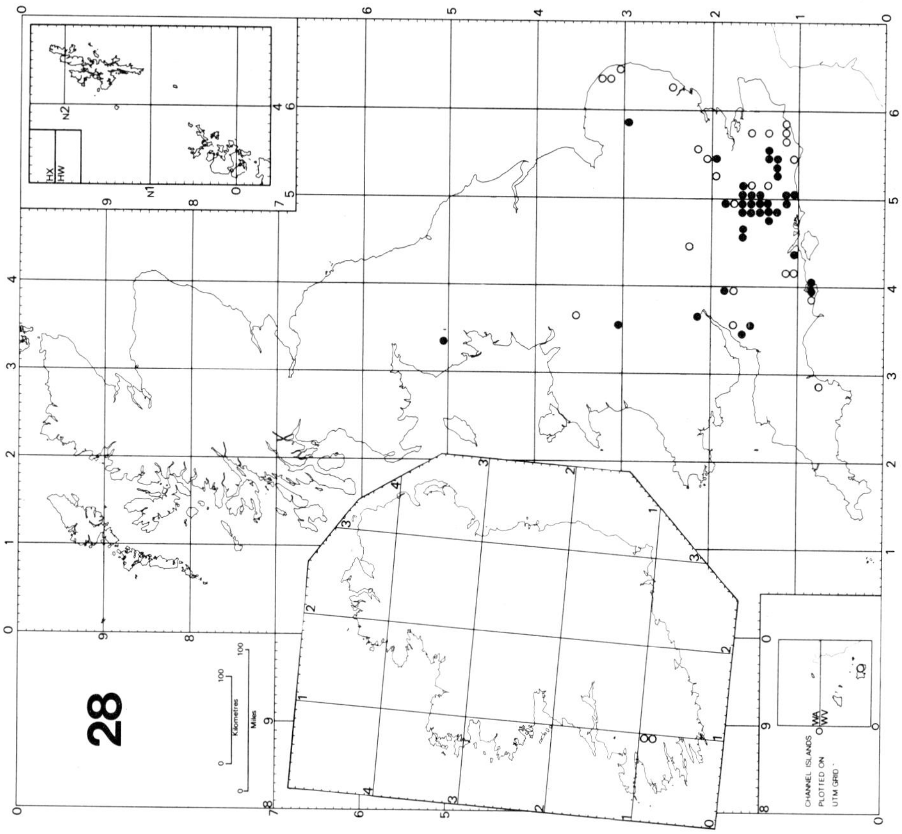

28

Kilometres

Miles

CHANNEL ISLANDS PLOTTED ON UTM GRID

Cordulia aenea

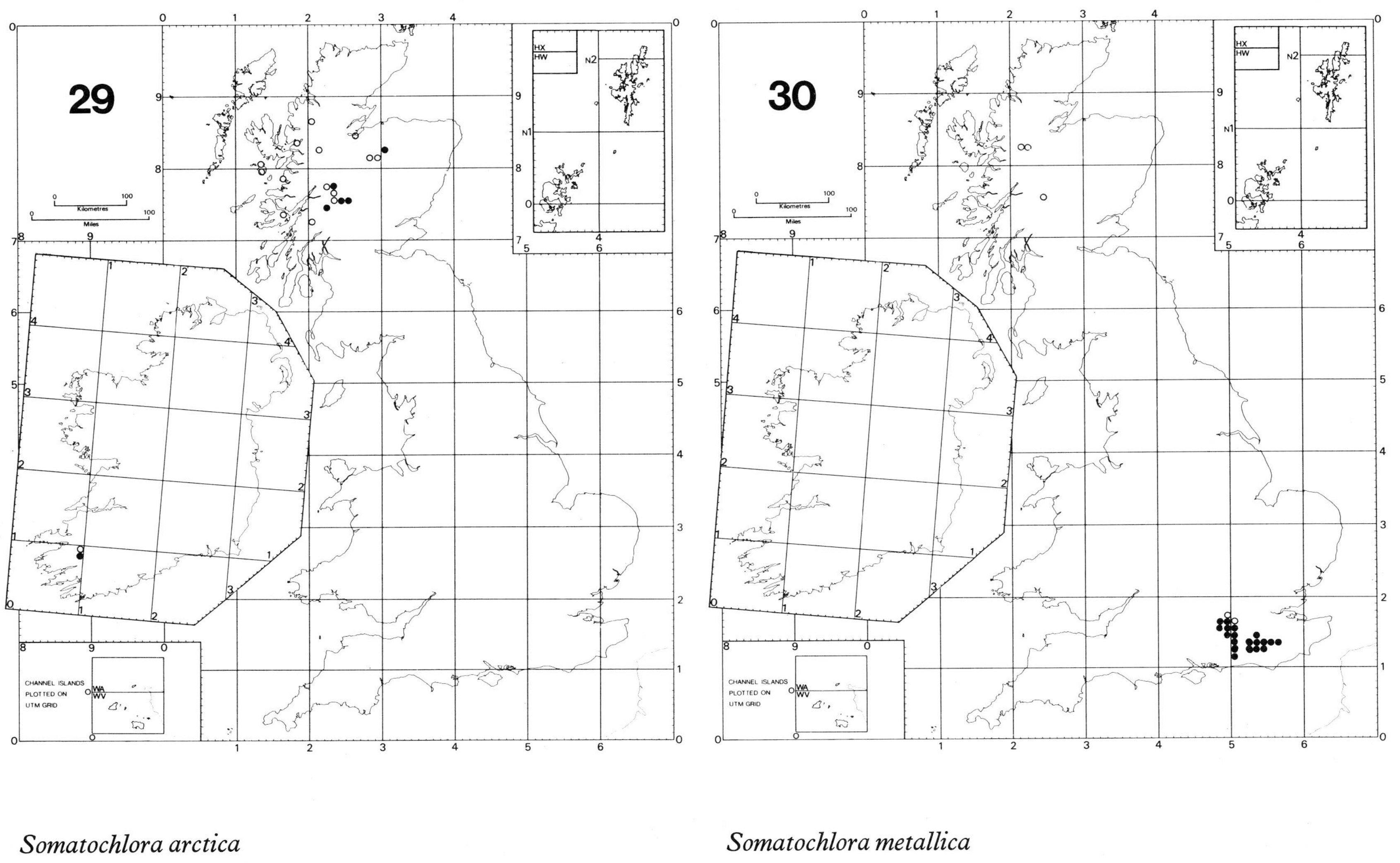

Somatochlora arctica

Somatochlora metallica

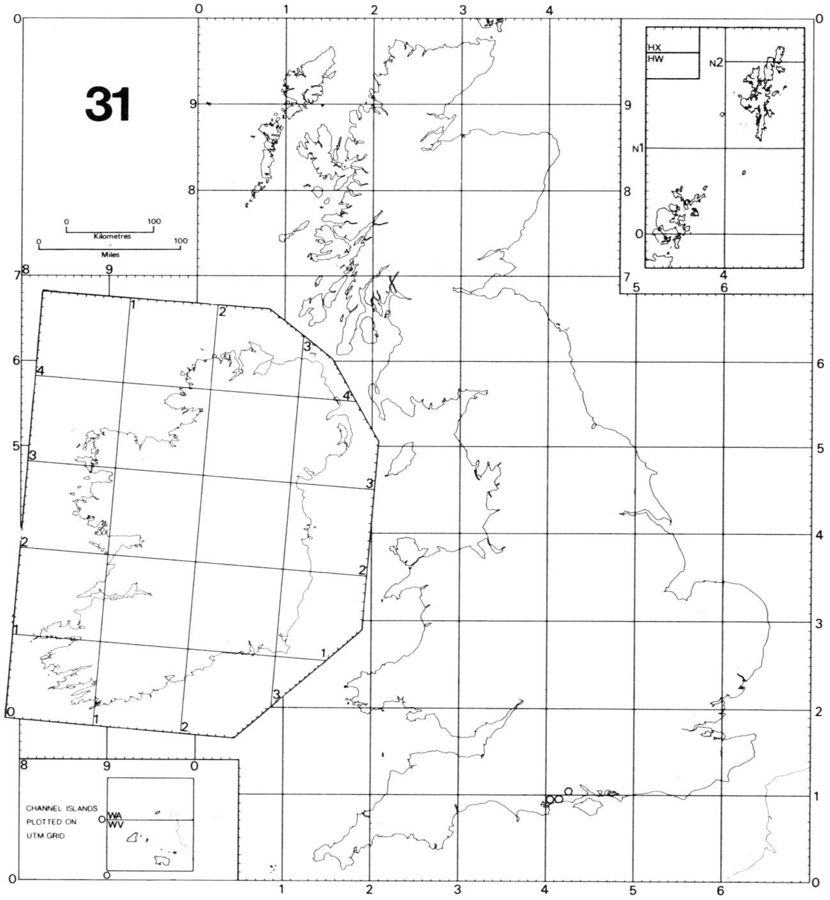

31

0 Kilometres 100
0 Miles 100

CHANNEL ISLANDS PLOTTED ON UTM GRID

Oxygastra curtisii

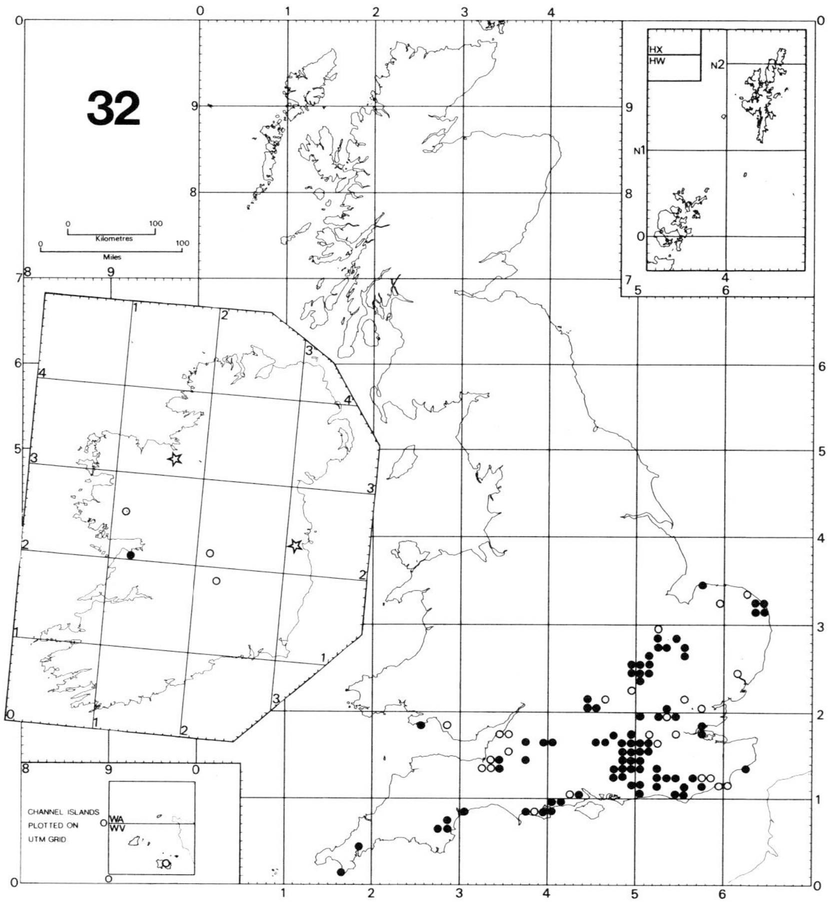

32

0 Kilometres 100
0 Miles 100

CHANNEL ISLANDS PLOTTED ON UTM GRID

Orthetrum cancellatum

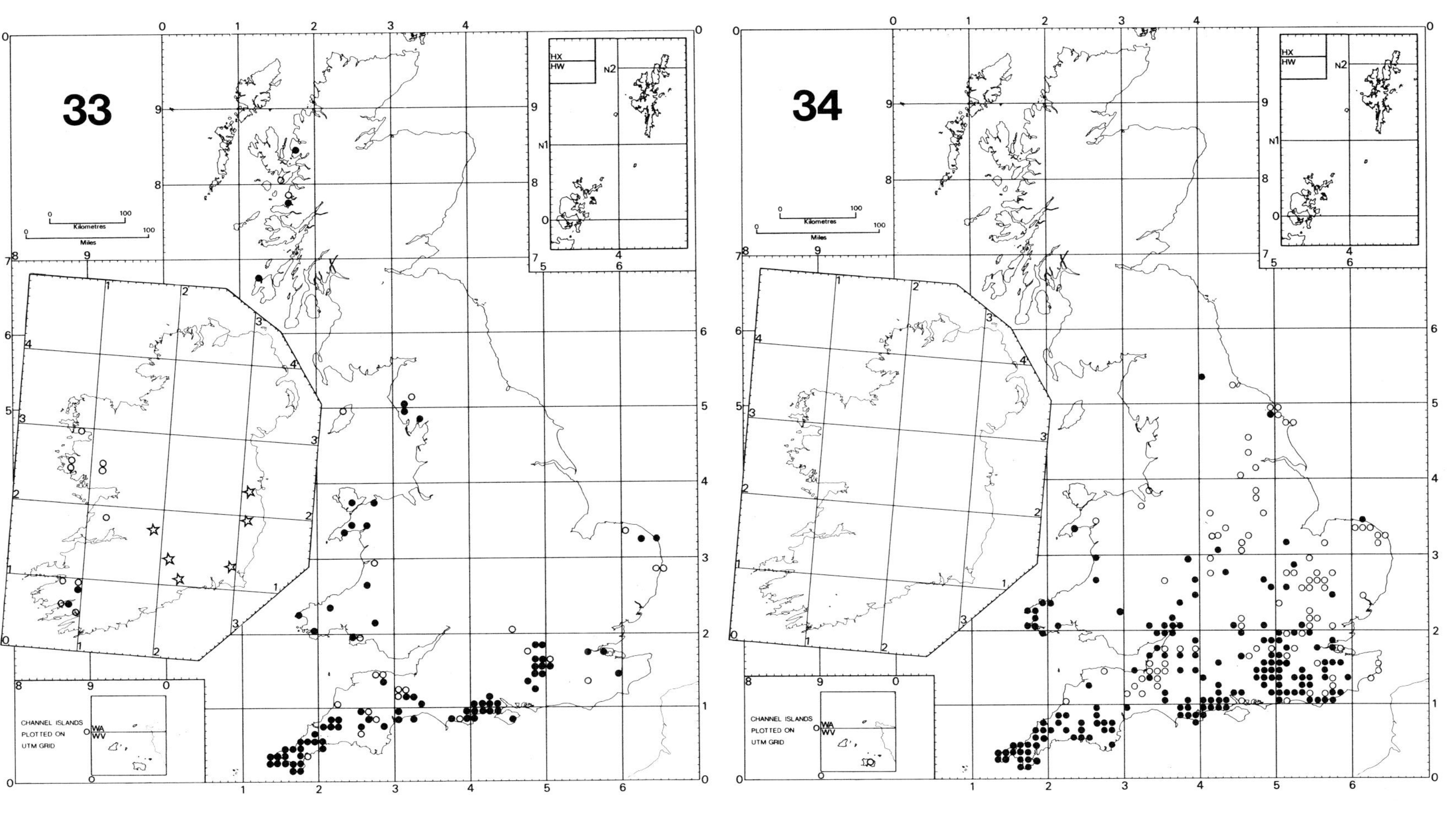

Orthetrum coerulescens

Libellula depressa

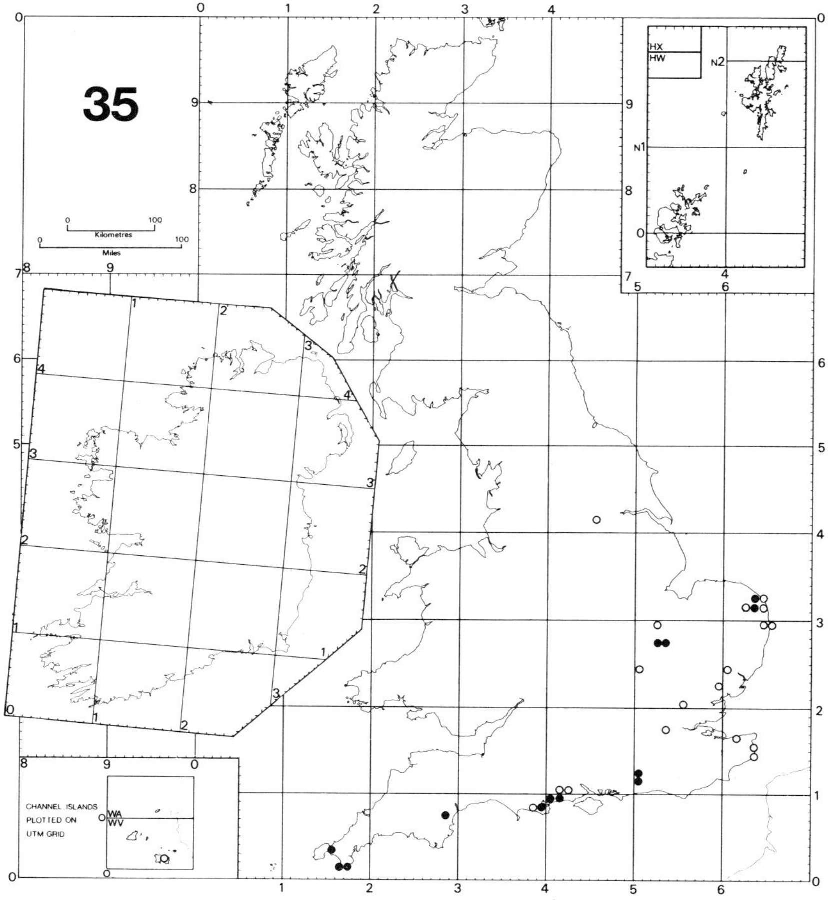

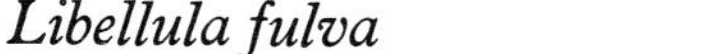

Libellula fulva

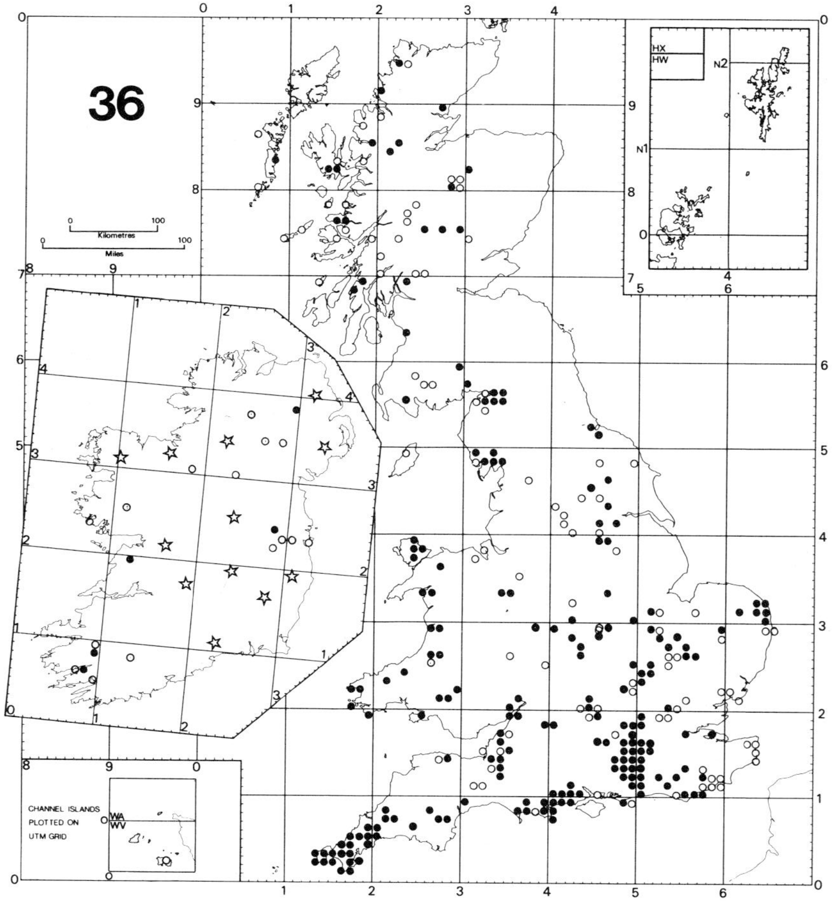

Libellula quadrimaculata

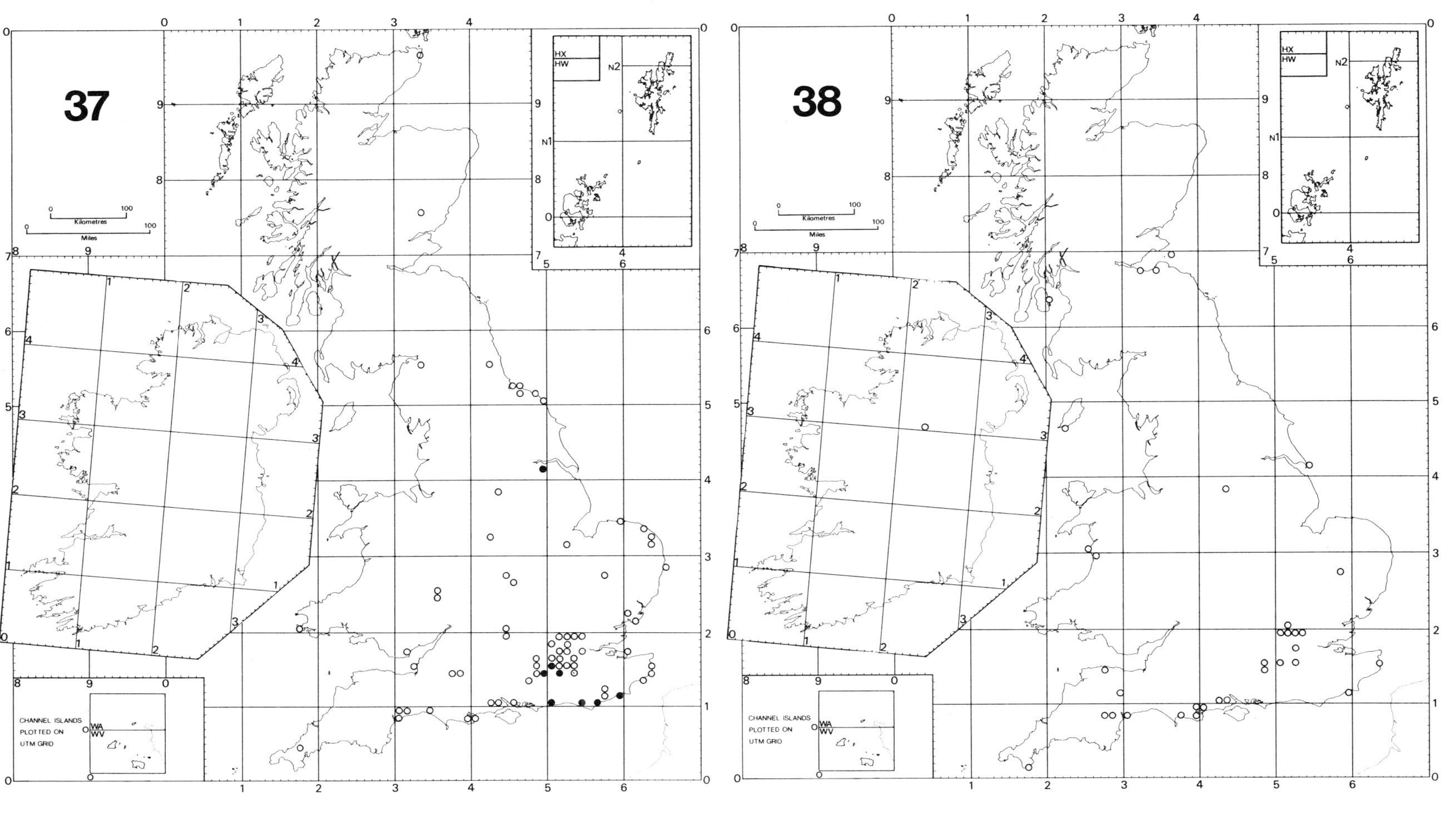

Sympetrum flaveolum

Sympetrum fonscolombei

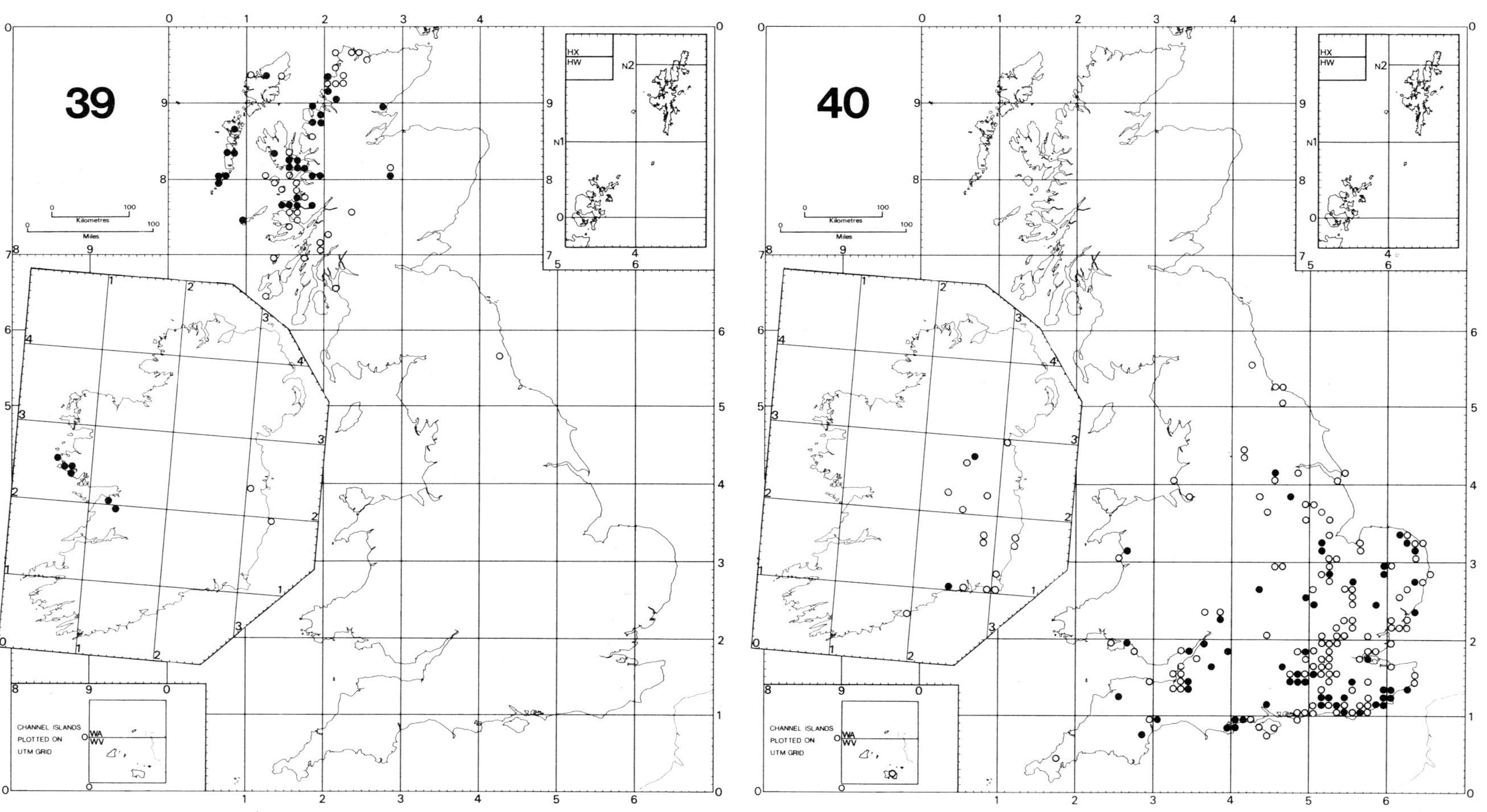

Sympetrum nigrescens

Sympetrum sanguineum

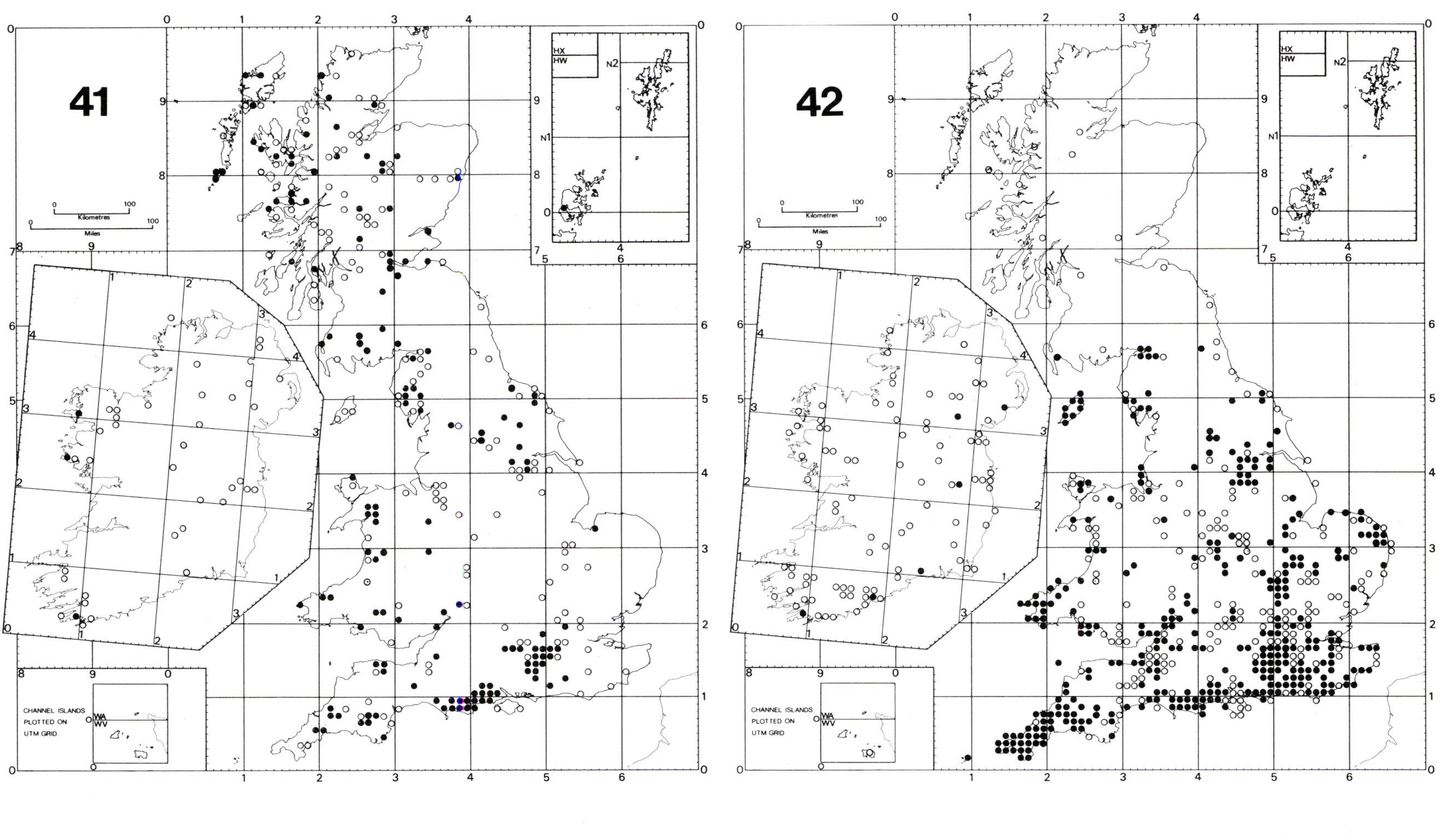

Sympetrum scoticum

Sympetrum striolatum

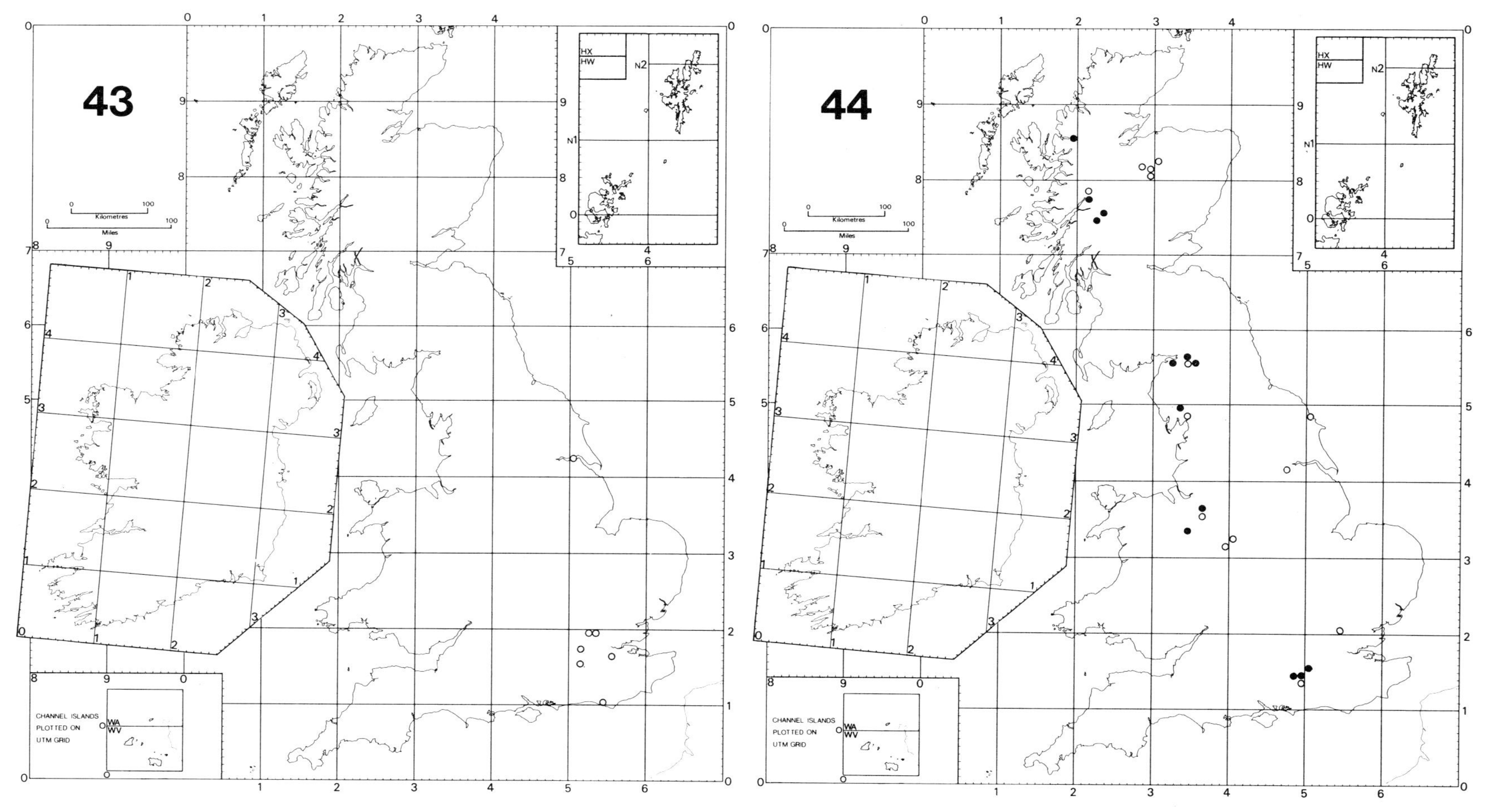

Sympetrum vulgatum

Leucorrhinia dubia

General Index

Principal entries are shown in **bold type** and plate references are given as (8:1–3). Where there are two entries in bold type, the second refers to the section on larvae. The index includes references to figures in the text as 84(Fig.17), to keys and maps.